Companion Guide

Based on the original Companion Guide by

Tana L. Pedersen

Copyright © 2007-2023 The Software MacKiev Company.
All rights reserved.

Family Tree Maker, the Family Tree Maker tree logo, FamilySync, the FamilySync logo, TreeVault, the TreeVault logo, Photo Darkroom, Next of Kin, Sync Weather Report, Turn Back Time, Emergency Tree, AlbumWALK, and Historical Weather are registered trademarks, and Software MacKiev, the Software MacKiev logo, SoundSpot, Smart Weather Sentences, and Smart Stories are trademarks of The Software MacKiev Company. All other trademarks are the property of their respective owners.

No part of this publication may be reproduced in any form without written permission of the publisher, except by a reviewer, who may quote brief passages for review.

2124-6-01

Contents

Welcome to Family Tree Maker xvii

What's New? xviii

Part 1: Getting Started 1

Chapter 1   Installing Family Tree Maker 3
Installing Family Tree Maker 4
Registering the Software 4
Getting Help 5
    Onscreen Help 5
    Companion Guides 7
    Technical Support 7
    Feedback 7

Chapter 2   Family Tree Maker Basics 9
Opening and Closing Family Tree Maker 9
The Family Tree Maker Interface 10
    Main Toolbar 10
Workspaces 10
    The Plan Workspace 10
    The People Workspace 12
    The Places Workspace 23
    The Media Workspace 24
    The Sources Workspace 25

vi   Contents

        The Publish Workspace 26
        The Web Search Workspace 27

Chapter 3   **Creating a Tree** **29**
        Before You Begin 29
        Creating a Tree 29
            Entering Your Information from Scratch 29
            Importing a Tree File 30
            Downloading a Tree from Ancestry 32
            Copying a Tree File from Another Computer 34
            Downloading a FamilySearch Tree Branch 36
        Choosing a Home Person 38

Part 2: Building a Tree 41

Chapter 4   **Entering Family Information** **43**
        Entering Basic Information for an Individual 43
            Adding a Spouse 45
            Adding a Child to a Family 47
            Adding Parents 48
        Adding More Details 49
            Adding a Fact 49
            Copying and Pasting Facts 52
            Adding a Note for an Individual 55
            Adding Web Links for an Individual 58
        Rich Color Coding 59
            Applying Color Coding to a Person 60
            Removing Color Coding 62
        Working with Relationships 62
            Using the Combined Family View 62

  Viewing an Individual's Family Relationships..... 63
  Adding Additional Spouses 64
  Choosing a Type of Relationship for a Couple 67
  Choosing a Status for a Couple's Relationship 67
  Choosing a Parent-Child Relationship................. 68
  Adding an Unrelated Individual 68
 Viewing a Timeline 68
 Creating Smart Stories™.. 69
  Creating a Smart Story as a Media Item.............. 71
  Creating a Smart Story as a Report....................... 71
  Including a Short Biography.................................. 72
  Including Facts 73
  Including Sources.. 74
  Including Notes 75
  Including Images 76
  Creating Timelines.. 76
  Editing Smart Stories Text 77

Chapter 5 Documenting Your Research 79

 Understanding Sources and Source Citations 79
 Creating Sources.. 81
  Adding a Source for a Fact..................................... 81
  Using Source Templates 82
  Creating a Source Using the Basic Format 85
 Creating Source Citations 87
  Adding a New Source Citation 87
  Attaching a Media Item to a Source Citation........ 92
  Adding a Note to a Source Citation...................... 93
 Using Source Repositories.. 94
  Managing Repositories.. 95

Chapter 6   Including Media Items 99
    Adding Media Items 100
        Adding a Media Item for an Individual 100
        Scanning an Image into Your Tree 101
        Changing the Display of an Image 102
    Entering Details for a Media Item 103
    Entering a Note About a Media Item 104
    Adding a Portrait for an Individual 105
    Editing Photos with Photo Darkroom® 107
    Linking a Media Item to Multiple Individuals 109
    Playing AlbumWALK® Files 111
    Managing Media Items 113
        Opening a Media Item from Family Tree Maker 113
        Changing a Media Item's File Name 113
        Arranging an Individual's Media Items 113
    Media Categories 115
        Creating a Category 115
        Assigning a Category to Multiple Items 115
    Creating a Slide Show 116
    Printing a Media Item 119

Chapter 7   Using Maps 121
    Viewing a Map 121
        Moving Around a Map 124
        Zooming In and Out on a Map 125
        Using Streetside View 126
        Finding Places of Interest 127
        Printing a Map 128
    Viewing Locations in Groups 129
    Viewing People and Facts Linked to a Location 129
    Creating Migration Maps 131

Creating a Migration Map for an Individual..... 131
Creating a Migration Map for a Family 132
Entering GPS Coordinates 133
Entering a Display Name for a Location 134

Chapter 8   Researching Your Tree Online 135
Ancestry Hints.. 135
FamilySearch Hints 136
Viewing Ancestry and FamilySearch Hints....... 136
Searching Ancestry 138
Searching FamilySearch.. 144
Matching a Person with FamilySearch 144
Merging FamilySearch Historical Records 147
Adding Records to a Tree 148
Searching Online with Family Tree Maker 151
Copying Online Facts... 152
Copying an Online Image 154
Copying Online Text to a Note 155
Archiving a Web Page.. 157
Managing Research Websites..................................... 158
Adding a Website to Your Favorites List 158
Sorting Your Website Favorites 159

Part 3: Creating Charts, Reports, and Books ...161

Chapter 9   Creating Family Tree Charts 163
Pedigree Charts.. 163
Standard Pedigree Charts.................................... 164
Vertical Pedigree Charts 164
Hourglass Charts 165
Standard Hourglass Charts 165
Horizontal Hourglass Charts............................... 167

Contents

Descendant Charts 168
Bow Tie Charts 169
Family Tree Charts 169
Fan Charts 170
Extended Family Charts 170
Relationship Charts 171
Creating a Chart 172
Customizing a Chart 172
    Choosing Facts to Include in a Chart 172
    Changing a Chart's Title 174
    Including Source Information with a Chart 175
    Adding Images to a Chart 175
    Changing the Header or Footer 180
    Changing Formatting for a Chart 181
Using Chart Templates 186
    Creating Your Own Template 187
    Using a Custom Template 187
Saving Charts 188
    Saving a Specific Chart 188
    Saving a Chart as a File 189
Printing a Chart 189
Large Chart Printing 190
Sharing a Chart 190
Charting Companion Plug-In 191

Chapter 10 Running Reports 193

Genealogy Reports 193
    Ahnentafel Report 193
    Descendant Report 194
Person Reports 195
    Custom Report 195

  Data Errors Report 195
  Individual Report 196
  LDS Ordinances Report 196
  LDS Ordinance Summary Report 197
  List of Individuals Report 197
  Notes Report 198
  Surname Report 198
  Task List 199
  Timeline Report 199
 Relationship Reports 200
  Family Group Sheet 200
  Kinship Report 201
  Marriage Report 201
  Outline Ancestor Report 202
  Outline Descendant Report 202
  Parentage Report 203
  Family View Report 203
 Place Usage Report 204
 Media Reports 204
  Photo Album 204
  Media Item Report 205
  Media Usage Report 206
 Source Reports 206
  Source Bibliography 206
  Documented Facts Report 207
  Undocumented Facts Report 207
  Source Usage Report 208
 Calendars 208
 Creating a Report 209
 Customizing a Report 209
  Choosing Facts to Include in a Report 209

Choosing Individuals to Include in a Report 212
Changing a Report's Title 213
Adding a Background Image 213
Changing the Header or Footer 214
Changing Fonts 215
Saving Reports 216
Saving the Settings for a Report 216
Saving a Specific Report 216
Saving a Report as a File 218
Printing a Report 219
Sharing a Report 219

Chapter 11 Creating a Family History Book 221
The Desktop Book-Building Tool 221
Starting a Family History Book 221
Accessing a Saved Book 222
Setting Up a Book 222
Adding Content to a Book 223
Adding Text 223
Adding Images 226
Adding a Chart or Report 228
Adding a Placeholder 228
Creating a Table of Contents 229
Creating an Index of Individuals 230
Organizing a Book 230
Changing an Item's Settings 231
Rearranging Book Items 232
Deleting a Book Item 233
Printing a Book at Home 233
Exporting a Book 233
Family Book Creator Plug-In 234

Part 4: Managing Your Trees 235

Chapter 12 Working with Trees 237

Managing Your Trees 237
    Using the Tree Browser 237
    Opening a Tree 240
    Viewing Information About a Tree..................... 240
    Renaming a Tree.. 241
    Deleting a Tree... 241
    Using Privacy Mode... 242
Exporting a Tree File... 242
Backing Up Tree Files 245
    Backing Up a Tree File 246
    Restoring a Tree from a Backup 247
Turn Back Time®.. 248
Compressing a Tree File 251
Uploading a Tree to Ancestry................................... 251
    Uploading and Linking a Tree to Ancestry 252
    Differences Between FTM and Ancestry Trees..... 254
Working with Linked Trees....................................... 256
    Setting Up Syncing.. 257
    Syncing Trees Manually...................................... 260
    Getting a Sync Weather Report® 260
    Resolving Conflicts Between Linked Trees 261
    Unlinking Trees... 262
    Changing Privacy Settings.................................. 262
    Inviting Others to View Your Ancestry Tree....... 264

Chapter 13 Using TreeVault® Cloud Services 267
Welcome to TreeVault..267
Creating a TreeVault Account......................................267
Emergency Tree® Restore Service 269
Next of Kin®..270
Family Tree Maker Connect 271
Historical Weather®..272
AlbumWALK Connection 273

Chapter 14 Tools and Preferences 275
Using Family Tree Maker Tools..................................275
    Soundex Calculator..275
    Relationship Calculator 276
    Date Calculator 277
    Name Converter...278
    Find Individual Tool..279
    Automatic Reference Numbers 280
    Global Birth Order Tool......................................281
    Research To-Do List 281
Setting Up Preferences..284
    General Preferences 285
    Date Preferences...289
    Name Preferences...291
    Warning and Alert Preferences 292
Managing Facts...294
    Creating a Custom Fact.......................................294
    Modifying a Predefined Fact 295
    Modifying a Fact Sentence..................................296
Managing Relationships 297

Managing Historical Events 298
Customizing the Tree Tab Editing Panel 299
Entering User Information 301

Chapter 15 Family Tree Problem Solver 303
Straightening Out Relationships 303
    Merging Duplicate Individuals............................ 303
    Removing an Individual from a Tree 307
    Removing a Marriage 307
    Detaching a Child from the Wrong Parents 308
    Attaching a Child to a Father and Mother 309
Fixing Text Mistakes 310
    Global Spell Checker 310
    Find and Replace Tool 311
    Merging Duplicate Facts 313
Running the Data Errors Report 314
Standardizing Locations 315
    Identifying a Single Location 315
    Identifying Multiple Locations 317
Finding Missing Media Items 318
    Finding a Single Missing Media Item 318
    Finding All Missing Media Items 319

Glossary 321

Index 327

About the Original Author 343

Welcome to Family Tree Maker

On September 30, 1989, Ken Hess and his company Banner Blue introduced the original edition of Family Tree Maker which quickly became the best selling family history software of all time. Three decades later to the day, Software MacKiev introduced Family Tree Maker 2019, which takes this grand old brand to places its original creators could only have dreamed of. Where changes you make to your tree on your Mac or PC are automatically backed up to a secure cloud vault every fifteen seconds, including your media collection. Where your tree can be instantly fact-checked by a relative half way around the world on their smartphone or tablet. Where you can turn back time to erase mistakes you made even a thousand changes ago. Where you can arrange for your tree to be passed on to a successor of your choice along with your Family Tree Maker license to ensure your legacy lives on. Welcome to the new world of Family Tree Maker. We think you're going to like it here.

🌱 What's New?

Dozens of new features and enhancements in Family Tree Maker 2019 (aka FTM 2019) make it easier than ever to discover your family history, build your family tree, and share your unique heritage. This symbol 🌱 appears wherever a new or improved feature is described in this guide. Here are the most notable new features you will find as you explore FTM 2019:

Turn Back Time. FTM 2019 now keeps track of every one of your last THOUSAND changes. Lopped off Uncle Harry's branch of the tree by mistake three days ago but your last full backup is three weeks old? No problem. Simply roll back to just before the accident with a single click. Then use the comprehensive Change Log to restore the moves you meant to make. See page 248.

FamilySearch Integration 2.0. Access to FamilySearch, the world's largest collection of genealogical records, was integrated into FTM 2017 so you can get hints, search, and merge the results into your tree, much like you do with Ancestry.com. And now, with FTM 2019 you can download an entire branch from FamilySearch tree into Family Tree Maker. (See page 36.) And now you can also get hints linked to more than six billion online FamilySearch historical records by "matching" people in the FamilySearch tree to yours. (See page 144.) A unique new source of records for Family Tree Maker users – for free.

Hints in the Index. Once found only on tree views, in FTM 2019 those little green Ancestry leaves and FamilySearch hints now appear in the people index too. No more scrolling through branches to find all the latest hints. And you can check for hints for a particular family name in the Index or in a saved list. See page 13.

What's New?   xix

 **Rich Color Coding.** One of the most frequent requests from genealogists using FTM 2017's color coding was for "rich" color coding – not just coding the home person's ancestors but each ancestor's descendants as well. With FTM 2019, you can assign up to eight colors to each person. See page 59.

 **Smart Filters.** In FTM 2017 we introduced the ability to save filtered lists. Now those lists just got a whole lot smarter. The new Smart Filters create lists in FTM 2019 that actively gather any new people you add to your tree who meet that filter's criteria as soon as they are added to your tree. For example, if your filtered list is for military service, when you add two more service men or women to your tree, they'll be added automatically to the military service list. Simple as that. See page 14.

 **Folder Counters.** You can stop peeking into folders to see if there's anything in there. Now numbers on your folder tabs show the quantity of items stored in each one. Simple idea. Big time-saver. See page 22.

 **Profile Picture Cropping.** Clean up the look of your tree with our new profile picture-cropping tool. Smart technology in FTM 2019 detects the person's face and zooms in just the right amount, then crops a perfect square so that it fits perfectly on each leaf of your tree, and your cropped profile pictures will sync with your Ancestry tree. Best of all, since the original photo is kept completely untouched, you can easily create several profile pictures from a single group photo and you won't have to squint anymore to see what your great-uncle Harry looked like. Perfect. See page 106.

xx   What's New?

Linking Media to Multiple Individuals. With just a few clicks, you can now link a group photo or a scanned document to any number of people in your tree, without having to start over for each person. See page 109.

Managing Relationships. Change one relationship or thousands at a time and get things back on track. For example, you can use this new tool to find all married people in your tree whose relationship is mistakenly shown as "Unknown", and change them all at once to "Spouse". If only fixing real relationships were that easy. See page 297.

Tree Browser. Get the tree you're looking for quickly with this new

window into your tree files. Search a family name and find all related trees wherever they are – on Ancestry, on your hard drive, or up in the clouds. And for each tree you'll have everything you need to know or do at your fingertips. Does that FTM tree have a linked Ancestry tree, and if so, under what name? No links to an Ancestry tree? Click Download in the browser to get it all synced up. See page 237.

TreeVault. With TreeVault, Family Tree Maker is no longer an

isolated desktop application, but rather the hub of a growing ecosystem of mobile apps and cloud services. View changes in your FTM tree in realtime on your smartphone or tablet. Know what the weather was like the day your grandfather was born. Sleep better knowing that an up to date copy of your tree is securely tucked away in the cloud, that someday will be passed on to the next generation for you. New cloud services will be added over time, but here's the starting lineup:

What's New?   xxi

- **Emergency Tree Restore Service.** TreeVault keeps an exact copy of your tree, updated every fifteen seconds with every change you've made, ready to hand back to you if your hard drive should crash or some other catastrophe strikes. You'll sleep better knowing that a copy of your family history is safely tucked away for you – with photos, voice recordings, videos, documents, and even your Turn Back Time log so you'll be able to undo your last thousand changes after your tree is restored. See page 269.

- **Family Tree Maker Connect** is a mobile app (for iPad, iPhone, and Android phones and tablets) that displays your latest FTM tree anywhere, any time – even when your computer is off. Handy for sharing your tree with relatives or for using your iPad as a second monitor with your continuously updated tree. See page 271.

- **AlbumWALK** is changing the way your family retells the stories behind old photos. Part of the Family Tree Maker ecosystem, AlbumWALK is a free mobile app for iOS and Android devices that uses patented tap-talk technology to create interactive talking photos. Just tap a face on a photo and talk about that person to create a SoundSpot™. Tap the next and talk. And when you're finished, AlbumWALK creates a mini-documentary with professionally scored background music that can be played back in the media center of FTM 2019. See page 111 and page 273.

Visit www.albumwalk.com for availability and pricing.

- **Historical Weather** provides the elements of a great family story with more than a BILLION historical weather records dating back to the 1800's. Did it snow on your parents' first Christmas Eve or rain at their wedding? See page 272.

- **Smart Weather Sentences**™ puts all those weather records from our Historical Weather database into plain English that you can just drop right into your Smart Stories and books.

- **Next of Kin** allows you to designate a successor to your TreeVault account to pass along your family tree. You will get a certificate that may be included with a will, providing instructions and passcodes for taking over your account along with your Family Tree Maker license. See page 270.

How the Guide Is Organized

As you read this book, you'll notice several features that provide you with useful information:

- Tips give you advice on the best ways to perform tasks.

- Notes offer you timely hints and explanations about how features work.

- Sidebars give you additional information on a variety of family history topics, such as using maps, that will enhance your ability to create a richer and more complete family tree.

- A glossary explains words you might not be familiar with, such as Family Tree Maker terms (family group view, Fastfields), and genealogy terms (GEDCOM, Ahnentafel).

If you still need help, a quick perusal of the Table of Contents should lead you right to the task you are trying to perform; if not, check the index in the back of the book.

Part One
Getting Started

Chapter 1: Installing Family Tree Maker................... 3

Chapter 2: Family Tree Maker Basics....................... 9

Chapter 3: Creating a Tree.. 29

Chapter One
Installing Family Tree Maker

This chapter lists the system requirements for Family Tree Maker, shows you how to install the software, and gives a quick introduction to available help resources.

Minimum System Requirements

To use FTM 2019, you'll need a computer that meets the specifications below. Keep in mind that the more family information you enter, the greater the amount of free hard disk space and available RAM you will need. If you have lots of images or videos, you'll need a substantial amount of hard disk space.

- macOS 10.10 "Yosemite" or later
- Any Intel or M1-based Mac
- 2 GB of memory (4 GB recommended)
- 900 MB of free disk space
- 1280×800 display resolution
- DVD drive (only if installing from a DVD)
- USB port (only if installing from a USB flash drive)

All online features require Internet access. Users are responsible for their Internet Service Provider (ISP) account, all Internet access fees, and phone charges.

Installing Family Tree Maker

To use Family Tree Maker the software must be installed on your computer's hard drive; you cannot run it directly from the DVD or the USB drive.

1. Insert the Family Tree Maker DVD into your Mac's drive, or double-click the .dmg file that you have downloaded or that is located on your Family Tree Maker USB Drive.
2. In the window that appears, double-click the **Family Tree Maker 2019** icon to launch the application installer.
3. Follow the onscreen instructions to complete the installation.

If you have an earlier version of Family Tree Maker installed on your computer, this new version will not replace it. While the installation process will not harm your existing Family Tree Maker files, it's always a good idea to back up your tree files on an external storage device or using a cloud storage service. See "Backing Up a Tree File" on page 246 for more information.

Note: If you experience any difficulties with installation, go to support.familytreemaker.com, type "installation" in the search field, and press **Return**.

Registering the Software

Before you create your first tree, take a couple of minutes to register the software. If you ever lose your copy of Family Tree Maker, you'll be glad you filled out the registration form. You'll also get to hear from us from time to time when there's a new edition or free updates.

When you open the application for the first time, the registration dialog opens automatically. If you choose not to register on the first run, but decide to do so some time later, choose **Register Family Tree Maker 2019** from the **Family Tree Maker 2019** menu, and then follow the onscreen instructions. Make sure your computer is connected to the Internet before you start.

Getting Help

Family Tree Maker has onscreen help, this companion guide, a TreeVault user guide, and online technical support. If you have questions about a feature or simply want to learn more about the application, check out one of these Help resources.

Onscreen Help

Family Tree Maker has convenient onscreen help to give you information on performing tasks and answer questions about the software. You can search help by typing in a topic or phrase. You can also print the resulting explanation.

Opening the Help Viewer

On the **Help** menu, choose **Family Tree Maker 2019 Help**. Family Tree Maker displays the Help Viewer (see fig. 1-1).

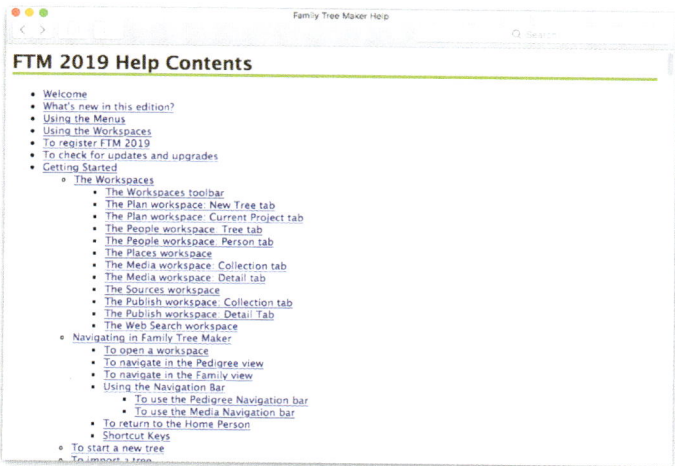

Figure 1-1. The table of contents for Family Tree Maker Help.

Searching in the Help Program

Searching is the quickest way to find the topic you're interested in. In the search field, type the word, phrase, or topic you want to know more about. Many useful pages can be found by entering keywords like "searching," "sources," "reports," and "notes."

When the search results appear, select a topic to open it. You can use the **Share** button and pop-up menu to print the current help page. Press the **Command** and "+" keys to enlarge the text and illustrations and the **Command** and "-" keys to make them smaller.

Tip: In many areas of Family Tree Maker you can press **Command+F1** (or **fn+F1**) to immediately open a Help topic for the area you are working in or you may click the **Help** button on windows that have them.

Navigating in the Help Program

The onscreen help makes use of links to take you to other related topics. These links are easily identified by their blue, underlined text. Simply click any link to go to a new topic. You can also use these buttons on the toolbar to move around within help:

- **Back and Forward buttons**—Click the **Back** button to return to a previous help topic; click the **Forward** button to move forward through the help topics you've already accessed.

> **Help Tags**
> If you want to know the name of a button or find out what it's used for, hold the pointer over it for a second or two and a help tag will appear.

Companion Guides

To view this *Companion Guide* as a PDF, choose **Companion Guide** from the **Help** menu. To view the *TreeVault User Guide* as a PDF, choose **TreeVault User Guide** from the **Help** menu.

Technical Support

Family Tree Maker has an online support center where you can get assistance with technical problems and answers to customer service questions. You'll start by searching our knowledge base of easy-to-understand articles with tips and step-by-step instructions. If that doesn't provide what you need, you can fill out an online support request and have an option to get an answer by email or be connected right away to our Live Chat service which is available 24 hours a day, 7 days a week. Choose **Family Tree Maker Tech Support** from the **Help** menu to get started.

> Tip: To open the live chat instantly, go to ftm.support/chat.

Feedback

We'd love to hear from you with comments, questions or suggestions. Please visit the Family Tree Maker product page online. Choose **Provide Family Tree Maker Feedback** from the **Family Tree Maker 2019** application menu or go to www.familytreemaker.com, and then use one of the feedback options available there.

Chapter Two
Family Tree Maker Basics

Family Tree Maker makes it easy for anyone to discover their family history and gather it into one convenient location. This chapter gives you the basic skills and knowledge you need to launch the program and navigate around the software.

Opening and Closing Family Tree Maker

To open the application, click the **Family Tree Maker 2019** icon in the Dock or locate the software in the Applications folder and double-click the **Family Tree Maker 2019** icon. To close the application, choose **Quit Family Tree Maker** from the **Family Tree Maker 2019** menu.

Saving and Backing Up When Quitting
There's no need to save your tree when quitting. Family Tree Maker automatically saves changes as you make them, and can also make an automatic backup (without media) when you quit (see page 285).

The Family Tree Maker Interface

To use any application effectively, the first step is to understand its unique interface and tools.

Main Toolbar

The main toolbar (fig. 2-1) at the top of the application window provides quick access to key features. Here you can select a tree to open, access TreeVault cloud services, and navigate between the seven main workspaces.

Figure 2-1. The main toolbar.

Workspaces

Family Tree Maker groups important features together into seven workspaces.

The Plan Workspace

The Plan workspace is the "control center" where you manage your family trees. On the New Tree tab you can start a new tree, import an existing tree file, download a tree from Ancestry or FamilySearch, or restore a tree from TreeVault.

The Current Tree tab on the Plan workspace (fig. 2-2) lets you view details about your tree, roll back changes to it, use TreeVault cloud services, manage your research to-do list, and, if you've linked the Family Tree Maker tree (FTM tree) on your computer to an online Ancestry tree, you can also manage how the trees are synced.

Chapter 2: Family Tree Maker Basics 11

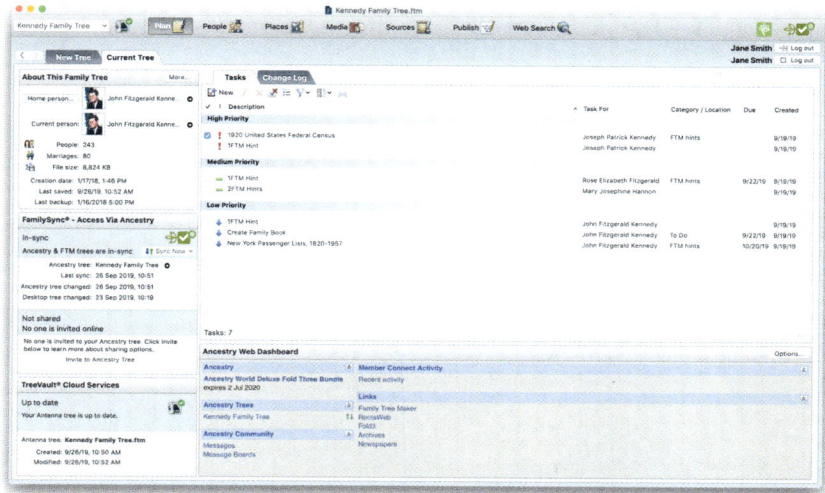

Figure 2-2. The Current Tree tab on the Plan workspace.

The Current Tree tab also contains the Ancestry Web Dashboard where you can see the status of your Ancestry subscription if you have one (click it to access your Ancestry account), open your Ancestry trees, and view your Member Connect activity.

What Is Member Connect on Ancestry?
Member Connect helps you stay in touch with others who are researching your ancestors. Ancestry scans public Ancestry trees and notifies you when there's activity around records you've saved or commented on.

The People Workspace

The People workspace is where you enter information about individuals and families in your tree—and where you will spend most of your time when using Family Tree Maker.

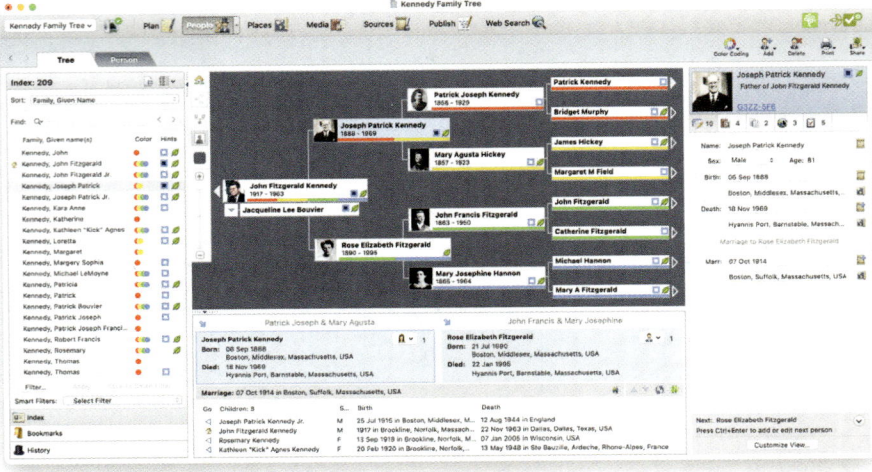

Figure 2-3. The Tree tab on the People workspace.

The Tree tab (fig. 2-3) provides a comprehensive view of your family. You can see several generations of your family at once and easily navigate to each person in your tree. Because you will use this tab often, its sections are explained here in detail.

The Index

The Index (fig. 2-4) lists all the individuals in your tree and is one of the easiest ways to locate the person you want to focus on. To view information for a specific individual, just click their name in the Index or enter it in the **Find** field to jump to their listing.

New Index Items. Ancestry and FamilySearch hints and FamilySearch IDs appear in the Index for the first time in FTM 2019.

Displaying Index Items. You can select which items are displayed using the **Index View** icon, including color coding and the date of one key life event at a time (birth, death, or marriage). Selecting **Lifespan** displays both birth and death.

Home Person. The house icon marks the individual who is the current home person in the tree. (You'll learn more about the home person in Chapter 3.)

Sorting the Index. Most of the time you will find it best to have the Index sorted alphabetically by family name, but you can sort by first name instead, or by birth, death or marriage dates using the **Sort** pop-up menu.

Alternate Views. Click the **Bookmarks** tab at the bottom of the Index pane to view the individuals you have bookmarked (Control-click a name in the Index and choose **Add Bookmark**), or click the **History** tab to see the individuals you have added or edited recently.

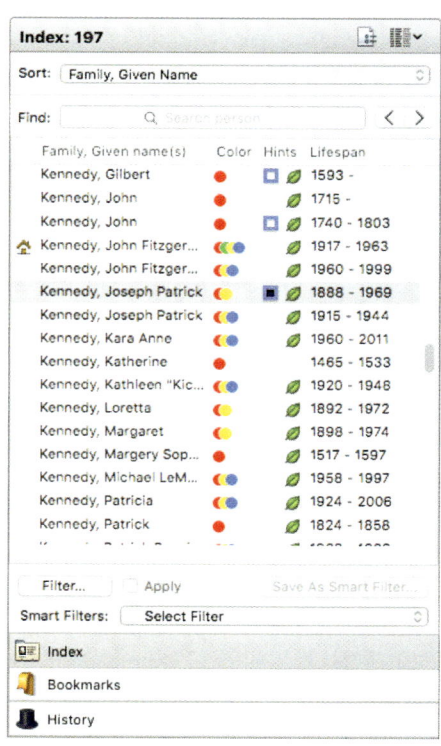

Figure 2-4. The Index.

Filtering the Index

You can temporarily limit the Index so it displays only certain individuals for analysis.

1   Click the **Filter** button. The **Filter Individuals** dialog appears.
2   Select a specific family line, an individual's descendants, or a group of your choice.
3   Click the **Apply** button to create a temporary filtered list.
4   To retain a temporary filter so you can apply it again later and edit it, save it by clicking the **Save As Smart Filter** button. In the dialog that appears, give the filter a name and, optionally, choose a color.

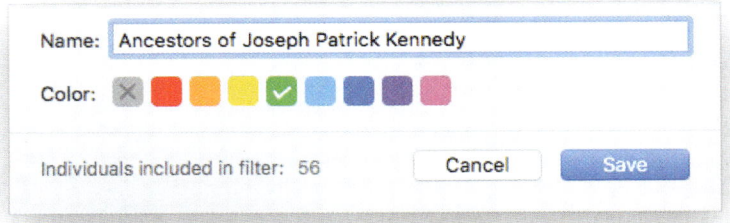

Figure 2-5. The Save Filter dialog.

Smart Filters

When you save a temporary filter you have constructed, the criteria are saved as a Smart Filter that you can apply later and edit. You may also create a Smart Filter from the start by selecting **New Filter** from the **Smart Filters** pop-up menu. Smart Filter lists are dynamic — when people who meet a Smart Filter's criteria are added to your tree, they are automatically added to the filtered list.

> **Smart Filter Color Coding**
> The color selected when saving or editing a Smart Filter will be displayed next to the names of all people in the filtered list—both in the Index and on their thumbnails in the tree viewer, exactly as colors assigned with color coding are. See "Color Coding" on page 59.

To create a Smart Filter from the start:

1 Choose **New Filter** from the **Smart Filters** pop-up menu.
2 Set the filter criteria in the **Filter Individuals** dialog that appears.
3 Click **Save**. In the dialog that appears, give the filter a name and, optionally, choose a color.

> Tip: Smart Filters are an excellent tool for tracking the people in your tree who are matched with the FamilySearch Family Tree. In the **Filter Individuals** dialog, click **Filter In**, then click the **All Facts** tab, and set the condition **Is Not Blank** for the **FamilySearch ID** fact.

Applying a Smart Filter

When you save a filter, it appears in the **Smart Filters** pop-up menu in the Index. To apply one of these Smart Filters, simply select it from the pop-up menu. You can also use Smart Filters to choose which people to include when exporting data from your tree or creating a chart or report.

Editing Smart Filters

Smart Filters make it easy to change the focus of your research without rebuilding the filter from scratch. You can instead simply duplicate a Smart Filter you have already created, edit one or more conditions, and save the result.

To edit the criteria of a Smart Filter, follow these steps:

1   Choose a filter you want to edit from the **Smart Filters** menu.
2   Click the **Edit Filter** button or choose **Edit Filter** from the **Smart Filters** menu. The **Filter Individuals** dialog (fig. 2-6) appears.

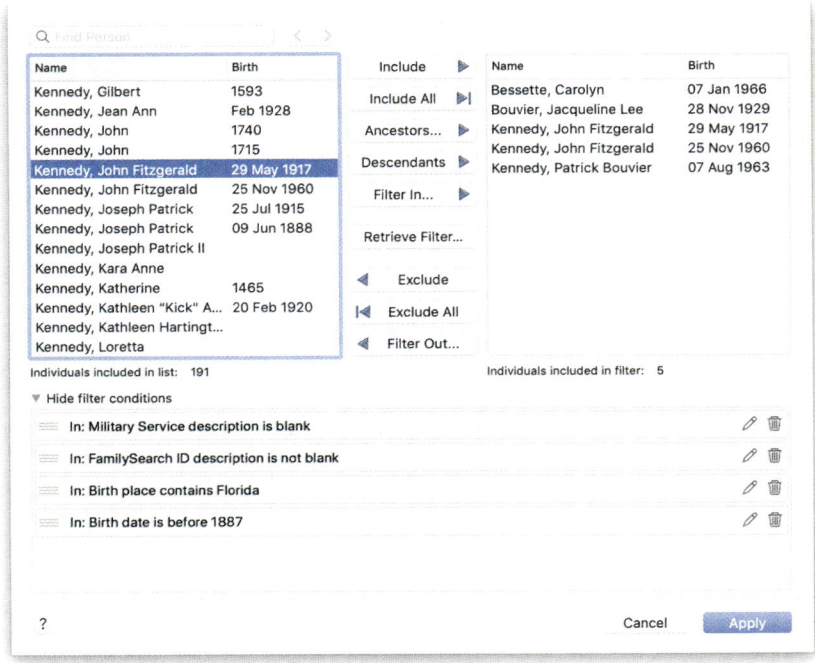

Figure 2-6. The Filter Individuals dialog.

3 At the bottom of the dialog is a list of the conditions that make up the filter. If you don't see the list, click the **Show filter conditions** disclosure triangle.

4 To add a new condition, use the controls in the top part of the dialog.

5 To remove a condition, click its trash can icon.

6 Some conditions can be edited. To edit a condition, click its pencil icon. The **Filter Individuals by Criteria** dialog appears. Use the dialog to edit the criteria, and then click **OK**.

7 When you have finished editing the filter conditions, click **Save**.

Adding Conditions from One Smart Filter to Another

To save time when creating a new filter, or to get a filter that produces narrower or broader results, you can reuse conditions from an existing Smart Filter and combine them with new conditions. You can also merge conditions from two or more Smart Filters.

1 Create a new filter by choosing **New Filter** from the **Smart Filters** pop-up menu or, in the **Manage Filters** dialog, duplicate an existing Smart Filter by selecting it and clicking the **Duplicate selected filter** button.

2 If you have duplicated a filter, the new copy is selected automatically. Type a name for the new filter in the **Name** field, and then click the **OK** button.

3 Click the **Smart Filters** pop-up menu, choose the filter you have just created, and then click the **Edit Filter** button or choose **Edit Filter** from the **Smart Filters** menu. The **Filter Individuals** dialog appears.

4 To add conditions from another Smart Filter, click the **Retrieve Filter** button. The **Retrieve Filter** dialog (fig. 2-7) opens.

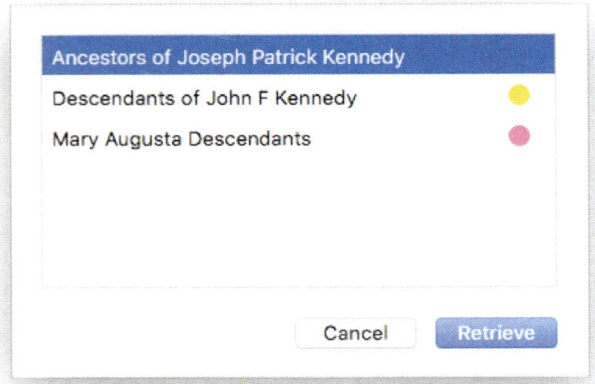

Figure 2-7. The Retrieve Filter dialog.

5 Select the filter from which you want to add conditions.
6 Click **Retrieve**. All the conditions from the selected filter are added to your new filter and appear in its list of conditions.
7 Delete or edit the added conditions as needed and set up any new conditions you want to include.
8 Click **Save**.

Managing Smart Filters

You can copy, delete, or change the name of a Smart Filter and change the color that is applied to the people in the list produced by the filter.

1 Choose **Manage Filters** from the **Smart Filters** pop-up menu. The **Manage Filters** dialog (fig. 2-8) appears.

2 Select the filter you want to work with.

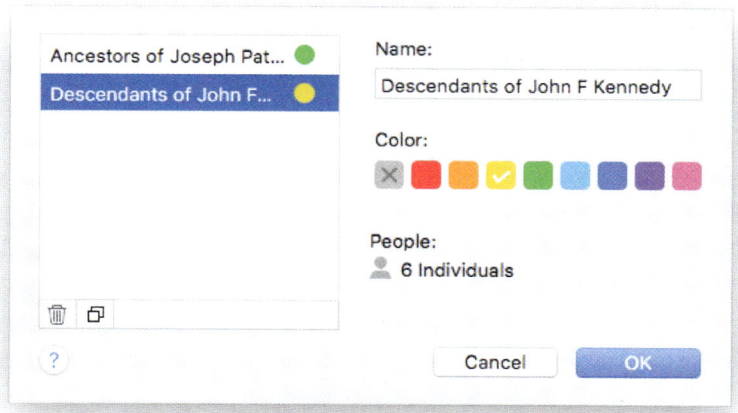

Figure 2-8. The Manage Filters dialog.

3 Do any of the following:
- To create a copy of the selected filter, click the **Duplicate selected filter** button.
- To delete the selected filter, click the "trash can" button.
- To change the name of the filter, type a new name in the **Name** field.
- To assign a color to the people in the filtered list, or to change a color you've already applied, select the color you want.

4 Click **OK** to apply your changes.

The Tree Viewer

The tree viewer (fig. 2-9) helps you navigate your family tree as well as add new individuals.

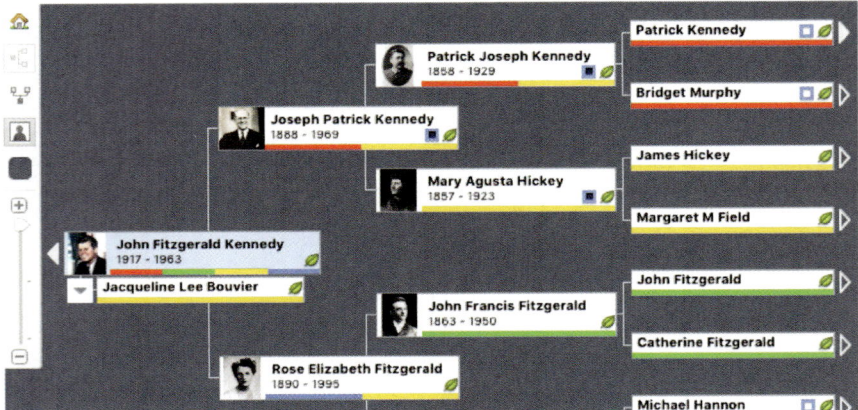

Figure 2-9. The pedigree view in the tree viewer.

These buttons will help you use the tree viewer:

 Go to home person. Makes the home person the primary individual or focus of the tree.

 Pedigree view. Shows a pedigree view of your tree. The primary individual or focus of the tree is on the left, with ancestors branching out to the right.

 Family view. Shows a family view of your tree. The primary individual is at the base of the tree, with ancestors branching above paternal on the left and maternal on the right.

 Include pictures. Displays portraits and lifespans for each individual in the pedigree view.

 Re-center on selected person. Adjusts the tree to focus on the currently selected person in the family view.

 Change background color. Lets you choose the tree viewer's background color.

The Editing Panel

The editing panel (fig. 2-10) is where you'll enter basic information about an individual, such as birth, marriage, and death, with fields for dates, places, and descriptions for each fact. At the top you'll find a portrait of an individual (if you've added one) and how he or she is related to the home person. Toolbar buttons under the portrait let you display media items, notes, Web links, and tasks associated with the individual.

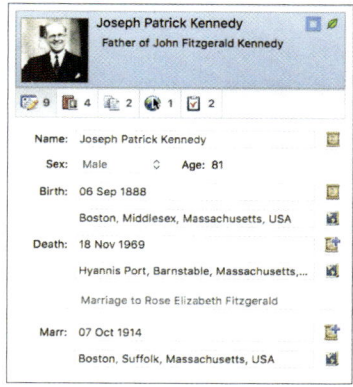

Figure 2-10. The editing panel.

The Family Group View

The family group view (fig. 2-11) lets you view an individual's spouse and children.

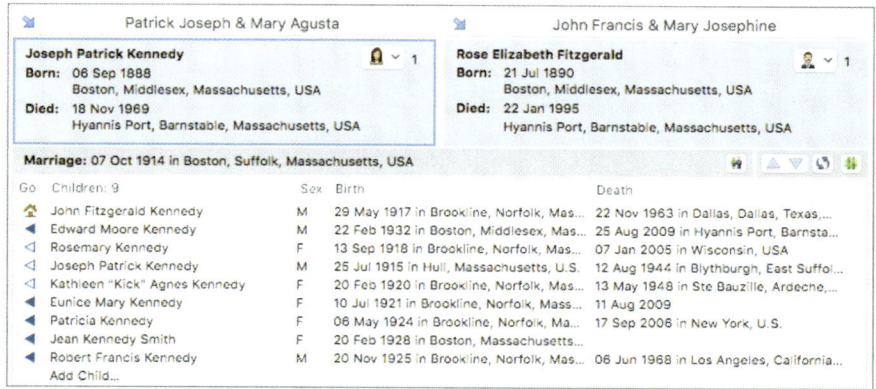

Figure 2-11. The family group view on the People workspace.

Click the "parents" button above the individual to display his or her parents and siblings. The toolbar buttons let you edit the couple's marriage fact, change the display order of their children, and view blended families.

The Person Tab

The Person tab on the People workspace (fig. 2-12) lets you add facts, media items, Web links, and notes for an individual. You can also view a timeline for the individual and their relationships to other family members.

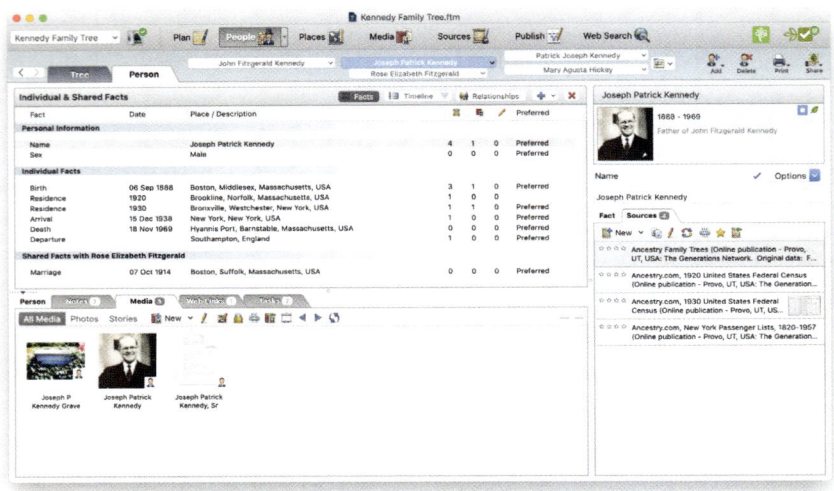

Figure 2-12. The Person tab on the People workspace.

 ### Folder Counters

New in FTM 2019, numbers on folder tabs show how many items there are for the selected person in each category. Previously the only way to find out if there were items in a folder was to open it. The folder counters can be seen on all folder tabs in FTM 2019, not only on the Person tab.

The Places Workspace

The Places workspace (fig. 2-13) helps you view the locations you've entered for events—and gives you the opportunity to view online maps of them. The Places panel on the left shows every location you've entered in your tree. When you select a place, it will be displayed on the map at the center of the workspace. The details panel on the right side shows the individuals who have life events associated with the location.

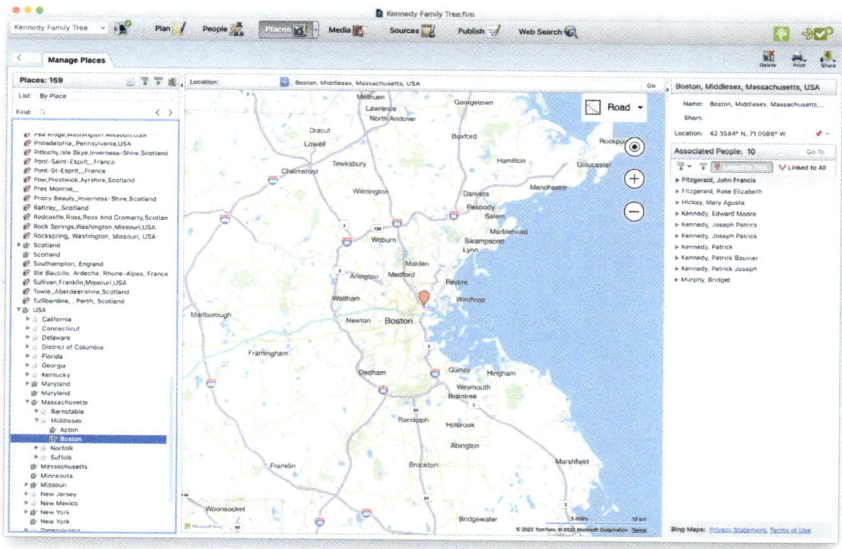

Figure 2-13. The Places workspace.

The Media Workspace

The Media workspace acts as a storage space for your photos, audio recordings, movies, family documents, and historical records. On the Collection tab (fig. 2-14) you can view thumbnails of your media items and enter information about them. On the Detail tab you can add notes for an item and link it to individuals and source citations.

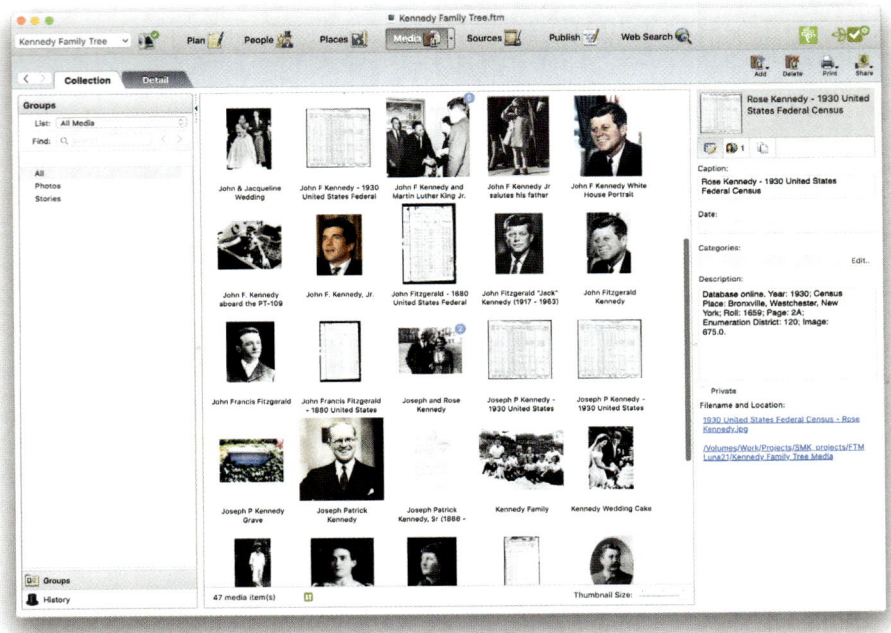

Figure 2-14. The Collection tab on the Media workspace.

The Sources Workspace

The Sources workspace (fig. 2-15) organizes your sources and source citations. The Source Groups panel on the left lets you sort sources by person, title, and repository; the sources display area shows which citations have been entered for a specific source. Tabs at the bottom of the window show the individuals linked to a source citation, related notes, and media items. In the editing panel, you can enter or update specific source citations.

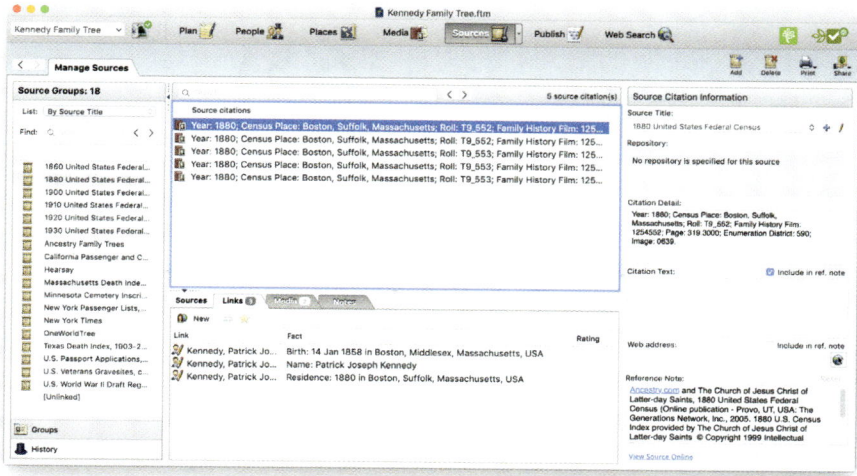

Figure 2-15. The Sources workspace.

The Publish Workspace

The Publish workspace offers a variety of charts and reports that you can view, print, and share. You can also create family history books. The Collection tab (fig. 2-16) shows the types of charts and reports that are available and gives an explanation of each.

On the Detail tab you can customize a chart or report using the editing panel and preview your changes.

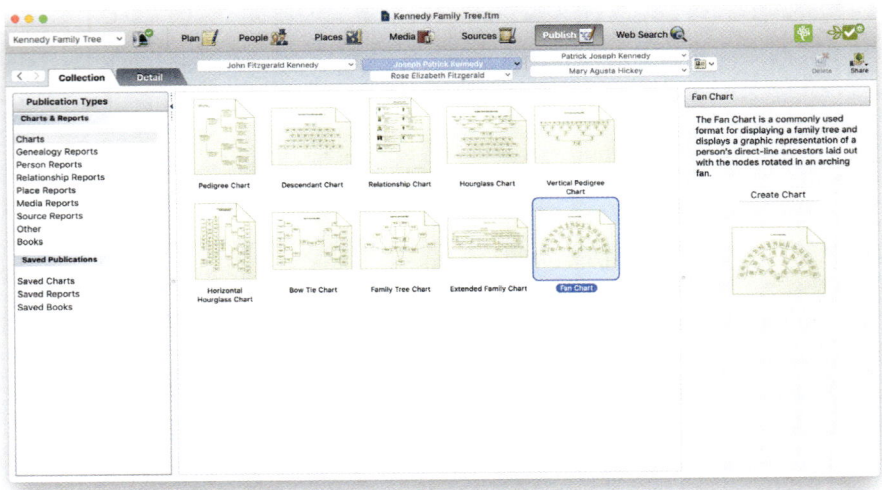

Figure 2-16. The Collection tab on the Publish workspace.

The Web Search Workspace

The Web Search workspace (fig. 2-17) lets you search billions of records on Ancestry and FamilySearch to find more information about your relatives—all without leaving Family Tree Maker. You can also search other websites and easily download discoveries into your tree.

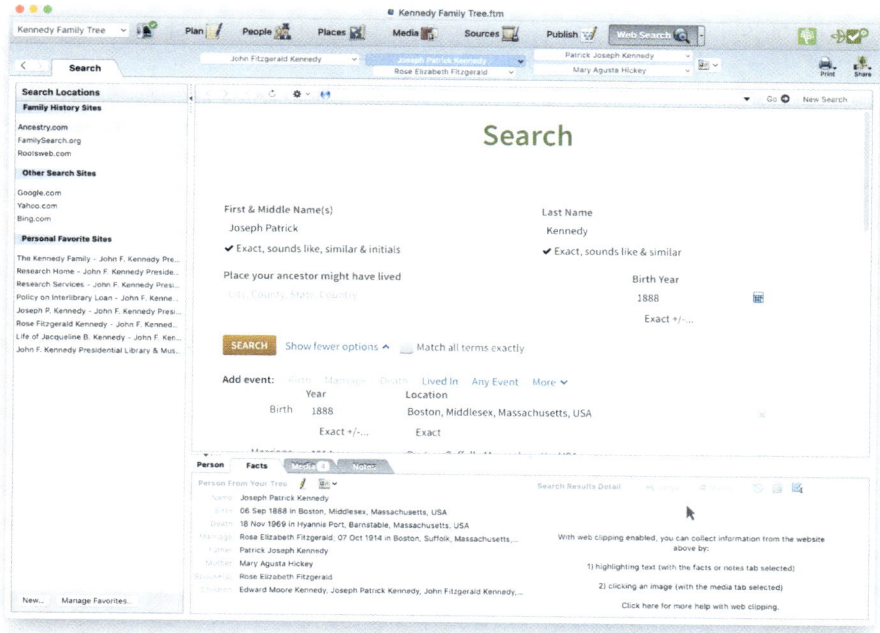

Figure 2-17. The Web Search workspace.

Chapter Three
Creating a Tree

Before You Begin

This chapter assumes that you have installed Family Tree Maker and read chapters 1 and 2. Once you've learned a few of the basic Family Tree Maker features, you're ready to create your first tree. Make sure you have some family information handy or have a file, such as a GEDCOM, or Ancestry tree, to use.

Creating a Tree

A tree is where you gather and enter your family facts and details. If you've received a family history file from another family member or researcher, you can import the file, creating a new tree. Then you can begin adding your own information. You can also create a tree by entering a few quick facts about yourself or by downloading a tree you've created on Ancestry or a branch of the FamilySearch Family Tree. Yet another way is to create a backup of an existing tree you have in FTM 2019 on another computer and move it to the current computer. This allows you to keep two FTM trees (or more if you wish) and a linked Ancestry tree in sync. See "Working with Linked Trees" on page 256.

Entering Your Information from Scratch

If this is your first time creating a family tree, you'll want to use this option. Enter a few facts about yourself and your parents, and you're on your way.

1. Choose **File > New**. The New Tree tab opens.
2. Select **Enter What You Know**.
3. Type your name and choose your gender. You can also enter your birth date and place and your parents' names.

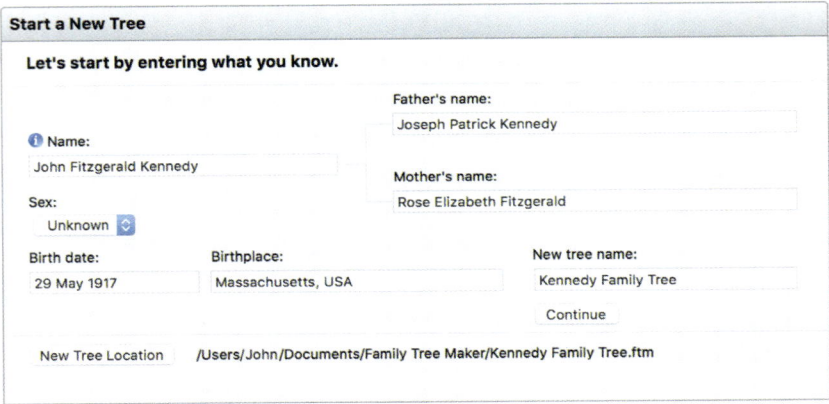

4. Enter a name for the tree in the **New tree name** field.
5. By default, your tree file will be saved to a Family Tree Maker folder in the Documents folder on your hard disk. To save the tree to another folder, click **New Tree Location**.
6. Click **Continue**. The tree opens on the People workspace, where you can start entering your family information.

Importing a Tree File

If you've already created a tree file or received one from a family member, you can import it. Tree files from Family Tree Maker for Mac (.ftm, .ftmm, and .ftmd), files from previous versions of Family

Tree Maker for Windows (.ftw, .ftm, and .fbk), and GEDCOMs (GEnealogical Data COMmunications format) are all compatible.

1 If you haven't already, copy the tree file you want to import to your computer.

2 Choose **File > New**. The New Tree tab opens.

3 Select **Import an Existing Tree**.

4 Click **Choose** to locate the tree file you want to import. If you are importing a Family Tree Maker file, a dialog will appear for you to save a copy of it with a different name, and then the tree will open on the People workspace. If you are importing a GEDCOM file, follow the steps below.

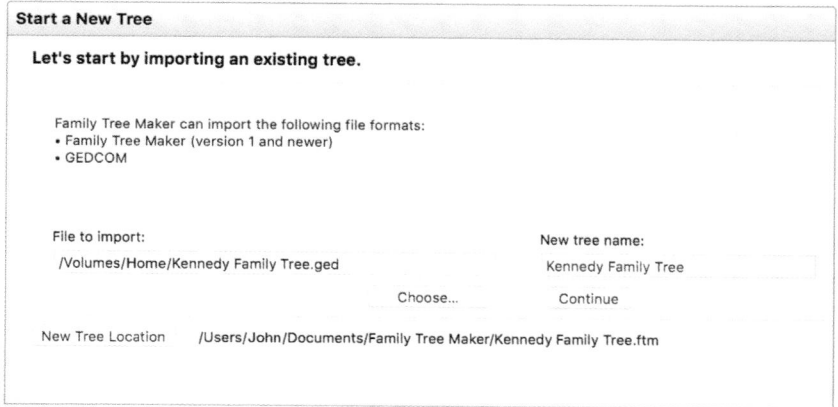

5 By default, your tree file will be saved to a Family Tree Maker folder in the Documents folder on your hard disk. To save the tree file to another folder, click **New Tree Location**.

6 If necessary, change the file's name in the **New tree name** field.

7 Click **Continue**. A dialog appears with statistics for the new tree, including the number of individuals, families, media items, and sources that were imported.

8   Click **Close**. The tree opens on the People workspace, where you can start entering your family information.

> **How Many Trees Should You Create?**
>
> When most beginners create a family tree, their first question is, "Should I create one large, all-inclusive tree or several small trees, one for each family?" The truth is, there is no right answer.
>
> The advantages to having one large tree are pretty clear. One computer file is easier to keep track of—one file to enter information in, one file to back up, one file to share. Also, you won't have to duplicate your efforts by entering some facts, sources, and media items in several trees. It's also a good idea to create your TreeVault Antenna tree from one large FTM Source tree so that it contains a maximum amount of your data and shows the broadest possible view of your extended family.
>
> Multiple trees can be useful too. The more trees you have, the smaller the tree files will typically be. If you have concerns about your computer's performance or have storage issues, smaller files might work best. Smaller tree files also make it easier to collaborate with other family members; you can send them only the family lines they're interested in.
>
> Regardless of which way you organize your trees initially, don't feel like you're stuck with a permanent decision. The flexible nature of Family Tree Maker means you can merge files anytime; you can even export parts of your tree to create a brand new tree.

Downloading a Tree from Ancestry

If you've created a tree on Ancestry, you don't need to start over in Family Tree Maker; you can download the tree to your computer. It will include all the facts, sources, and images you have attached to individuals.

Note: To download an Ancestry tree, you must be the tree's owner; you can't download trees you've been invited to view or edit.

Downloading and Linking a Tree in Family Tree Maker

When you download a tree from Ancestry, you create a link between your online Ancestry tree and its corresponding tree on your computer. This means that additions, deletions, or edits you make in your Family Tree Maker tree will be duplicated in your Ancestry tree (and vice versa) when you sync. (For more information see "Differences Between FTM and Ancestry Trees" on page 254 and "Working with Linked Trees" on page 256.)

Note: When you download your Ancestry tree, a new FTM tree will be created and linked to your Ancestry tree. You can merge the new FTM tree with another FTM tree later if you wish, but not during the download.

1 Go to the **New Tree** tab on the **Plan** workspace and make sure you are logged in to your Ancestry account (if necessary, click the **Log In** button in the upper-right corner of the workspace).

2 Click **Download a Tree from Ancestry**. A list of your trees on Ancestry appears.

3 Select the tree that you want to download. A summary of the tree status appears to the right of the list of trees.

4 Click the **Download Tree** button.

5 If you want to change the name of the tree, enter the new name in the New FTM Tree field.

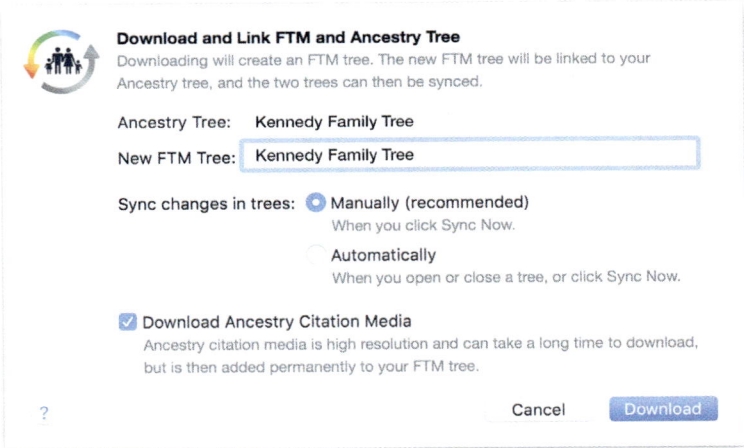

6 Choose whether your Ancestry and FTM trees will be synced manually or automatically. (For help, see "Setting Up Syncing" on page 257.)

7 Select the **Download Ancestry Citation Media** checkbox to also download Ancestry record images attached to your tree.

Note: Ancestry Citation Media will not be downloaded unless you have a current paid Ancestry subscription. You can check your subscription status in the Web Dashboard. See page 11.

8 Click **Download**. When the tree has been downloaded successfully, click **Close**.

Copying a Tree File from Another Computer

If you already have a tree on Ancestry and on one of your computers, you can move a copy of it to a different computer on which FTM 2019 is installed and keep all of the trees in sync. To do so, create a full backup of your existing FTM tree, copy it to your other computer using a flash drive, and then restore the tree there.

On the computer with the tree that you want to copy, do this:

1   In Family Tree Maker, open the tree that you want to copy.

2   Sync your FTM tree with the Ancestry tree.

3   Choose **File > Backup**.

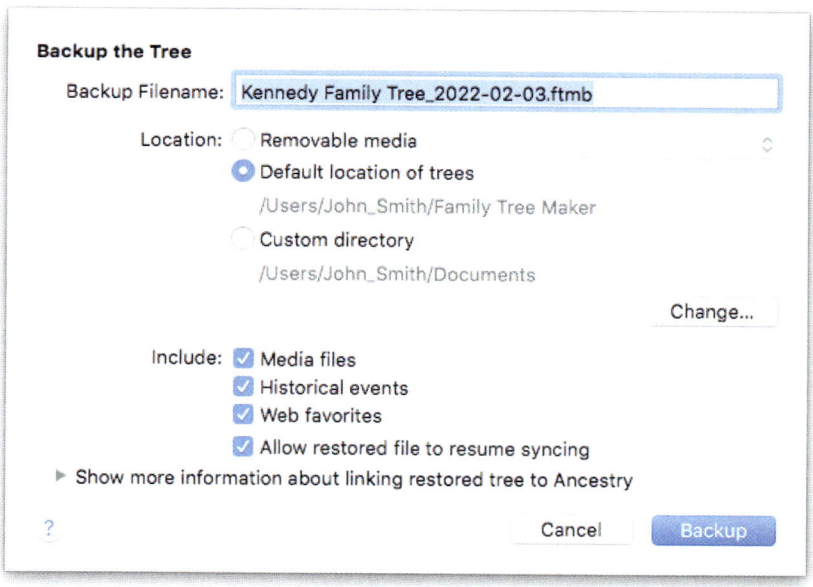

4   Select the checkboxes to include media files, historical events, and Web favorites in the backup.

5   Make sure that the **Allow restored file to resume syncing** checkbox is selected.

6   Choose a location on your computer to save the backup file.

    Note: If backing up directly to a flash drive fails with an error, try to back up to your computer and then copy the backup file to your flash drive.

7   Click **Backup**.

Now copy the backup file onto your flash drive and then copy it from the flash drive onto the other computer.

On the computer to which you have moved the backup file, do this:

1   Choose **File > Restore**.
2   Select the backup file and click **Open**.
3   Choose the location where you want Family Tree Maker to store your copied tree.
4   Click **Save**.
5   In the dialog that appears, make sure that the **Allow restored file to resume syncing** checkbox is selected, and then click **Restore**.

Downloading a FamilySearch Tree Branch

With FTM 2019, you can download a branch of the FamilySearch Family Tree to your computer to create a new FTM tree. All individuals in your new FTM tree will be matched to the same individuals in the FamilySearch Family Tree. This means that you will not have to search for these people on FamilySearch each time, and FamilySearch hints to historical records about these individuals will appear in Family Tree Maker. See "Matching a Person with FamilySearch" on page 144 for more information.

Chapter 3: Creating a Tree   37

1. Make sure you are logged in to FamilySearch in Family Tree Maker.

2. Click the **Plan** button on the main toolbar to open the Plan workspace.

3. On the New Tree tab, click **Download a Tree from FamilySearch**.

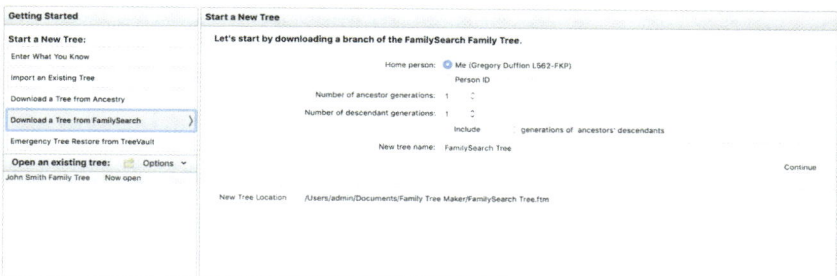

4. Set a home person for the new FTM tree. Select **Me** if you want the home person to be you (that is, the FamilySearch person associated with the account you are logged in to in Family Tree Maker), or select **Person ID** and then enter the relevant FamilySearch Person ID if you want it to be someone else.

5. In the **Number of ancestor generations** and **Number of descendant generations** fields, specify how many generations of ancestors and descendants of the home person will be included in your new tree.

6. If you want to include the descendants of each ancestor as well, select the **Include generations of ancestors' descendants** option and then enter a number in the field. For example, if you choose 1 generation of descendants, the immediate children of each ancestor will be included. Choosing 2 generations of descendants will include the children and grandchildren of each ancestor, and so on. If you want to include only ancestors in direct ascending line

from the home person, leave the option unselected.

Tip: Downloading a tree branch from FamilySearch may be time-consuming if it's large and includes many generations of ancestors and ancestors' descendants. It's better to download smaller branches from FamilySearch and then merge the resulting trees into your FTM tree.

7   If necessary, change the file's name in the **New tree name** field.
8   By default, your tree file will be saved to a Family Tree Maker folder located in the Documents folder on your hard disk. If you want to save the tree file to another folder, click **New Tree Location**.
9   Click **Continue**.

Choosing a Home Person

Each tree has a home person. By default, this is the first person you enter in a tree. If you're creating a tree based on your family, the home person will most likely be you. However, the home person can be anyone in your tree.

Occasionally, you may want to switch the home person. For example, if you're working on a specific family line, you may want to make someone in that ancestral line the home person.

Changing the Home Person on the Plan Workspace

1   Click the **Plan** button on the main toolbar. At the top of the **Current Tree** tab, you'll see the current home person.
2   Click the **Home person** button.

3   The Index of Individuals opens. Select the individual you want to be the home person and click **OK**. This individual becomes the new home person.

Changing the Home Person on the People Workspace

1   Click the **People** button on the main toolbar; then click the **Tree** tab.

2   Find the appropriate person in the family group view or Index; then Control-click and choose **Set As Home Person** from the shortcut menu.

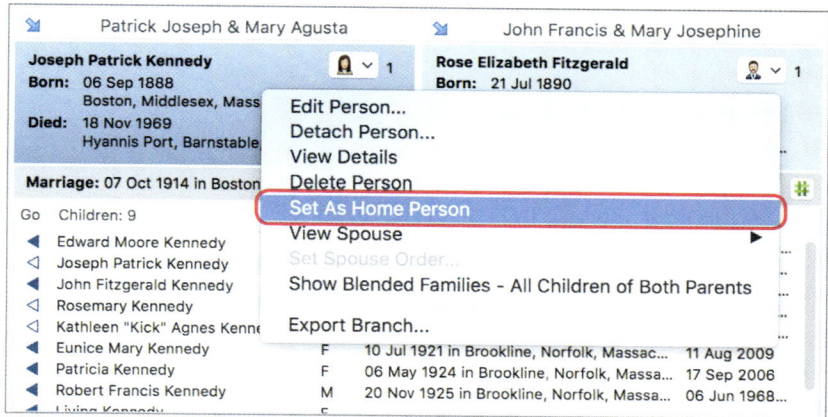

Part Two
Building a Tree

Chapter 4: Entering Family Information 43

Chapter 5: Documenting Your Research 79

Chapter 6: Including Media Items 99

Chapter 7: Using Maps 121

Chapter 8: Researching Your Tree Online 135

Chapter Four
Entering Family Information

Much of your time using Family Tree Maker will be spent entering the names, dates, and events that you've uncovered about your family. The simplest way to build your tree is to begin with what you already know—basic details about yourself, your spouse, your children, and your parents. As your tree grows, your focus can turn to ancestral lines, such as your grandparents and great-grandparents.

When you've entered basic birth, marriage, and death information for your family, you can expand your tree by adding marriage details, immigration stories, medical histories, and more.

Entering Basic Information for an Individual

You can enter facts about an individual (such as birth and death dates) on the Tree tab in the People workspace.

1 Click the **People** button on the main toolbar to open the People workspace.

2 Select an individual in the tree viewer or Index. The person's name and gender will be displayed in the editing panel.

3 In the editing panel, enter a date in the **Birth** field.

Entering Dates

Family Tree Maker automatically converts dates to the standard format used by genealogists: day, month, year. For example, 26 Jun 1961. If the application can't interpret the date you entered, a message asks for clarification. Simply retype the date in the standard format.

If you don't know the date for an event, you can leave the Date field blank or type "Unknown". If you have an approximate date, you can indicate this by typing "About 1920" or "Abt. 1920".

4 Click the **Birth Place** field below and type the location where the individual was born.

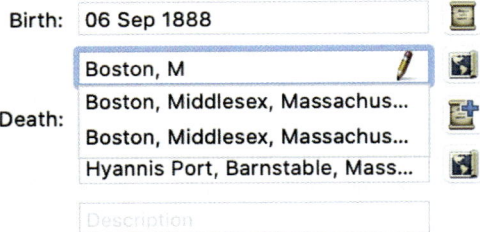

Tip: As you type a place name, you'll notice that a list of possible matches appears. To use a suggested location, select it. To ignore the suggestion, continue typing.

5 In the **Description** field, enter any additional information you may have for the Birth fact (e.g., birth weight, time of day).

6 If you know an individual's death date and place, enter those too, as well as a description if possible. You can now continue by adding marriage or other facts for the individual, entering additional family members, or adding photographs.

Entering Locations

Recording locations accurately and completely is an important part of your family history. Generally, you'll enter a location from the smallest to largest division. For example, in the USA, you would enter city or town, county, state, country (Haddam, Washington, Kansas, USA). For foreign locations, you would enter city or town, parish or district, province or county, country (Witton, Aston, Warwickshire, England).

- To help you enter locations quickly and consistently, Family Tree Maker has a locations database that includes more than 3 million place names. When you type a location, Family Tree Maker checks the name against the database and suggests possible matches. You can select a location from the list or add your own place name.
- Click the **Go to Place** icon next to a place field to open the Places workspace and center the map on the corresponding location.

Adding a Spouse

1 Click **Add Spouse** in the family group view. In the field that appears, type the spouse's name (first, middle, and last). Don't forget to use maiden names for women.

2 Choose a gender from the pop-up menu and click **Done**. The spouse is now the focus of the tree viewer and editing panel.

> **Entering Names**
>
> To keep names in your tree consistent, you'll want to follow these guidelines:
>
> - Be sure to use a woman's maiden name (her last name before she was married). This helps you trace her family and keeps you from confusing her with other people in your tree.
>
> - You may have last names (surnames) that are not a single word. You'll need to identify these names with backslashes (\); otherwise, Family Tree Maker will read only the last word as the surname. Here are some examples:
>
>   George \de la Vergne\   Teresa \Garcia Ramirez\

3 Enter any basic facts (such as birth and death) you have for the new spouse.

Entering Details About a Relationship

After you've added a spouse for an individual, you'll want to include any additional information you have about the couple. You can enter shared facts (such as marriage or divorce), notes, and media items (such as wedding photos).

1 Go to the **Tree** tab on the People workspace and select the appropriate individual.

2 To add a marriage date, place, and description, simply enter the information in the appropriate fields.

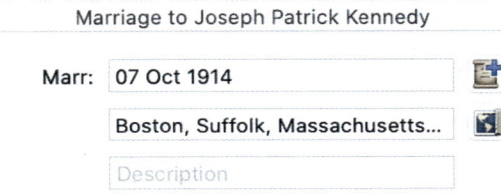

3 To enter more information for the couple, click the **Marriage to** button; then click a tab to enter facts, notes, or media items.

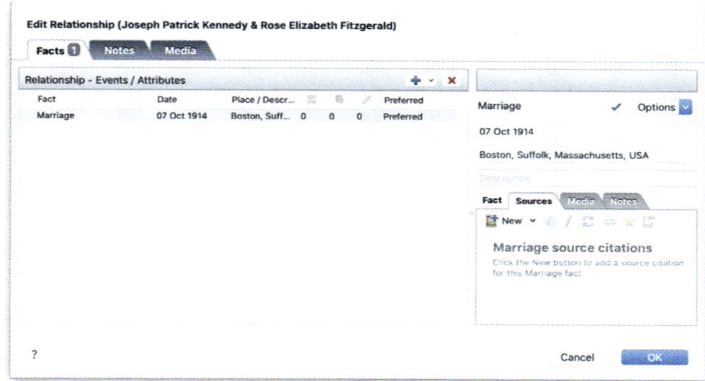

Adding a Child to a Family

1 In the family group view, click **Add Child**. Then type the child's name (first, middle, and last) and click **Done**.

> Tip: Family Tree Maker assumes that a child has the same last name as the father and automatically fills it in for you. You can ignore the suggested name by typing over it.

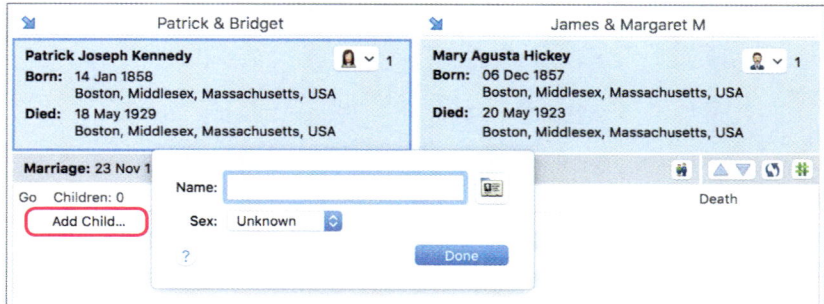

2 In the editing panel, select a gender and type any birth and death information you have for the child.

Changing the Sort Order of Children

You can change the order in which children appear in the family group view. For example, your direct ancestor can be displayed at the top of the list regardless of his or her birth order, or you can display all children by birth order. You can change the sort order of children only when the **Show blended families** option is turned off (see page 62 for more information).

1   Go to the **Tree** tab on the People workspace and select the appropriate family.
2   Select a child in the family group view.
3   Do one of the following:
    - Click the **Move child up** and **Move child down** buttons to move a child to a specific place in the order.
    - Click the **Sort children by birth order** button to display the children in their birth order. Choose whether you want to sort this family only or all children in your tree. Then click **OK**.

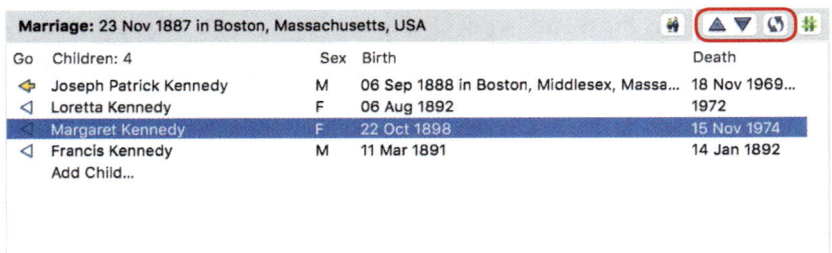

Adding Parents

When you've added your spouse and children to your tree, you'll want to continue with your parents, grandparents, great-grandparents, and so on.

1. Go to the **Tree** tab on the People workspace. In the Index or tree viewer, select the individual you want to add a father or mother to.

2. Click **Add Father** or **Add Mother** in the tree viewer.

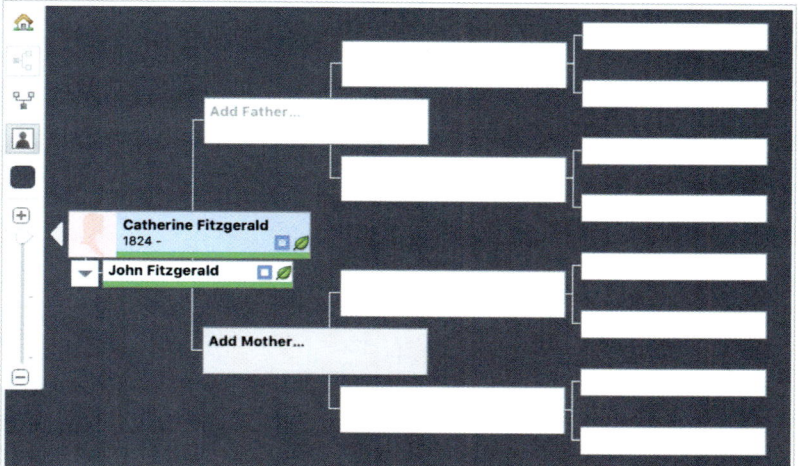

3. Type the parent's name (first, middle, and last) and click **Done**. Don't forget to use maiden names for women.

4. In the editing panel, select a gender and type any birth and death information you have for the individual.

Adding More Details

So far, you've only entered basic facts for a person. Now you can add more details and notes.

Adding a Fact

In addition to birth and death events, you can add facts such as christening, immigration, and occupations.

Note: You'll want to record the source of each fact. A source is what you learned the information from—a book or historical record, for example. For more information see Chapter 5 (page 79).

1 Go to the **Tree** tab on the People workspace and select the appropriate individual. Then click the **Person** tab.

2 Click the **Facts** button to open the **Individual & Shared Facts** pane, which shows the facts you've already entered for the individual.

3 Click the **Add Fact** button in the top-right corner of the Individual & Shared Facts pane. The Add Fact dialog opens.

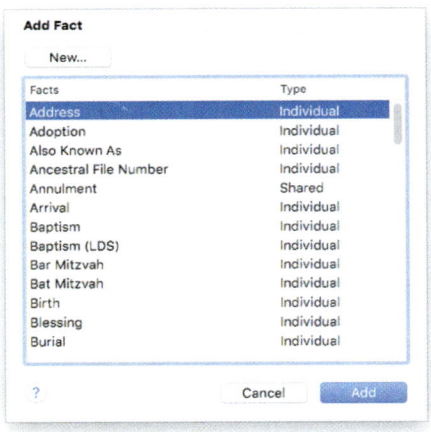

4 Select a fact in the list and click **Add**.

Tip: You can add your own fact types (for example, college graduation) by clicking the **New** button.

Notice that the editing panel on the right side of the workspace displays the appropriate fields for the fact.

5 Fill in the **Date**, **Place**, **Description**, and **Value** fields as necessary.

Note: Don't forget to add a source for each fact. For instructions see "Creating Sources" on page 81.

Common Facts

In addition to birth, marriage, and death events, here are some facts you will probably encounter as you record your family history:

- **Address.** Addresses can be useful for keeping contact information for living relatives or for recording where an ancestor lived.
- **Also Known As.** Use this fact if an individual was known by a nickname rather than his or her given name.
- **Baptism and Christening.** Birth records are not always available, so these records become useful because they may be the earliest available information you can find for an ancestor.
- **Burial.** If you can't find a death record for an individual, but you have a burial record, you can use this information to estimate a person's death date.
- **Cause of Death/Medical Condition.** Knowing your family's health history may help you prevent and treat illnesses that run in families. You can record an individual's cause of death or enter details you know about an individual's medical history, from long-term illness to simple things such as "suffers from allergies."
- **Emigration/Immigration.** Emigration and immigration records are the first step in finding your ancestors in their homeland. Use these facts to record dates, ports of departure and arrival, and even ship names.
- **Physical Description.** Although not necessarily beneficial to your research, a physical description of an ancestor can be a fascinating addition to any family history.
- **Title.** If an individual has a title, such as Captain, you can use it to tell the difference between the individual and others with the same or similar names.

Copying and Pasting Facts

You can copy a fact from one person and paste it into the facts for another person. This is useful if several family members share the same fact (such as residence), and you don't want to create a new fact for each person.

1   Go to the **Tree** tab on the People workspace and select the appropriate individual. Then click the **Person** tab.

2   Click the **Facts** button.

3   Control-click the fact you want to copy and choose **Copy** from the shortcut menu.

4   Use the mini pedigree tree above the workspace to go the person you want to add the fact to.

5   Control-click the **Individual & Shared Facts** pane and choose **Paste**. A list of immediate family members appears.

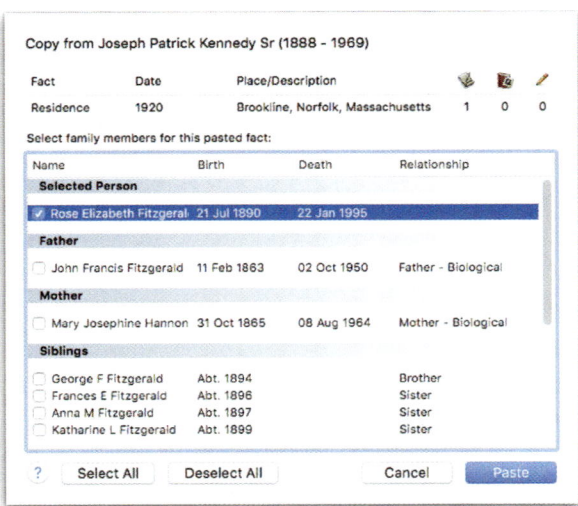

6 Select the checkbox next to each person you want to add the fact to; then click **Paste**.

Adding Alternate Facts

As you add facts, you may discover conflicting information about the same life event, such as two birth dates. When you have multiple facts for the same event, one fact will be "preferred," and the others will be "alternates." In figure 4-1 the birth has one preferred fact and one alternate fact.

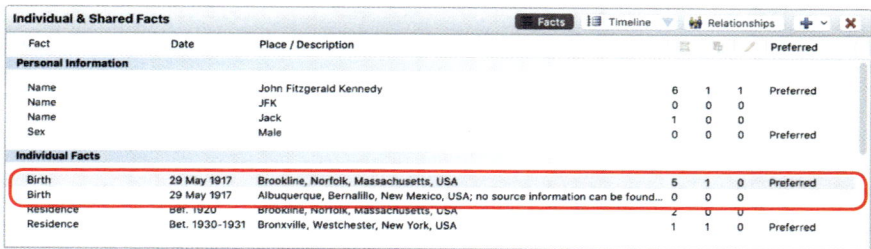

Figure 4-1. Alternate facts on the Person tab.

Note: An alternate fact doesn't have to include conflicting information. For example, you may have three Address facts for an individual, all of which are correct.

Choosing a Preferred Fact

When you enter multiple facts for the same life event, you'll have to choose which fact is preferred. Typically, this is the fact that is the most accurate or complete. Preferred facts are shown by default in the editing panel, charts, and reports.

1 Go to the **Tree** tab on the People workspace and select the appropriate individual. Then click the **Person** tab.

2 Select the fact you want to make preferred.

3 In the editing panel, click the **Options** button and choose **Preferred** from the pop-up menu.

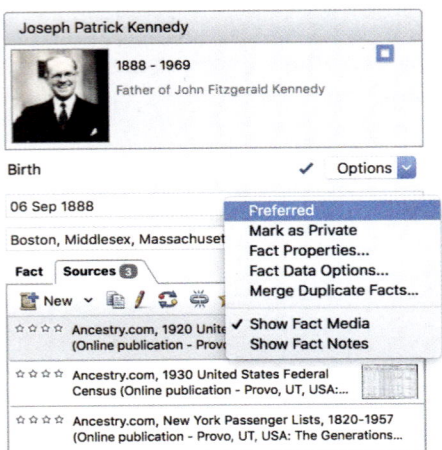

The Preferred column in the **Individual & Shared Facts** pane now shows the fact as preferred.

Tip: You can also set a preferred fact by Control-clicking the fact and choosing **Set As Preferred** from the shortcut menu.

Making a Fact Private

You may enter facts that you don't want to share with other family members or researchers. If you make a fact private, you can choose whether or not to include it in reports and when you export a tree.

1 Go to the **Tree** tab on the People workspace and select the appropriate individual. Then click the **Person** tab.

2 Click **Facts**; then select the fact you want to make private.

3 In the editing panel, click the **Options** button and choose **Mark as Private** from the pop-up menu.

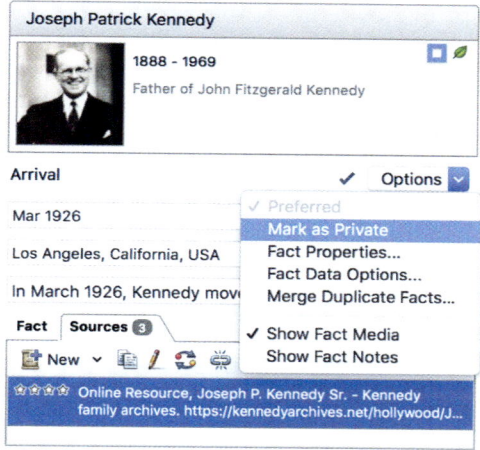

A lock icon 🔒 will appear next to the private fact in the Individual & Shared Facts pane (fig 4-2).

Figure 4-2. A lock icon indicates that a fact is private.

Adding a Note for an Individual

You may have family stories, legends, or research resources that you want to refer to occasionally. Family Tree Maker lets you enter this type of information in notes—up to 1MB of space, or about 200 printed pages, per note.

Tip: If you are entering notes from another document on your computer, you can "copy and paste" so you don't have to retype existing text.

Entering a Personal Note

Personal notes may be as simple as a physical description or as lengthy as a transcript of an interview with your grandmother.

Note: You should *not* record source information on the Notes tab; if you do, the information won't be included in source reports.

1. Go to the **Tree** tab on the People workspace and select the appropriate individual. Then click the **Person** tab.

2. Click the **Notes** tab at the bottom of the **Person** tab. Then click the **Person note** button in the notes toolbar.

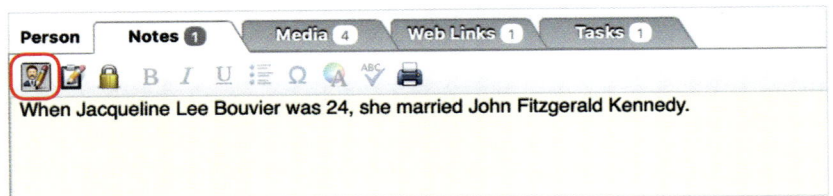

3. Place the cursor in the notes area and enter your text. You can press **Return** to start a new paragraph.

Entering a Research Note

Sometimes a record or family story will give you clues that can help you learn more about your family. You can create research notes to remind you of the next steps you want to take.

1. Go to the **Tree** tab on the People workspace and select the appropriate individual. Then click the **Person** tab.

2 Click the **Notes** tab at the bottom of the Person tab. Then click the **Research note** button in the Notes toolbar.

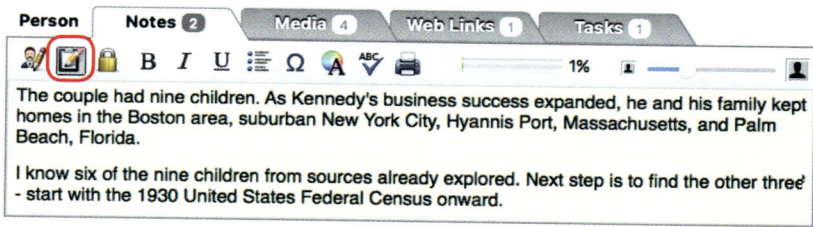

3 Place the cursor in the notes area and enter your text.

Changing a Note's Display Size

You can resize your notes to make the text larger and easier to read or make the text smaller to fit more words on the tab. Simply drag the slider on the right side of the Notes toolbar (fig. 4-3). This only changes how the note is displayed; it does not change how it prints.

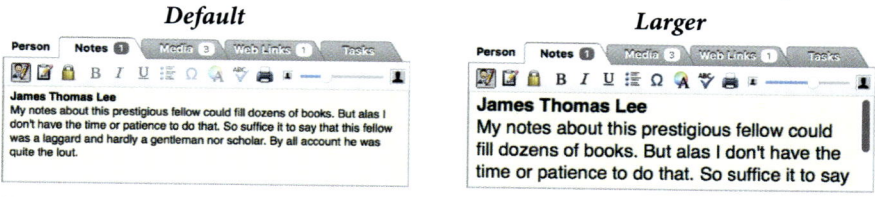

Figure 4-3. A slider on the Notes tab lets you resize the text.

Printing a Note

To print a note, click the printer button on the Notes toolbar. Select your printing options and click **Print**.

Tip: You can also create a report of any notes you've entered in your tree. Go to the Publish workspace and select **Person Reports**. Then double-click **Notes Report**.

Making a Note Private

You may have information about a relative that you don't want to share with other researchers. If you make a note private, you can choose whether or not to include it in reports and when you export a tree.

After entering a note, click the **Mark as Private** 🔒 button in the notes toolbar. You can tell the note has been marked as private because the lock icon will have a border around it.

Not Private *Private*

Figure 4-4. The Mark as Private button in its two states.

Adding Web Links for an Individual

If you want to keep track of a website you found about an ancestor or an interesting collection of online maps, you can create a Web link so you can easily access it again.

1 Go to the **Tree** tab on the People workspace and select the appropriate individual. Then click the **Person** tab.

2 Click the **Web Links** tab at the bottom of the **Person** tab. Then click the **New** button in the toolbar.

3 Enter the address for the website, a name for the link, and then click **Add**.

Note: While Family Tree Maker Web links cannot be synced with Web links in your Ancestry tree (see "Differences Between FTM and Ancestry Trees" on page 254), you can use TreeVault cloud services to view created Web links from your FTM tree in the free Family Tree Maker Connect app on a smartphone or tablet.

Rich Color Coding

When you are working on a large tree, it can sometimes be difficult to trace family lines through the generations without creating a relationship report. To help you see lineages at a glance, Family Tree Maker allows you to use color coding to mark not only all the direct-line ancestors and descendants of any given person, but each ancestor's descendants as well. The coloring scheme is based on the classic four-color system created by Mary E. V. Hill, but has been further extended to give you more coloring options.

You can highlight a selected person's descendants with one color and his or her ancestors with another. Or, for ancestors and their descendants, you can use a four-color system to apply different colors to four different lineages: the paternal father's line, the paternal mother's line, the maternal father's line, and the maternal mother's line.

You can apply one of the four color choices to one parent, and another four color palette to another parent, producing the full eight colors in the tree viewer. You can also mark any individual with a color. This can be useful to highlight a person for whom additional research is needed, for example, or conversely, a person whose information you consider to be complete.

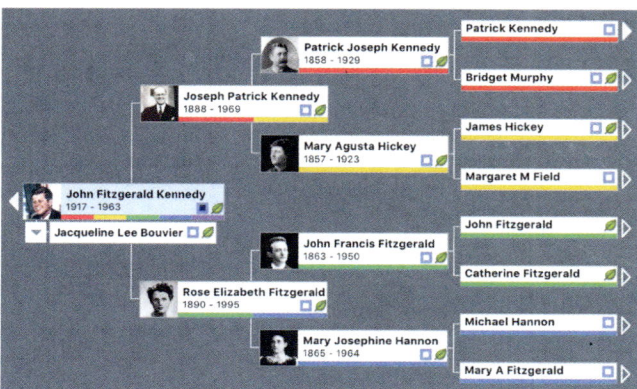

Applying Color Coding to a Person

1 Go to the **Tree** tab on the **People** workspace.

2 Select the person you want to highlight or whose ancestors and descendants you want to highlight.

3 Click the **Color Coding** button above the editing panel.

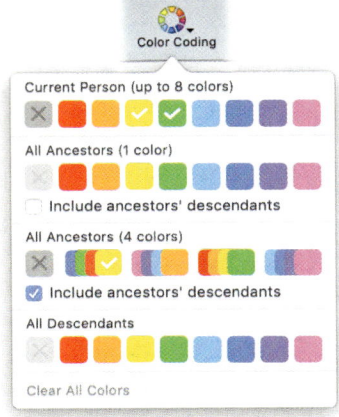 

4 Click a color or a color group for the type of individuals to whom you want to apply color coding: **Current Person, All Ancestors (1 color), All Ancestors (4 colors),** or **All Descendants.** For the Current Person, you can select up to eight different colors.

5 For ancestors, color coding is applied to all those in direct ascending line from the selected person. If you want to apply color to all descendants of all ancestors as well, select the **Include ancestors' descendants** checkbox.

Colored bars now appear on all the relevant person thumbnails in the tree viewer. Colored dots are also shown next to the corresponding names in the Index and in the lists of people on the Places, Media, and Sources workspaces. If you don't want the colored dots to appear in the Index, click the **Show additional data in index** button in the top-right corner of the Index, and then click the **Color Coding** option so that the checkmark next to it disappears.

If you have applied color coding for several selected individuals in your tree, there may be some people who belong to more than one family line—in this case all the corresponding colors will be displayed on those individuals' thumbnails. To find out why a person is marked with a particular color, hold the pointer over the colored bar on his or her thumbnail. A help tag will appear with the explanation.

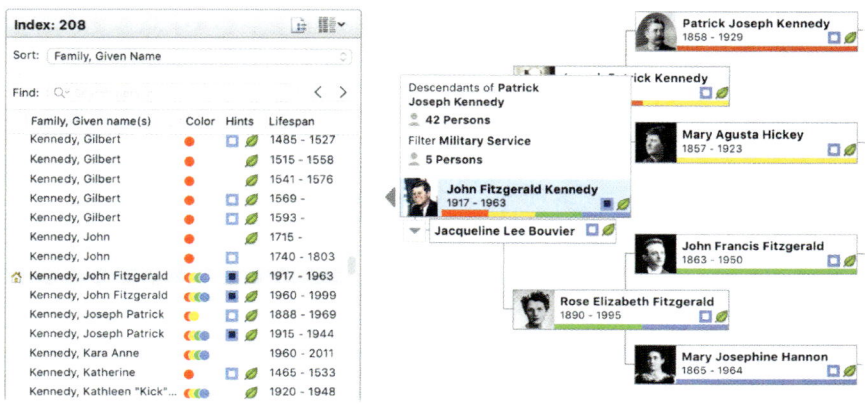

Another great way to use Color Coding is as an attribute of a certain criterion—in other words, an additional, at-a-glance filter. For example, you can create a filter of all individuals who served in the military, or lived in a certain location, then assign a color to that attribute and save your filter. That allows you to easily see the people who satisfy that criterion both in the Index panel, and in the tree viewer. To learn more about creating filters, see page 14.

Tip: For more information, visit ftm.support/color.

Removing Color Coding

1. On the **Tree** tab of the **People** workspace, select a person to whom color coding has been applied.
2. Click the **Color Coding** button above the editing panel.
3. Click the **No Color** ✖ button for the color coding that you want to remove.

To remove all color coding from your tree, including color coding added with Smart Filters, click the **Color Coding** button above the editing panel, and then click **Clear All Colors**.

Working with Relationships

As you dig deeper into your family history you will discover individuals who marry multiple times, divorces, adoptions, and other special situations. Family Tree Maker can handle all different types of relationships.

Using the Combined Family View

The family group view on the People workspace displays a couple and their mutual children. You can change this view so it displays all children associated with the couple, including children from previous marriages and relationships.

Note: When you display a "blended family" in the family group view, you cannot change the sort order of the children; they will be listed chronologically by birth date.

1. Go to the **Tree** tab on the People workspace and select the appropriate family.
2. Click the **Show blended families** button in the family group view.

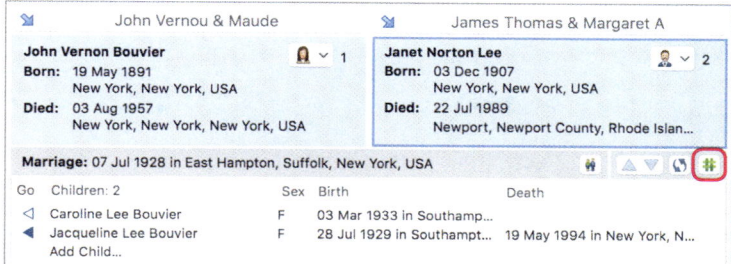

The combined family group view now displays all the children of both individuals. An icon to the left of the child's name indicates whether he or she is the child of the father, the mother, or both parents.

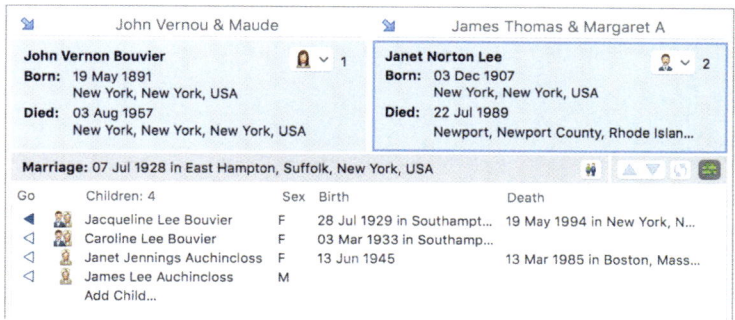

3 To return to the traditional family group view, simply click the **Show blended families** button again.

Viewing an Individual's Family Relationships

You can see all the members of an individual's family at a glance—spouses, children, parents, and siblings.

1 Select the appropriate individual and go to the **Person** tab on the People workspace.

2 Click the **Relationships button.** You can now see parents, siblings, spouses, and children entered for the individual.

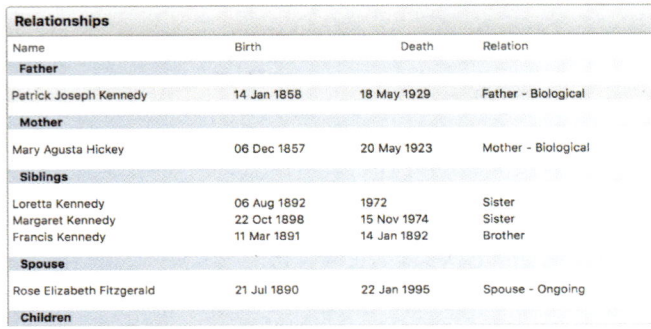

Adding Additional Spouses

If an individual in your family has been married more than once, you'll want to enter all additional spouses.

1 Go to the **Tree** tab on the People workspace and select the appropriate individual.

2 In the family group view, click the **Choose spouse** button next to the individual. From the pop-up menu, you can view the existing spouse or add a new spouse.

3 Choose **Add Spouse**.

4 Type the name of the new spouse and click **Add**. Family Tree Maker displays a new family group view—this time with the new spouse.

5 To view the first spouse again, click the **Choose spouse** button and choose his or her name from the pop-up menu.

Choosing a Preferred Spouse

If you enter more than one spouse for an individual, you need to indicate who is the preferred spouse. (Usually this is the spouse whose children are in your direct family line.) The preferred spouse will become the default spouse displayed in the family group view, tree viewer, and charts and reports.

1 Go to the **Tree** tab on the People workspace and select the appropriate individual.

2 Click the **Person** tab; then click the **Relationships** button. You should see two or more names listed under the Spouses heading.

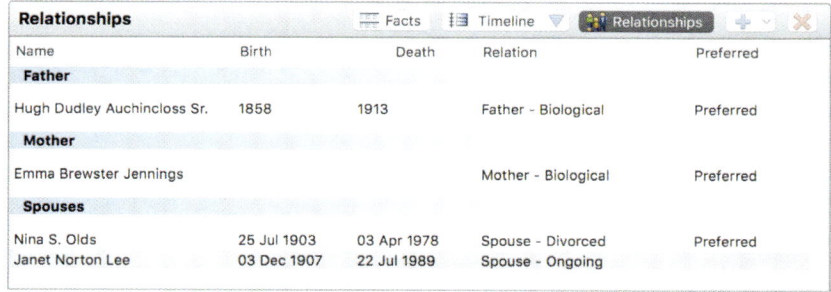

3 Select the individual you want to be the preferred spouse. Then, in the editing panel, select the **Preferred spouse** checkbox.

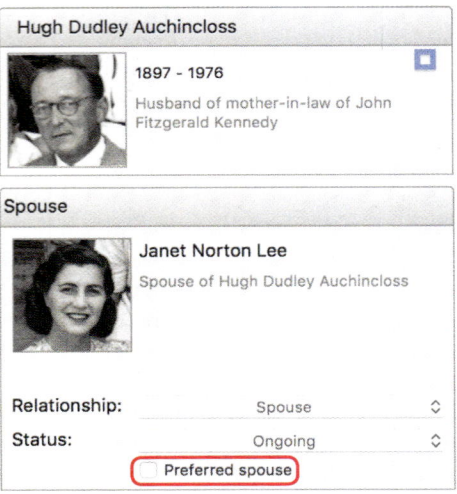

Switching Between Spouses

Family Tree Maker displays a person's preferred spouse by default, but you can switch to other spouses when necessary.

1 Go to the **Tree** tab on the People workspace and select the appropriate individual.

2 In the family group view, click the **Choose spouse** button next to the individual. From the pop-up menu, choose the spouse you want to view.

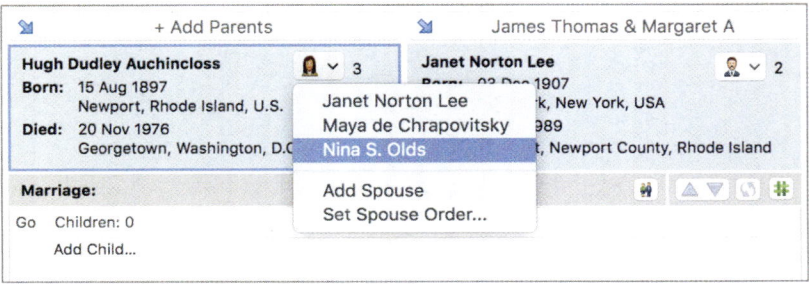

Choosing a Type of Relationship for a Couple

You can choose what type of relationship a couple has (e.g., partner, friend, spouse).

1   Go to the **Tree** tab on the People workspace and select the appropriate couple.
2   Click the **Person** tab; then click **Relationships**.
3   Select the spouse's name. Then, in the editing panel, choose a relationship type from the **Relationship** pop-up menu.

Choosing a Status for a Couple's Relationship

The status of a couple's relationship will be "Ongoing" by default. If necessary, you can change this status. For example, if a couple gets a divorce, you can indicate this with their relationship status.

1   Go to the **Tree** tab on the People workspace and select the appropriate couple.
2   Click the **Person** tab; then click **Relationships**.
3   Select the spouse's name. Then, in the editing panel, choose a status from the **Status** pop-up menu.

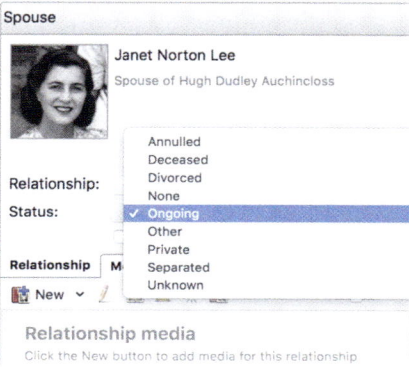

Choosing a Parent-Child Relationship

You can indicate a child's relationship to each of his or her parents (e.g., biological, adopted, foster).

1. Go to the **Tree** tab on the People workspace and select the appropriate individual.
2. Click the **Person** tab; then click **Relationships**.
3. Select the father's or mother's name. Then, in the editing panel, choose a relationship from the **Relationship** pop-up menu.

Adding an Unrelated Individual

As you search for family members, you might find a person you suspect is related to you, but you have no proof. You can add this person to your tree without linking them to a specific family. Later on, if you find out that they are related, you can easily link them to the correct family.

1. Click the down arrow next to the **People** button on the main toolbar, and then choose **Add Person** > **Add Unrelated Person** from the pop-up menu.
2. Type the person's name (first, middle, and last). Then choose a gender from the pop-up menu and click **Add**.

Viewing a Timeline

Timelines can be a great tool to put the life of your ancestor in context—historical and otherwise. Family Tree Maker has three timeline variations: events in an individual's life; events in the lives of their immediate family (such as birth, marriage, and death); and historical events.

1. Select the appropriate individual on the **Tree** tab of the People workspace, and then click the **Person** tab. Click **Timeline**.

A chronological list of events is displayed—along with the person's age at the time of each event.

2   To display events for immediate family members, click the arrow next to the **Timeline** button and choose **Show Family Events**. Events for the individual are indicated by green markers, and events in his or her family are indicated by pink markers.

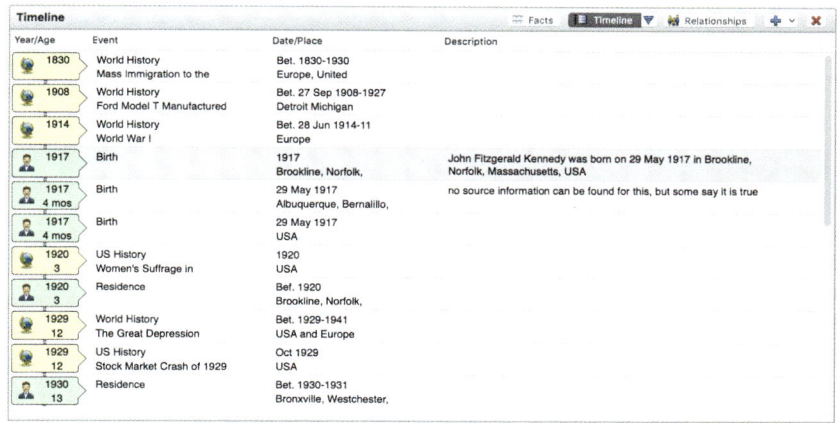

3   To display historical events, click the arrow next to the **Timeline** button and choose **Show Historical Events**. Historical events are indicated by yellow markers.

4   To learn more about a historical event, select the event. A description appears on the right side of the workspace.

Note: Family Tree Maker comes with default historical events that you can edit, delete, and add to. To learn more, see "Managing Historical Events" on page 298.

Creating Smart Stories

Smart Stories is a tool that helps you quickly create stories about individuals and families using the facts, notes, and photos in your tree. You can also use the TreeVault Historical Weather service with Smart Stories to add automatically generated descriptions of what the weather was like when events in the story occurred. Smart Stories are linked to the tree, so you can edit a fact and the text in your story will be updated automatically. For example, if you find out that grandfather's birth date is different than you thought, change it in your tree and the story will be updated at the same time.

Family Tree Maker can automatically generate a Smart Story for an individual. It will have an image of the person (if you've added a portrait), the individual's immediate family (children, spouses, parents, and siblings), and their life events. You can also create your own Smart Stories, starting with a blank page and adding your own images and text.

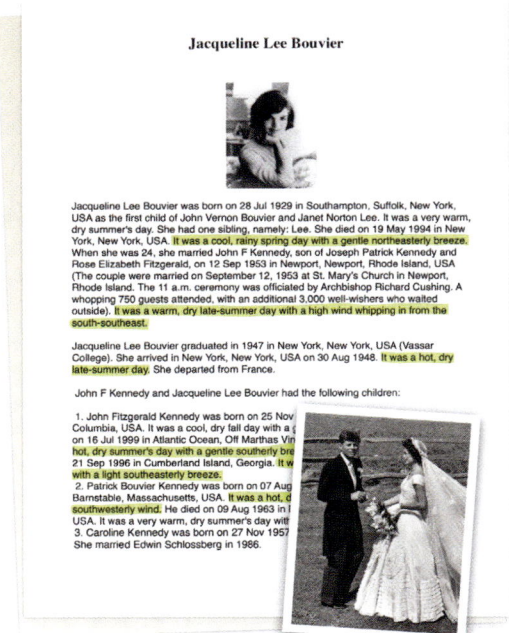

You can create Smart Stories on an individual's Media tab, the Media workspace, or the Publish workspace. All stories can be printed, exported, and included in family history books; however, if you upload your tree to Ancestry, Smart Stories created on the Publish workspace are considered reports and won't be uploaded.

Creating a Smart Story as a Media Item

1 Select the individual you want to create a Smart Story for.
2 Do one of the following:
   - Go to the **Person** tab for an individual and click the **Media** tab at the bottom of the window. Click the arrow next to the **New** button and choose **Create a New Smart Story** from the pop-up menu.
   - Go to the Media workspace. Then Control-click a media item and choose **Create a New Smart Story** from the pop-up menu.

3 If you want Family Tree Maker to generate the story for you, click **Auto-populate Smart Story**. To create your own story, click **Start with blank page**.
4 Click **OK**.

Creating a Smart Story as a Report

1 Go to the **Collection** tab on the Publish workspace. In **Publication Types**, click **Other**.

2 Double-click the **Smart Story** icon. The editor opens.

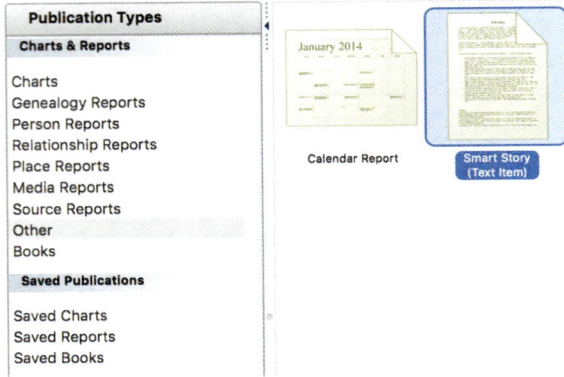

Tip: To access this Smart Story later, go to the Publish workspace and select **Saved Reports**.

Including a Short Biography

1 Place the cursor where you want to add a biography.

2 Click the **Facts** button on the Smart Stories toolbar. Then choose **Personal Biography** from the pop-up menu.

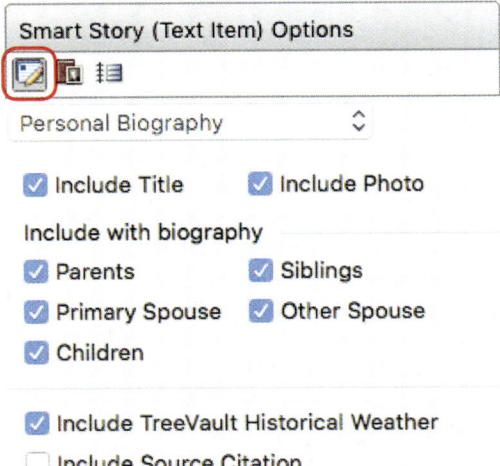

3 By default, a title, photo, and the individual's immediate family (children, spouses, parents, and siblings) will be included. Deselect the checkboxes for items you don't want to include.

4 If you want to include historical weather reports in the biography, make sure the **Include TreeVault Historical Weather** checkbox is selected. A brief summary of the weather conditions on the day of the event will be included after the main fact sentence—for example, "It was a hot summer's day."

5 Click the **Insert** button.

Including Facts

1 Place the cursor on the page where you want to add a fact.

2 Click the **Facts** button on the Smart Stories toolbar. Then choose **Facts** from the pop-up menu.

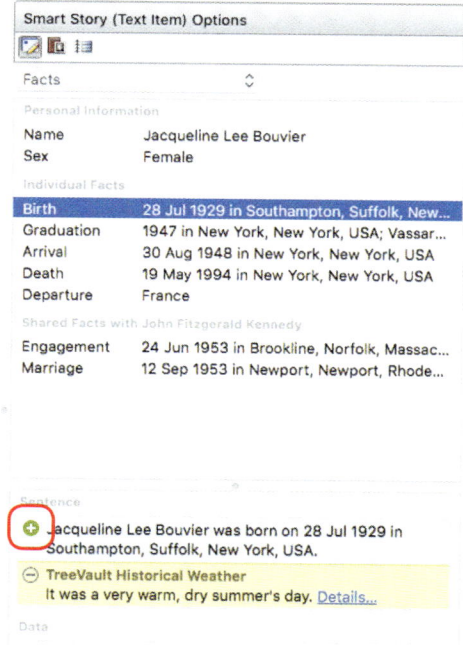

74   Part 2: Building a Tree

3   Select the fact you want to add to your story. Below the fact, you'll see options of how the fact will be entered. You can create a sentence or add specific details.

 4   If historical weather data is available for the date and place of the fact, the TreeVault Historical Weather block will appear just below the fact sentence. Click the "plus" button to reveal the historical weather summary. Click **Details** to open the Historical Weather window showing the fact's location on a map and more detailed weather information for the given date.

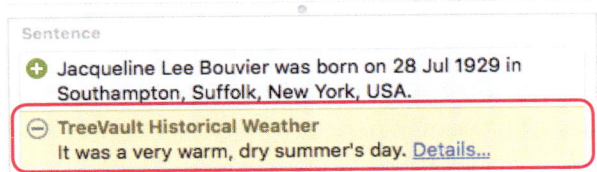

5   Drag the text to your document or click the "plus" button.

Tip: To include the facts, media items, or notes from another person in your tree, click the Index of Individuals icon next to the Pedigree Navigation bar at the top of the window and choose a different person.

Including Sources

1   Place the cursor on the page where you want to add a source.

2   Click the **Facts** button on the Smart Stories toolbar. Then choose **Fact Sources** from the pop-up menu.

3   Click the fact that has the source you want to add to your story. Below you'll see any associated source citations. If more than one source citation exists for a fact, you can choose it from a pop-up menu.

Chapter 4: Entering Family Information   75

4 Drag the text to your document or click the "plus" button.

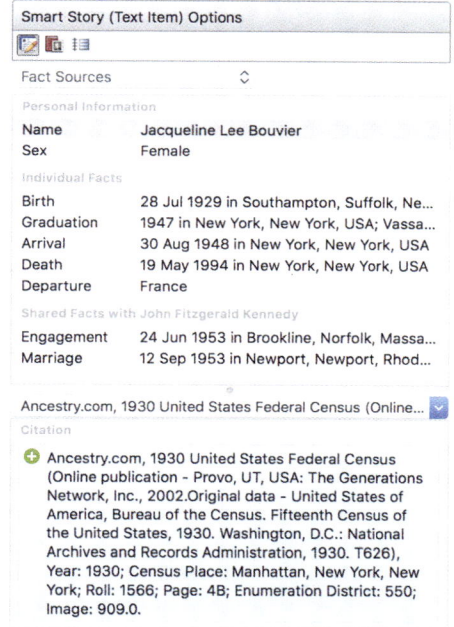

Including Notes

1 Place the cursor on the page where you want to add a note.

2 Click the **Facts** button on the Smart Stories toolbar. Then choose **Notes** from the pop-up menu.

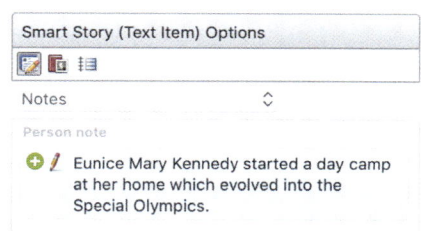

3 Drag the text to your document or click the "plus" button.

Including Images

1. Place the cursor on the page where you want the media item.
2. Click the **Media** button on the Smart Stories toolbar.

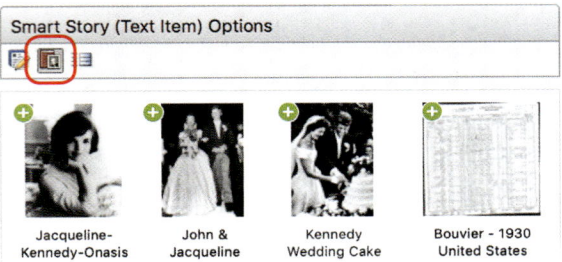

3. Drag the image to your document or click the "plus" button.

Creating Timelines

You can use facts in a person's life and historical events to create a timeline.

1. Place the cursor on the page where you want to add an event.
2. Click the **Timeline** button on the Smart Stories toolbar. Then choose an event type from the pop-up menu.
3. Click the event you want to add to your story. Below the event, you'll see options of how the event will be entered. You can create a sentence or add specific details.

 4. If historical weather data is available for the date and place of the event, a TreeVault Historical Weather block will appear in the event sentence section on the right. Click the "plus" button to reveal the historical weather summary. Click **Details** to open the Historical Weather window showing the location of the event on a map and more detailed weather information for the given date.

5 Drag the text to your document or click the "plus" button.

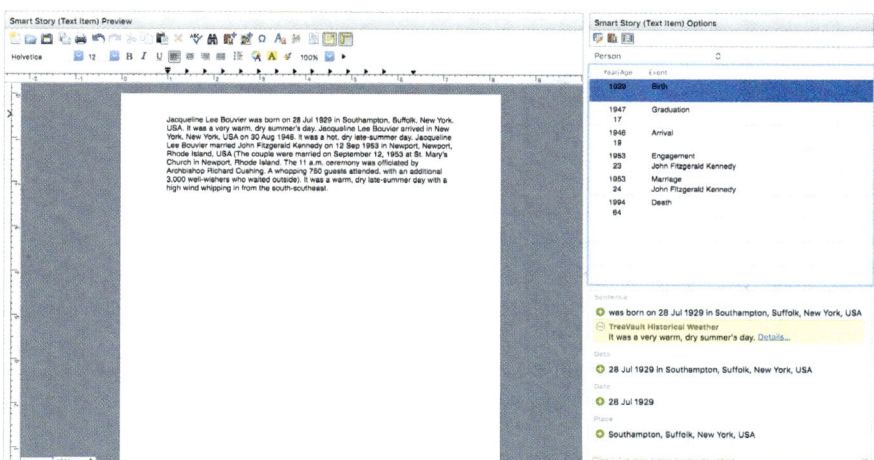

Editing Smart Stories Text

Smart Stories pulls text directly from your tree. That means you don't have to worry about continually redoing your story; if information in your tree changes, your story will be updated automatically.

You can also edit text in Smart Stories. But, be aware that the text will no longer be linked to your tree and will not be updated automatically.

1 Move the cursor over the text you want to add, edit, or delete. You can identify which text is linked to your tree because it will be highlighted.

> Jacqueline Lee Bouvier was born on 28 Jul 1929 in Southampton, New York as the second child of John Vernon Bouvier and Janet Norton Lee. She had one sibling, namely: Lee. She died on 19 May 1994 in New York. When she was 23, she married John Fitzgerald Kennedy, son of Joseph Patrick Kennedy and Rose Elizabeth Fitzgerald, on 12 Sep 1953 in Newport, Newport, Rhode Island, USA (The couple were married on September 12, 1953 at St. Mary's Church in Newport, Rhode Island. The 11 a.m. ceremony was officiated by Archbishop Richard Cushing. A whopping 750 guests attended, with an additional 3,000 well-wishers who waited outside).

2. Double-click the text block. A message asks whether you want to convert the text to free form text (text that can be edited but is not linked to your tree).
3. Click **Yes** and edit the text.

Chapter Five

Documenting Your Research

Documenting sources—recording where you discovered a fact—is one of the most important aspects of your research. Sources are valuable for many reasons. When you cite a source, you are proving to others which records you based your facts on; if you eventually share your research with your family or other researchers, your family history may be judged for accuracy based on your sources. If your sources are detailed and correct, others will be able to follow your research footsteps.

Each time you add information to your tree, you'll want to create a source and source citation that describe where you found the info. For example, if you find your father's birthplace on his World War I draft card, you'll create a source for the record when you add his birth date and birthplace.

Understanding Sources and Source Citations

If you're new to family history, you may not be familiar with sources and source citations. This section gives an explanation of each and also shows you some examples.

- A source is the unchanging facts about an item; for example, the author, title, and publication information for a book.

- Source citations are individual details that explain where you found a fact, such as the page number in a book.

To help you understand how sources and source citations work together, let's look at an example from the 1930 United States Federal Census. First, you would create a source for the census that includes information like this:

- A title—1930 United States Federal Census
- Where you located the source—www.ancestry.com
- Publishing details—Bureau of the Census. Washington, D.C.: National Archives and Records Administration, 1930.

As you can see, these details about the 1930 census won't change regardless of who or what you find in the records. However, because you'll find families and individuals in different locations throughout the census, each census fact will need its own source citation. A source citation for an individual in the 1930 census might include this information:

- Source—1930 United States Federal Census
- Source citation—Harold Reed household, Santa Clara Township, Santa Clara County, California. Roll: 219; Page: 14A; Enumeration district: 110.

A source citation for a different individual in the 1930 census might look like this. (Notice the source is the same as the previous example.)

- Source—1930 United States Federal Census
- Source citation—Michael Reed household, Kokomo Township, Beaver County, Oklahoma. Roll: 1892; Page: 5B; Enumeration district: 26.

Both individuals can be found in the 1930 census (the source), but the source citation for each individual has changed because the individuals were recorded in different places in the source.

Creating Sources

Family Tree Maker lets you create sources in two ways: using templates or a basic format. Source templates are useful because you don't have to guess which details need to be entered. Choose the type of source you're creating (for example an obituary) and Family Tree Maker displays the relevant fields. If you don't want to use a template (for example, because you have your own system of citation or you can't find a matching template), you can create a source by completing the standard fields (author, title, and publisher) in the basic source format.

Adding a Source for a Fact

Usually, you will add a source as you create a source citation for a fact or event. This section focuses on adding a source while entering facts on the Tree tab in the People workspace.

Note: You need to create only one source for each item; you can use a source for as many source citations as necessary.

1   Go to the **Tree** tab on the People workspace.

2   In the editing panel, click the **New source citation** button next to the fact you want to add a source to. Then choose **Add New Source Citation** from the pop-up menu.

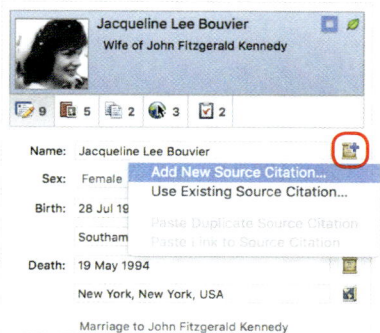

3 The Add Source Citation dialog opens. To create a source using a template, follow the instructions in "Creating a Source from a Template" below. To create your own source, refer to the "Creating a Source Using the Basic Format" section on page 85.

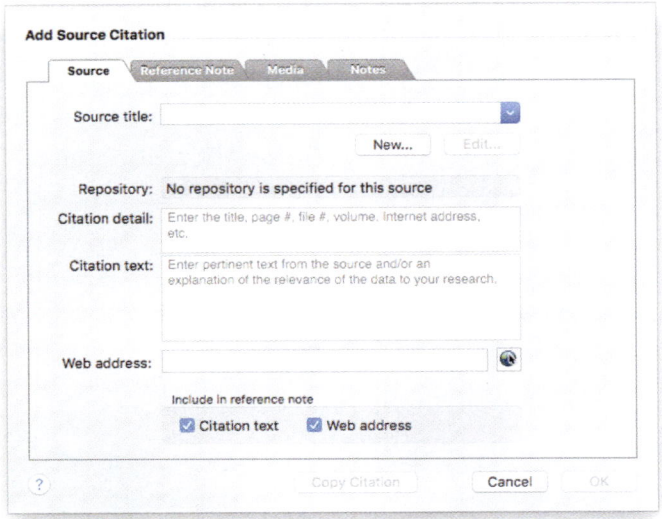

Using Source Templates

Family Tree Maker has more than 170 templates to help you source everything from embroidered samplers and other artifacts to online databases and vital records. These source templates are based on the QuickCheck models used in Elizabeth Shown Mills' book *Evidence Explained*—the premier reference for citing genealogy sources.

Creating a Source from a Template

Using a source template is simple. To determine which template you should use, type keywords and choose from a list of suggestions, or view a list of all available templates and choose the one that fits best.

To choose a template using keywords

1 Open the Add Source Citation dialog and click **New**. The Add Source dialog opens. (See "Adding a Source for a Fact" on page 81.)

2 Type a keyword in the **Source Template** field and choose a template from the pop-up menu. To narrow the list, type multiple keywords. For example, "property" brings up eleven results, while "property grant" brings up one result.

3 The fields that appear now reflect the template you've selected. Complete these fields as necessary and click **OK**.

Note: Some fields may be mandatory.

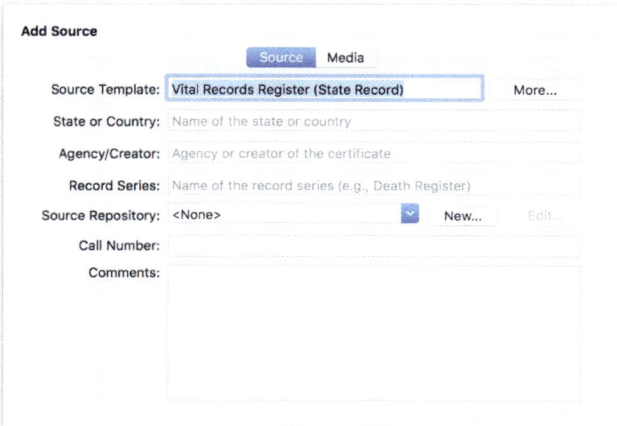

You can now add a source citation for the fact (see page 87).

To choose a template from a list

1 Access the Add Source Citation dialog and click **New**. (If you need help, see "Adding a Source for a Fact" on page 81.) The Add Source dialog opens.

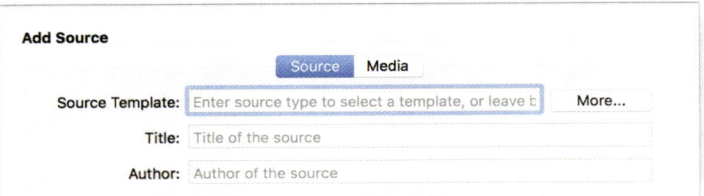

2 Click **More**.
3 In **Source group** select the group that most closely matches the item you're sourcing. The categories list changes to reflect the selected source group.

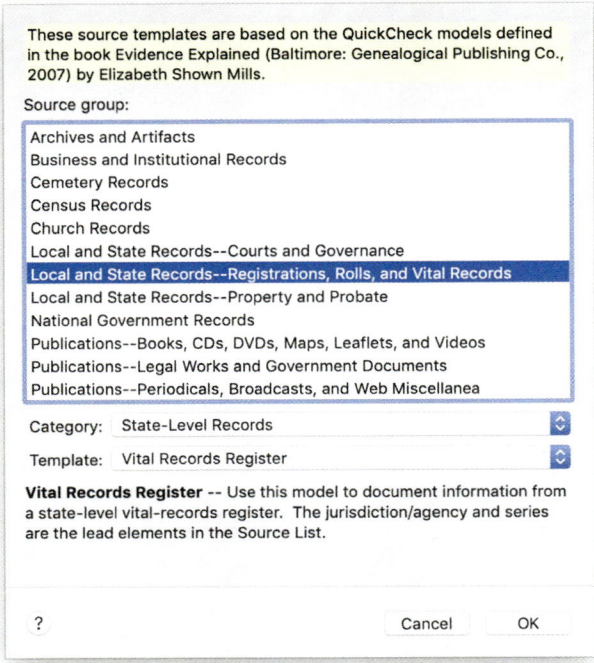

4 Choose the appropriate category from the **Category** pop-up menu. The templates list changes to reflect the selected source group and category.

5 Choose a template from the **Template** pop-up menu. A description of the template is displayed beneath its title.

6 Click **OK** to return to the Add Source dialog; the fields that appear now reflect the template you've selected. Complete these fields as necessary and click **OK**. You can now add a source citation for the fact (see page 87).

Creating a Source Using the Basic Format

If you don't want to use a source template, you can create a source by completing some standard fields (such as author, title, and publisher) in the basic source format.

1 Access the Add Source Citation dialog and click **New**. (If you need help, see "Adding a Source for a Fact" on page 81.) The Add Source dialog opens.

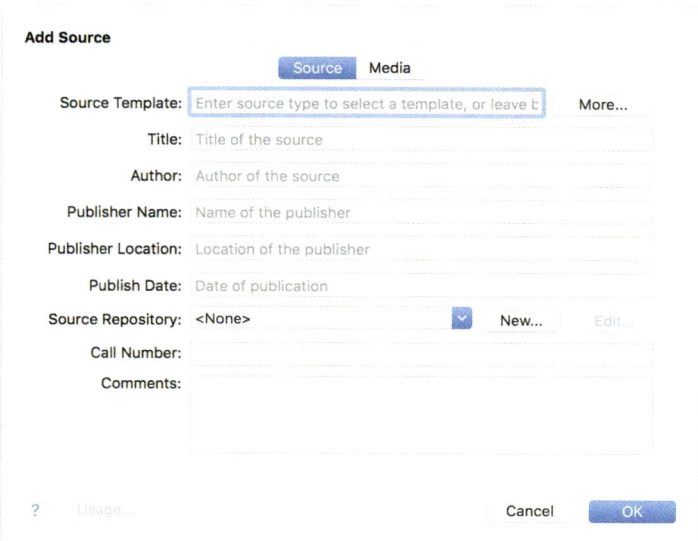

2 Complete the source fields as necessary:

- **Title.** Type the title of the source exactly as it appears in the source.
- **Author.** Type the author or originator's name.
- **Publisher Name.** Type the name of the publishing company.
- **Publisher Location.** Type the place of publication (for example, London, England).
- **Publish Date.** Type the copyright date for the source (usually only a year).
- **Source Repository.** Create a new repository or choose one from the pop-up menu.

  A repository is the location where an original source exists. This could be a library, archive, county courthouse, or cousin's home. To create a repository, click **New**. Then type the name, address, email, and phone number for the location.
- **Call Number.** Type a call number, if one exists.

  The call number is the number assigned to the source at the repository where you found the item. It could be a microfilm number, a Dewey Decimal system number, or some other numbering system unique to a particular library or archive.
- **Comments.** Type any comments about the source and the information found in it. This information will not print on your reports; it is for your personal reference. You might include a description of the item or even information about its legibility.

3 Click **OK**. You can now add a source citation for the fact (see page 87).

Creating Source Citations

After you create a source, you're ready to identify where in the source you found information by creating a source citation. Family Tree Maker lets you create source citations in a variety of ways; you'll need to decide which method is most effective for you.

Note: You can have more than one source citation for the same fact. For example, you might find an immigration date for your great-grandmother on a naturalization record and a census record. You should make source citations for both records.

Adding a New Source Citation

Each time you add a fact to your tree, you should take a minute to document where you discovered the information, whether it's a book in a library or a record you found online. When you create a new source citation, you'll link it to a source and add any additional identifying information such as page or volume number.

1 Access the Add Source Citation dialog. (If you need help, see "Adding a Source for a Fact" on page 81.)

2 Change the citation as necessary:

- **Source title.** From the pop-up menu, choose the source where you found the information.
- **Citation detail.** Type details about where you found the information in the source, such as a page number.
- **Citation text.** Type any additional information. For example, you might type a quote from a book or add a paraphrased summary of the source text.
- **Web address.** For online sources, type the URL where the information was found.

- **Include in reference note.** Select the **Citation text** checkbox to include text in the Citation text field in printed reference notes. Select the **Web address** checkbox to include the source's URL in printed reference notes. (The source title and citation detail are always included in reference notes.)

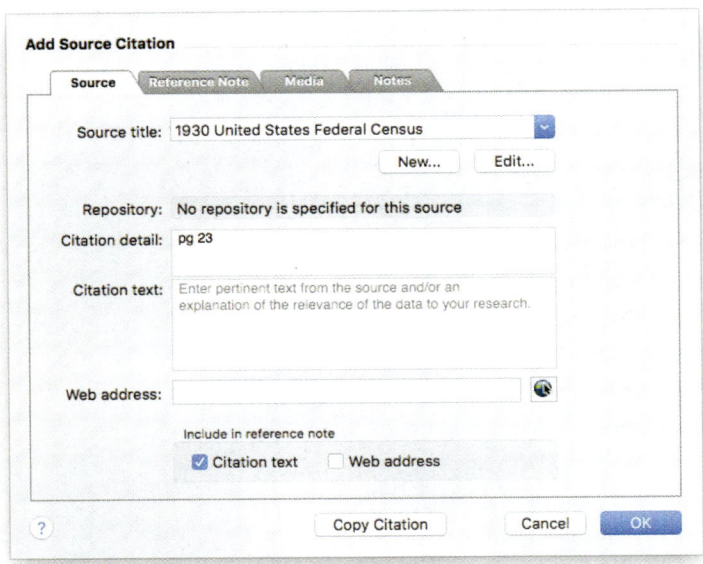

You can include a media item or note as part of a source citation. For instructions, see "Attaching a Media Item to a Source Citation" on page 92 and "Adding a Note to a Source Citation" on page 93.

3 Click **OK**.

Linking a Fact to an Existing Source Citation

If you've already created a citation for a source, such as a death certificate, you don't have to create another source citation for each fact or individual in the source. For example, if you find your grandparents' names and birthplaces in your aunt's death certificate, you don't have to create a new source citation for the death certificate; you can simply link these facts to the citation you already created.

1   Go to the **Tree** tab on the People workspace and select the appropriate individual. Then click the **Person** tab.

2   Select the fact you want to add a source citation to.

3   On the **Sources** tab of the editing panel, click the down arrow next to the **New** button and choose **Use Existing Source Citation** from the pop-up menu.

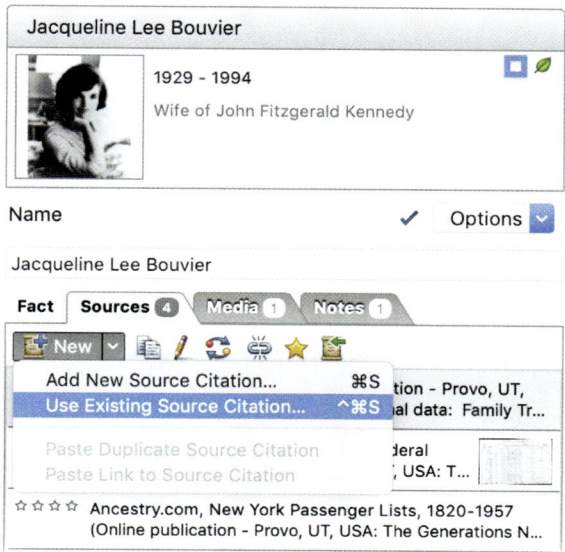

The **Find Source Citation** dialog opens.

4   Select the citation you want to link to from the list.

5   Click **Link to Citation**. The citation information now appears on the Sources tab.

Copying and Updating a Source Citation

If you need to create a source citation that is similar to one already in your tree, don't make a new citation. Simply copy the old one and update details as necessary (such as a page number). For example, if several family members are in the same city directory for Cleveland, Ohio, you can create a source citation for one family, then copy and update the source citation for other families in the directory.

1   Go to the **Tree** tab on the People workspace and select the appropriate individual. Then click the **Person** tab.

2   Select the fact you want to add a source citation to.

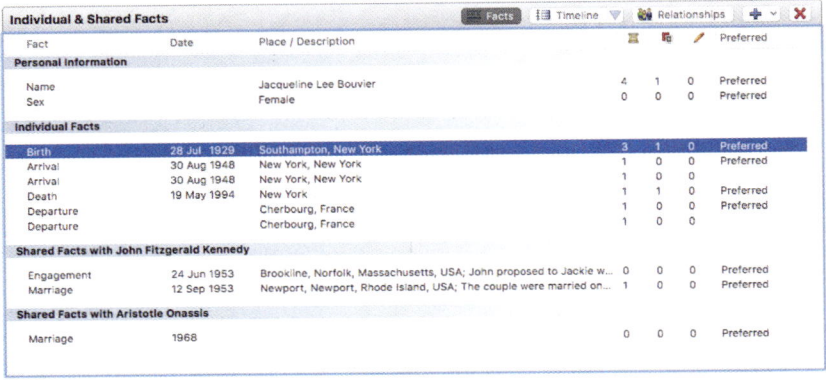

3   On the **Sources** tab of the editing panel, click the down arrow next to the **New** button and choose **Use Existing Source Citation** from the pop-up menu. The Find Source Citation dialog opens.

Chapter 5: Documenting Your Research   91

4 Select the citation you want to copy from the list.

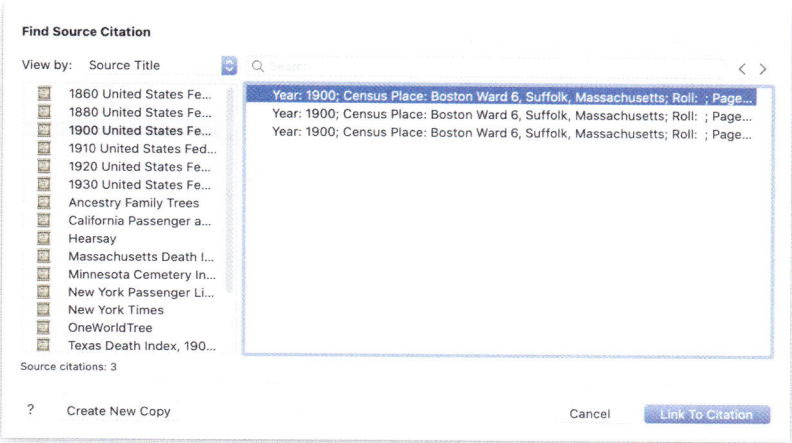

5 Click **Create New Copy**. A citation link appears on the **Sources** tab. Now you can edit the citation without affecting the original.

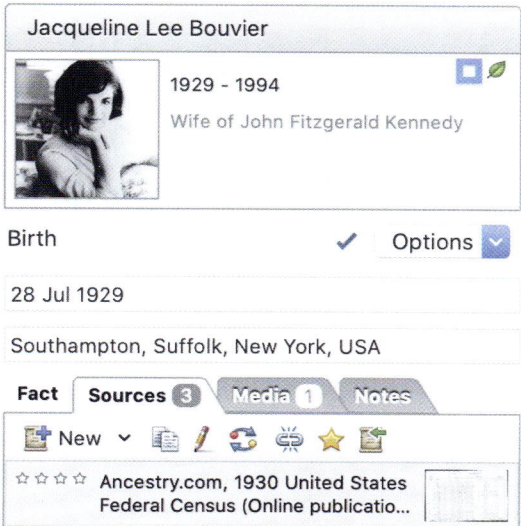

6 Double-click the source citation to open it in an editing dialog. Make any necessary changes and click **OK**.

Replacing a Source Citation

If you need to replace a source citation with another one that is already in your tree, follow the same steps as for linking a fact to an existing citation (see page 89), but click the **Replace source citation** button on the **Sources** tab.

The **Find Source Citation** dialog will open, and you will be able to choose another citation.

Attaching a Media Item to a Source Citation

If you have an image or recording of a source, you can link it to a source citation. For example, you might have a scan of a marriage certificate or census record that you want to add to the source citation.

1 Double-click the source citation you want to add the media to.
2 Click the **Media** tab.

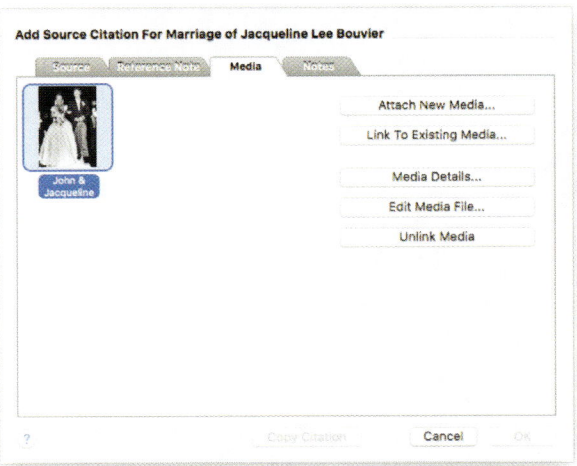

3 Do one of the following:
- If the media item is already in your tree, click **Link To Existing Media**. Select the item you want then click **OK**.
- To add a media item, click **Attach New Media**. Use the file management dialog to navigate to the media item. Then click **Open**.

4 In the **Copy to Media Folder** dialog that appears, choose whether you want to create an additional copy of the file in your tree's media folder or to link to the file on your computer only, and then click **OK**.

5 Click **OK**.

Adding a Note to a Source Citation

You can use the Notes tab for additional information about a source that you weren't able to include elsewhere. For example, you can type a note about how you discovered a source or where the source is located.

1 Click the **Notes** tab in a source citation.

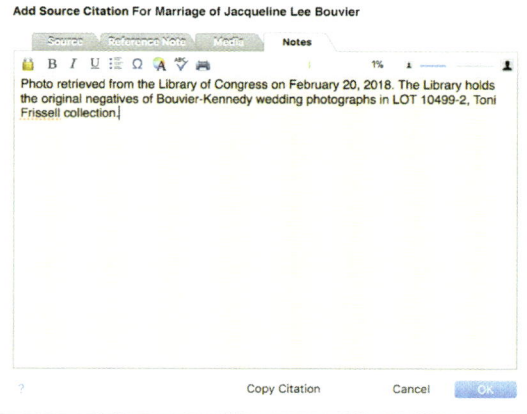

2 Type a note and click **OK**.

Using Source Repositories

With most sources, it's possible to specify the physical location where the original source can be found. This could be a library, county courthouse, or an individual's home. This location is called the source's repository. Naturally, more than one source may reside in a repository. Therefore, you only need to enter information on each repository once. You can then link the appropriate sources to it rather than retyping the information for each source you create.

Adding a Repository

1   In the **Add/Edit Source** dialog (see "Adding a Source for a Fact" on page 81), click the **New** button next to the **Source Repositories** pop-up menu.

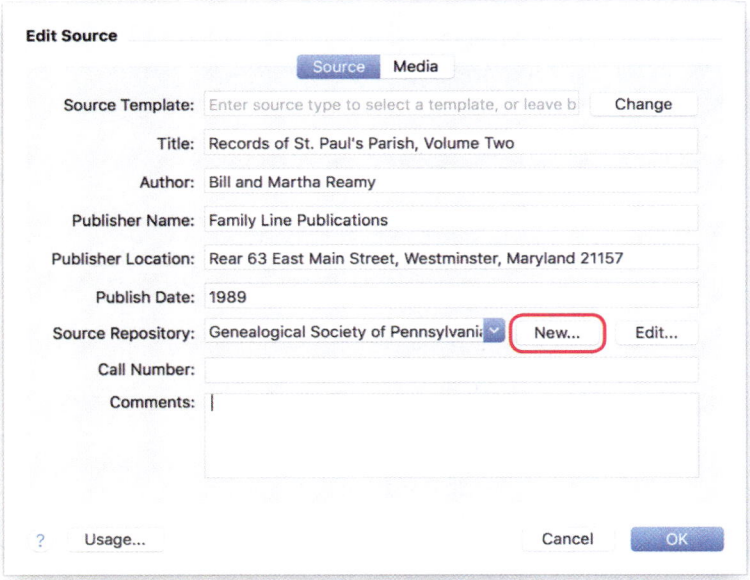

2 In the dialog that appears, enter the name, address, phone number, and email address of the location, and then click **OK**.

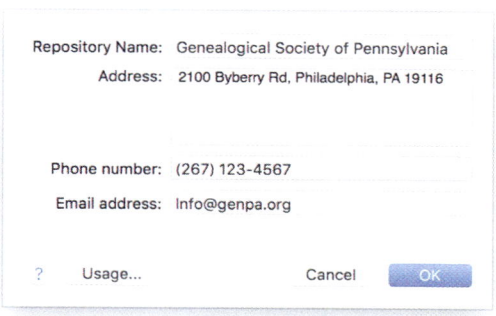

Managing Repositories

You can monitor the usage of repositories in your tree, as well as edit repository information, delete repositories, and add new ones. Changes you make to a repository are automatically applied to all the sources that are linked to it.

Reviewing Usage of a Repository

You may need to know how much information in your tree is sourced from a specific repository or to check that a repository has the correct sources linked to it. To do that, follow these steps:

1 Open the **Repositories** dialog (fig. 5-1 on the next page) by choosing **Manage Repositories** from the **Edit** menu.

2 Select a repository and click **Usage**. The **Repository Usage** dialog will appear with a list of sources linked to the selected repository and citations for these sources.

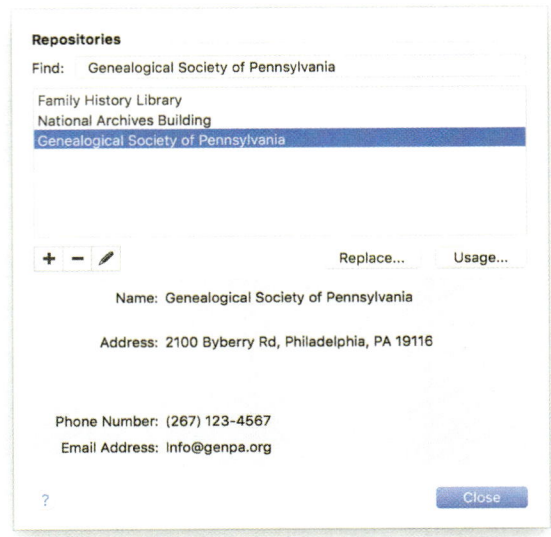

Figure 5-1. The Repositories dialog.

3 When done, click **Close**.

Replacing a Repository

You can change all of the occurrences of one repository to another repository. This merges the two repositories together as the second repository and deletes the first repository. All of the sources previously linked to the first repository will now be linked to the second repository. This allows you to combine duplicate repositories into a single repository without reassigning each source.

1 In the **Repositories** dialog, select the repository you want to replace.

2 Click the **Replace** button.

3 In the dialog that appears, select the repository to which you want to link all sources from the first repository.

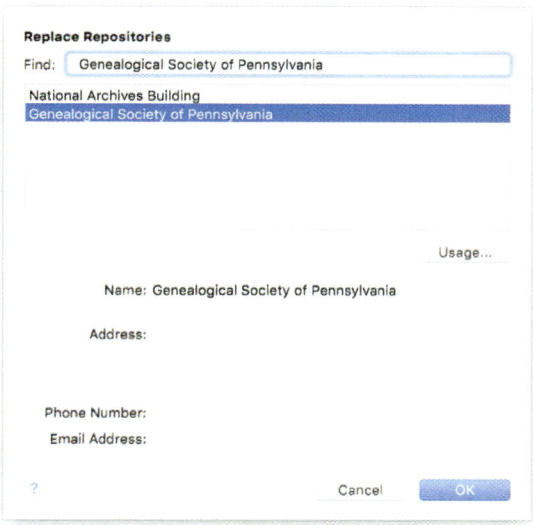

4 Click **OK**.

5 Click **Replace** in the confirmation dialog.

6 When done, click **Close**.

Editing Repository Information

To update or correct information about a particular repository, follow these steps:

1 Open the **Repositories** dialog by choosing **Manage Repositories** from the **Edit** menu.

2 Select the repository you want to edit.

3 Click the **Edit (pencil)** button.

4 Change the name, address, phone number, and/or email address, and then click **OK**.

5 When done, click **Close.**

Deleting a Repository

1 In the **Repositories** dialog, select the repository you want to delete.

2 Click the **Delete** (–) button.

3 In the message that appears, click **Delete and Unlink** to unlink all sources from the repository and delete it.

4 When done, click **Close.**

Chapter Six
Including Media Items

As you gather names, dates, and facts, you'll realize that they tell only part of your family's story. In order to really bring your ancestors to life, you'll want to illustrate your family history with photographs, important documents, and video and sound clips.

What Media Items Can I Add to My Tree?
Photographs are usually the first thing that comes to mind when you want to illustrate your family history. But don't limit yourself. Here are some items you might want to add to your tree:

- Important records, such as birth and marriage certificates, censuses, paяwork, quilts, christening outfits, and furniture
- Images of ancestral houses and hometowns, businesses, maps, cemeteries, and headstones
- Family documents, such as letters, funeral books, diaries, Christmas cards, and newspaper and magazine articles
- Audio clips of oral histories and family stories
- AlbumWALK talking photos with embedded SoundSpot recordings

Family Tree Maker helps you organize your multimedia items in one central location. You can link media items to specific individuals; record important notes about each item; use images in family tree charts; and more.

Adding Media Items

If you have a baby picture of your grandmother or a photo of your grandfather's military uniform, you'll want to add it to your tree. You can add photos, audio files, and videos from your computer, scan documents directly into Family Tree Maker, or instantly import photos from your camera.

Adding a Media Item for an Individual

1 Go to the **Tree** tab on the People workspace and select the appropriate individual. Then click the **Person** tab.

2 Click the **Media** tab at the bottom of the workspace.

3 Click the down arrow next to the **New** button and choose **Add New Media** from the pop-up menu.

Note: When you add a media item to Family Tree Maker, the original file is not moved from its location on your computer.

4 Use the file management dialog to navigate to the media item you want to add to your tree. Then click **Choose**.

Tip: You can select multiple media items by Command-clicking on each file.

A message asks whether you want to link the file to your tree or create a copy of the file.

5   Select **Copy this file** to create an additional copy of the file in the Family Tree Maker media folder, or select **Link to this file** to link to the file where it is on your computer.

Tip: Make copies of your media items if you want all your heritage photos and other media items saved in one central location on your computer. This makes them easier to find and easier to back up.

6   Select the checkbox for the category you want this item to belong to; you can select multiple categories. (For more information see "Media Categories" on page 115.)

*Tip: Select the **Always use this selection without prompting me** option to remember your choice.*

7   Click **OK**. The item is added to the individual's Media tab.

Scanning an Image into Your Tree

If you have images you'd like to add to your tree that aren't already on your computer, you can scan them directly into your tree.

When you scan an image, you'll choose the resolution in which the item will be saved. The higher the resolution, or DPI (dots per inch), the sharper your image—and the larger the file size that will be created. If you plan on viewing your images online or sharing them via email, scan images at a lower resolution such as 72 to 150 DPI; if you want to print images in charts and reports, use a higher resolution such as 200 to 300 DPI.

1   Make sure your scanner is connected to your computer and turned on.

2. Click the **Media** button on the main toolbar. Then click the down arrow next to the button and choose **Scan Media** from the menu that appears. Family Tree Maker automatically searches for connected scanners.

3. Change any settings and click **Scan**.

4. In the dialog that appears, select the checkbox for the category you want this item to belong to; you can select multiple categories. (For more information see "Media Categories" on page 115.)

5. Click **OK**. The item is added to the Media workspace.

Changing the Display of an Image

When you're viewing a photo, you can change how it's displayed by rotating the image or zooming in and out on it.

Go to the **Collection** tab on the Media workspace. Double-click a photo, or select the photo and then click the **Detail** tab.

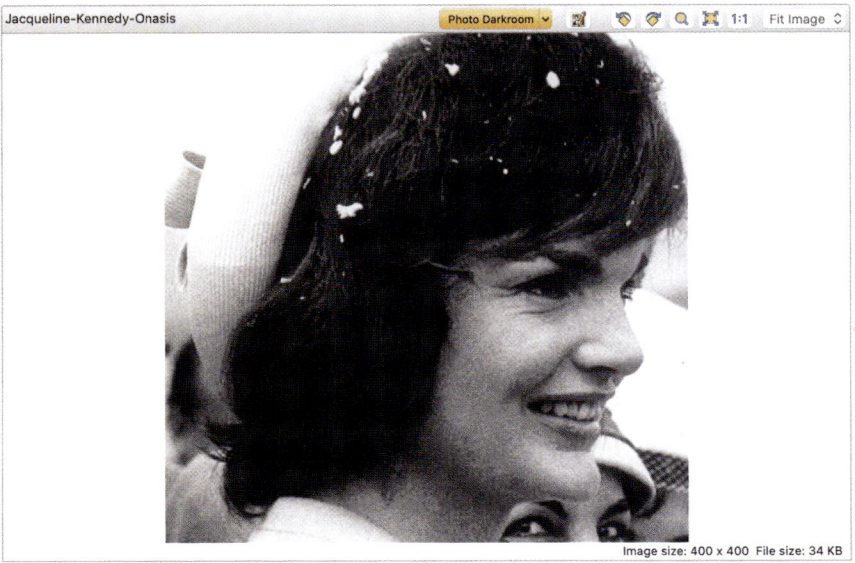

Use these buttons in the image toolbar to change the display:

 Click the **Rotate right** button to move the image clockwise; click the **Rotate left** button to move the image counterclockwise.

 Click the **Magnifier** button to turn the pointer into a magnifying glass when viewing an image.

 Click the **Size to fit** button to display the entire image in the current view.

 Click the **Show actual size** button to show the actual size of the image. You can also choose a specific percentage from the **Fit Image** pop-up menu.

Entering Details for a Media Item

After you add a media item, it's a good idea to enter details about it such as a caption, date, and description.

1 Go to the **Collection** tab on the Media workspace. Click the image to select it.

2 Change the image's details as necessary:

- **Caption.** Type a brief title for the item.

- **Date.** Type a date for the item. (Typically this is the date the item was created.)
- **Description.** Describe the media item in detail. For photos you can enter the names of individuals or info about the location depicted; for heirlooms you may want to explain what the item is and its significance to your family.

3 Select the **Private** checkbox to keep this media item from being exported or uploaded to your online Ancestry tree.

4 To assign a category to the item, click the **Edit** button next to the Categories field. Select the checkbox for the category you want this item to belong to; you can select multiple categories, add new ones (by clicking "+") or delete existing ones (by clicking "-"). Click **OK** when you're finished.

Tip: You can click the Filename and Location links to open the file or the folder where the media item is.

Entering a Note About a Media Item

If you have details that won't fit in a media item's description, you can enter it in the item's notes. For example, a photo of your grandmother in her graduation robes may include notes about her college education and how you found the image.

1 Go to the **Collection** tab on the Media workspace. Double-click the media item you want to add a note to, or select the image and click the **Detail** tab.

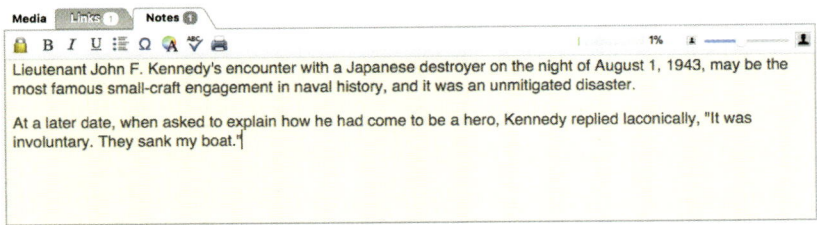

2 Click the **Notes** tab at the bottom of the workspace and type the information.

Note: For more information about using notes, see "Adding a Note for an Individual" on page 55.

Adding a Portrait for an Individual

If you want to display a photo of an individual in charts, reports, and the People workspace, you'll need to add a portrait for them. When you add a photo, you can zoom and crop it. This allows you to easily add quality portraits that show the people in your tree clearly without having to modify the images in a separate photo editor first. Any cropping and zooming you do to a photo to make portraits will not affect the original media file.

1 Click the **People** button on the main toolbar. Make sure the individual you want to add a portrait to is the focus of the Tree tab or Person tab.

2 In the editing panel, Control-click the person silhouette and do one of the following:

- If the photo is already in your tree, choose **Link to Existing Picture**. The Find Media Item dialog opens. Select the photo you want, and then click **OK**.

- If you're adding a new image, choose **Add New Picture**. Use the file management dialog to navigate to the image you want. Then click **Choose**.

3 If the image is a new one, choose whether you want to copy it to the media folder for your tree or just make a link to the file. Then click **OK**.

Profile picture cropping

Smart technology introduced in FTM 2019 is able to detect individual faces on photos and suggest possible profile pictures, even when there are several people in the photo.

1. In the **Edit Profile Picture** dialog that appears after you complete the steps above, move the pointer over the people in the photo to see squares framing the detected faces.

2. Click the face of the person for whom you are adding a profile picture or use the **Auto Zoom** button. Family Tree Maker zooms in to suggest the cropping area for the portrait.

3. To adjust the zoom level and cropping area manually, drag the photo and use the **Zoom** slider so that the person's face is in the center of the view. When you are satisfied with how the portrait looks, click **Apply**.

Tip: Adjustments to profile portraits using cropping are synced between your FTM and Ancestry trees.

Editing Photos with Photo Darkroom

Old photos may fade and deteriorate with time and wear. Fortunately, Family Tree Maker now comes with a photo repair tool integrated into your genealogy toolkit, to quickly and effortlessly edit your vintage photos without needing to switch to an external image editor. Family Tree Maker's Photo Darkroom is all you need to revive and enhance old photos.

1 Go to the **Collection** tab on the **Media** workspace. Double-click the photo you want to repair, or select the photo and click the **Detail** tab.

2 Click the **Photo Darkroom** button. The photo opens in Photo Darkroom.

3 To view before and after images side by side as you are editing, click the two-pane button in the view control. Both the Result and Original will be displayed.

4. Use the Faded Photo Repair Tool to make the image clearer. Depending on the degree of fading, click the **Light**, **Moderate**, or **Intensive** tool. Click the tool several times to increase the effect.

5. If you want to make further changes to the photo, open the **Advanced Settings** section by clicking the disclosure triangle, scroll down, and then drag the **Brightness**, **Contrast**, **Saturation**, and **Sharpness** sliders while observing the changes in the Result view.

6. If you don't like the result of your changes, click the **Undo** button to discard them step by step. You can click the **Restore to Original** button to undo all the changes that you have made to the photo.

7. Click **Done** to apply your changes and return to the **Detail** tab of the **Media** workspace.

Note: The original photo is not modified. It is stored in the **Darkroom Originals** folder in your tree's media folder. If you want to use the original photo in your tree, without the changes that you have made to it, just open the photo in Photo Darkroom at any time, and then click the **Restore to Original** button.

Linking a Media Item to Multiple Individuals

You may have a family photo that includes several individuals in your tree. You don't have to add the picture to each individual; simply add it once to the Media workspace, then link it to the necessary individuals. You can also link media items to specific facts. For example, if you have a photograph of the ship on which your grandparents immigrated to America, you can link the picture to your grandparents and their immigration fact.

1 Go to the **Collection** tab on the Media workspace. Then double-click the item you want to link to multiple individuals, or select the item and click the **Detail** tab.

2 Click the **Links** tab at the bottom of the workspace. Then click the **New** button and choose **Link to Person**.

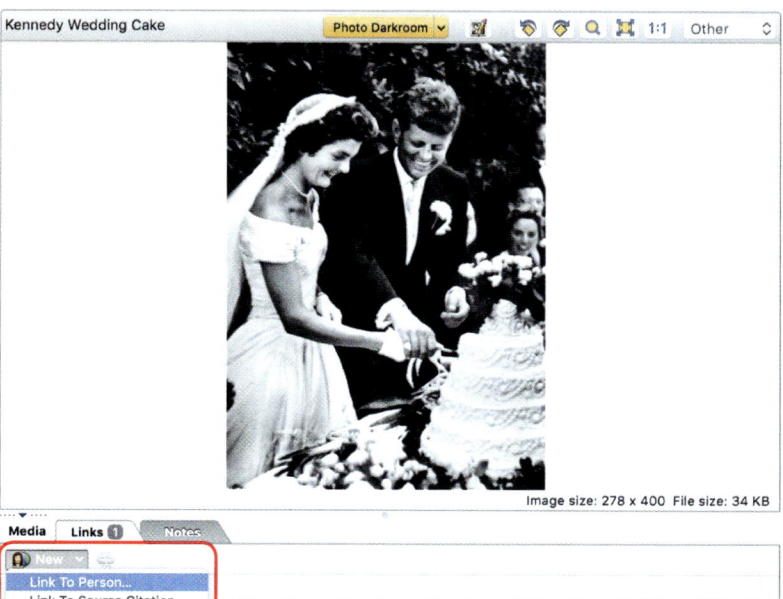

3 Do one of the following:

- To link the item to one or more people, click **Link to selected individuals**. Then, in the list on the left, select the individual you want and click **Include**. Repeat until all the people you want to link appear in the list on the right.

    Tip: To quickly add a person together with their parents, children, siblings, and spouses, select the person and click the Family button.

- To link the item to a specific fact (such as birth), click **Link to person's fact**. Then select a person in the list on the left and click the fact you want in the list on the right. To link the item to more facts, repeat the process.

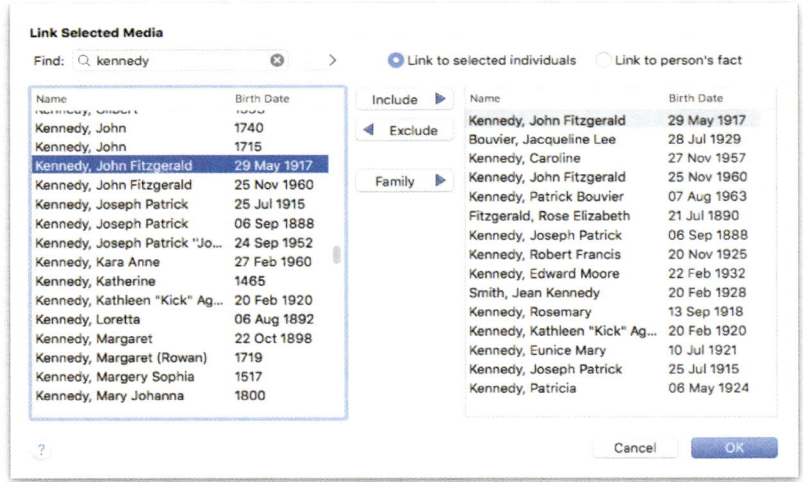

4. Click **OK**.

Tip: If you mistakenly link a media item to an individual, you can unlink it on the Links tab. Select the appropriate individual and then click the **Unlink** button on the Links toolbar.

Playing AlbumWALK Files

Every photo has a story or two to tell. AlbumWALK makes it easy to capture the memories of those who were there when the photograph was taken. Using AlbumWALK's patented tap-talk interface, just tap a face in a photo on your mobile device and talk about that person. Then tap the next face and talk. When you have finished, AlbumWALK creates a mini-documentary, zooming in on each person as they are mentioned, along with professionally scored background music. So the next time you look through old photos with a relative, say "Let's go on an AlbumWALK" and create talking photos that will retell their stories for generations to come.

To play AlbumWALK .tap files on your computer:

1 Go to the **Collection** tab on the Media workspace and find an AlbumWALK media item you have added (it has a small badge with the number of SoundSpot recordings on it).

Tip: A new AlbumWALK media category has been added to allow you to categorize your .tap files from the app easily.

Tip: If you have used the list of people from your Antenna tree to assign names to SoundSpot recordings in an AlbumWALK photo, the photo will be automatically linked to those people as soon as you add it to the Source tree in FTM 2019.

2 Double-click the item or click the **Detail** tab. The photo opens with the SoundSpot recordings—which appear as circles around faces in the photo—ready to be played.

3 Now you can do the following:
- Double-click **a face with a SoundSpot** to listen to the recorded narration about that person.
- Click the **Play** button to play the whole mini-documentary. Playback starts with the Intro sound (if one has been recorded), which provides a general description of the event and place pictured, and then the SoundSpot recordings are played one by one.
- Click the **Next** or **Previous** button to stop playing the current SoundSpot and skip to the next one or go back to the previous one.
- To stop playback, click the **Stop** button.

Managing Media Items

Occasionally you might need to do some maintenance tasks for your media items such as change file names or assign categories.

Opening a Media Item from Family Tree Maker

If you need to edit an image or open a document in your tree, you can open it in its default application without leaving Family Tree Maker.

Go to the **Collection** tab on the Media workspace. Double-click a media item or select the item and click the **Detail** tab.

 Click the **Open file** button in the image toolbar. The media item opens in the file's default application. If you edit the media item and save your changes, the modified file will be linked to Family Tree Maker.

Changing a Media Item's File Name

Family Tree Maker lets you change a media item's file name on your computer. This can be useful if you've imported a tree and its media files have generic names; you can use Family Tree Maker to change their file names to something more identifiable.

1 Go to the **Collection** tab on the Media workspace. Control-click a media item and choose **Rename Media File** from the shortcut menu, or select a media item, click the down arrow next to the **Media** button, and then choose **Rename Media File** from the pop-up menu.

2 Type the new name for the file and click **Rename**.

Arranging an Individual's Media Items

When you add media items for an individual, they are arranged in alphabetical order (by caption). You can change the order in which they appear on the individual's Media tab. For example, you may want to display the pictures by date.

1 Go to the **Person** tab on the People workspace and select the appropriate individual.

2 Click the **Media** tab at the bottom of the workspace. The tab shows thumbnails of any media items you've linked to this individual.

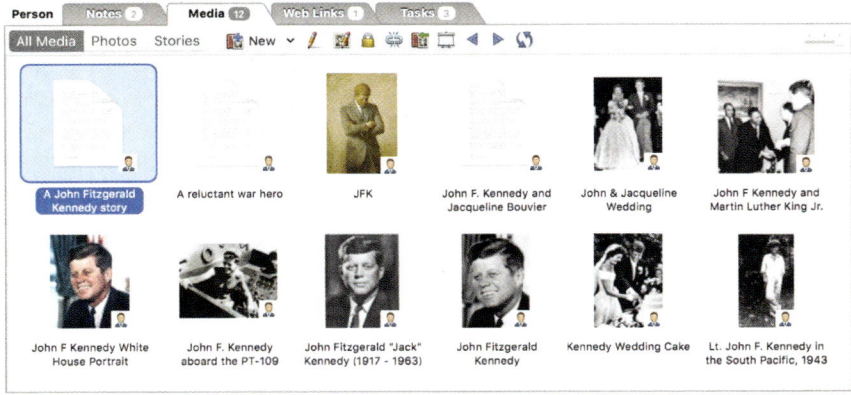

Use these buttons in the media toolbar to change the display order:

Select the item you want to move. Then click the **Move Media Forward** and **Move Media Backward** arrows to rearrange the media items. The items will remain in the order you've chosen.

Click the **Auto Sort Media** button to arrange media items alphabetically (by caption) again.

Click the **Photos** and **Stories** buttons to view only images or only text items respectively. Click the **All Media** button to display all of the media items linked to the individual.

Media Categories

As you add each media item to your tree, you can assign it to categories. These categories make your media items easier to search for, sort, and view.

Creating a Category

You can use the default categories, modify them, or create your own. If you decide to create your own categories, you might want to set up a system before you add your media items. For example, you may want to have event categories (e.g., Weddings, Birthdays, Travel) or categories based on item types (e.g., Photos—Portraits, Movies—Holidays).

1 Go to the **Collection** tab on the Media workspace. In the media editing panel, click the **Edit** button next to the **Categories** field. The Categories dialog opens.

2 Click the **Add** (+) button.

3 Type a name for the category and click **OK**.

Assigning a Category to Multiple Items

Family Tree Maker lets you assign categories to a group of items at the same time.

1 Go to the **Collection** tab on the Media workspace.

2 Select the media items you want to assign a category to. You can select multiple media items by Command-clicking on each one you want.

3 Click the down arrow next to the **Media** button on the main toolbar and choose **Categorize Media** from the pop-up menu.

4   In the Categorize Media dialog, you can choose categories for each media item one by one or for all selected media items at once.

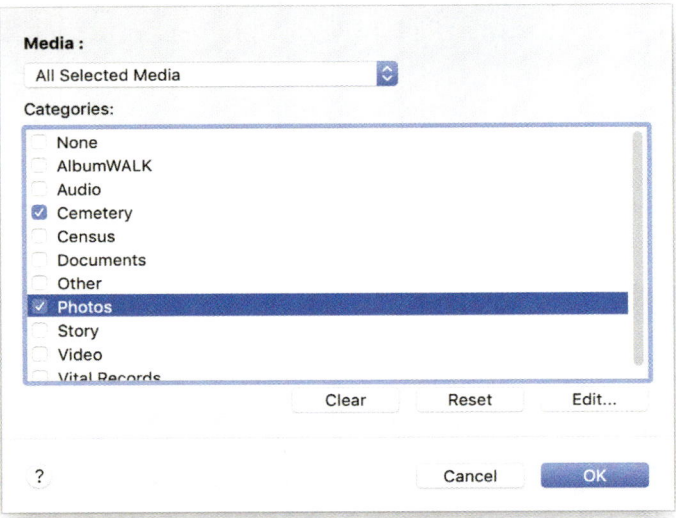

Creating a Slide Show

You can create a slide show of pictures you've included in your tree, and even add a soundtrack. You can view your completed slide shows using *QuickTime*.

1   Click the **Media** button on the main toolbar. Then click the down arrow next to the button and choose **Create Slide Show** from the menu that appears.

   Tip: You can create a slide show for a specific individual by clicking the **Create Slide Show** button on the individual's Media tab.

2   Change the slide show options as necessary:
   - **Title.** Type a name for the slide show. (This will be the item's file name on your computer also.)

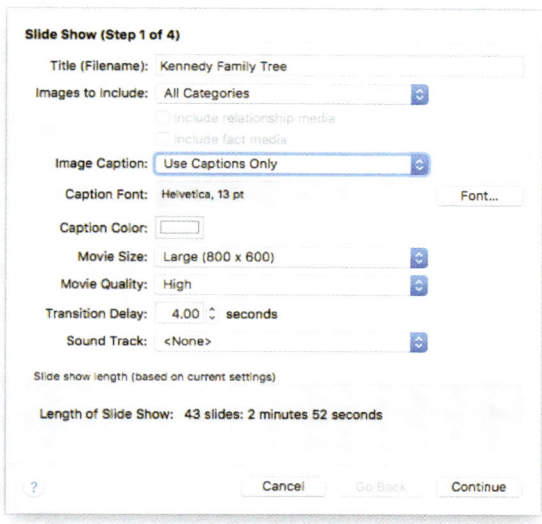

- **Images to Include.** To include pictures from a specific category, choose the category from the pop-up menu. If you opened this dialog by clicking the **Create slide show** button on an individual's Media tab, select the **Include relationship media** checkbox to include images linked to the person's relationships and select the **Include fact media** checkbox to include images linked to facts associated with the person.

- **Image Caption.** Choose what text is displayed for images. Choose **None** to hide captions displayed; choose **Use Captions Only** to display image captions; choose **Use Filenames Only** to display file names; choose **Use Captions or Filenames** to display captions (if no caption has been entered, the file name will be displayed).

  Click the **Font** button to select a font style, size, and color for captions and file names used in the slide show.

- **Movie Size.** Choose the display size from the pop-up menu.

  Note: The larger the movie, the more memory required.

- **Movie Quality.** Choose the display quality from the pop-up menu.

  Note: The higher the movie quality, the more memory required.

- **Transition Delay.** Choose the number of seconds an image is displayed.

- **Sound Track.** To add music to the slide show, click **Sound Track** and choose **Browse** from the pop-up menu. Then locate the audio file (MP3) you'd like to use and click **Open**.

3 Click **Continue**. Now you can change the order in which images appear or delete images you don't want.

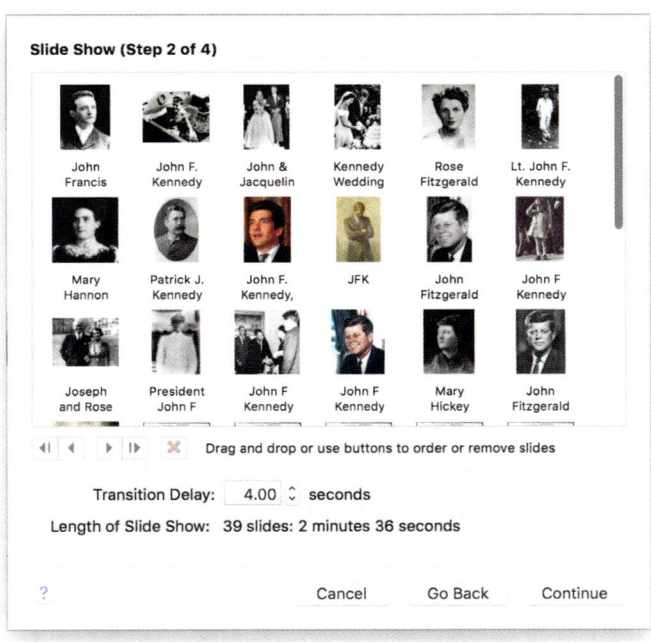

4 Click **Continue**. A preview of the slide show opens.

5 Do one of the following:

- To view the finished slide show in *QuickTime*, select **Launch slide show with Finder**.

- To save the slide show to your tree, select **Add slide show to the media collection**.

6 Click **Finish**.

7 If you have selected the **Add slide show to the media collection** checkbox, the **Save to Media Folder** dialog appears. Click the checkbox for the category you want this slide show to belong to; you can select multiple categories. Click **OK** to add the slide show to the Media workspace.

8 If you have not selected the **Add slide show to the media collection** checkbox, the **Save movie** dialog appears. Choose a location and click **Save**.

Printing a Media Item

1 Go to the **Collection** tab on the Media workspace and select the item you want to print.

2 Click the **Print** button below the main toolbar and choose **Print Media Item** from the pop-up menu.

3 When prompted choose a printer, select the number of copies, and choose a page range.

4 Click **Print**.

Chapter Seven
Using Maps

As you gather the names and dates of important events in your ancestors' lives, you'll also record the locations where these events took place—the towns, cities, and countries that shaped their daily lives.

Often, these places exist only as names in a report or on a pedigree chart. Family Tree Maker brings these ancestral homelands to life by letting you virtually visit each place in your tree. For example, you can see satellite images and maps of the town in Denmark where your grandfather was born, the apartment in Chicago where your great-grandparents lived, or even the lake where you went swimming with your cousins every summer.

Each time you enter a location for a fact or event, Family Tree Maker adds it to a "master list" of locations. To view this master list, simply go to the Places workspace. You can then view maps and satellite images of a location, identify individuals in your tree who are associated with certain locations, and more.

Viewing a Map

The interactive online maps in Family Tree Maker are easy to navigate using a few simple tools. You can zoom in and out on the map, change the type of map you're viewing, and more.

Note: You must be connected to the Internet to view these maps.

1. Click the **Places** button on the main toolbar. To view a map, select a location in the **Places** panel.

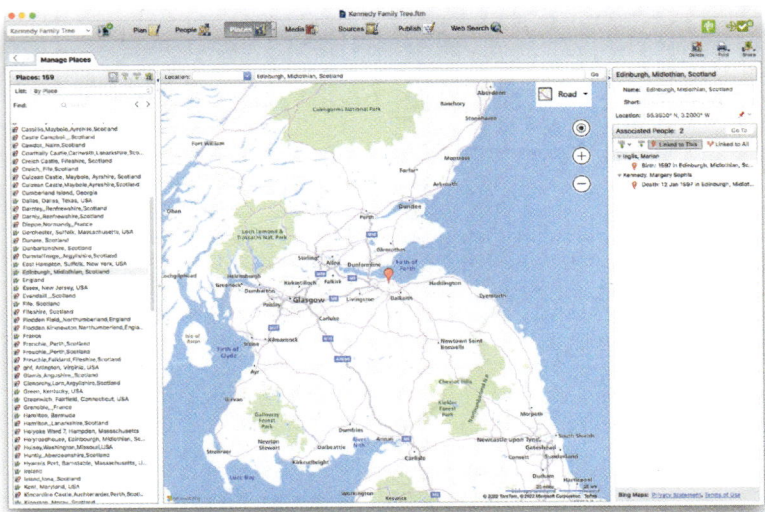

There are four map types. The **Road** map type appears by default with the location centered and identified with a red marker. **Aerial** looks straight down at the location. **Bird's eye** provides a 3D angled view. And **Streetside** is the view you'd have standing there. To change the map type, click the map view pop-up menu in the upper-right corner and choose the view you want.

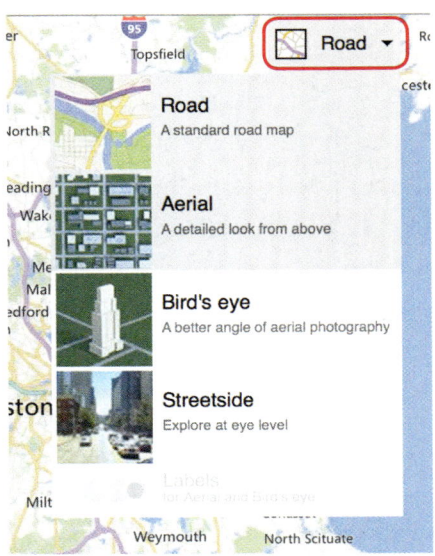

Chapter 7: Using Maps   123

2   Choose **Aerial** to view a satellite image of the location.

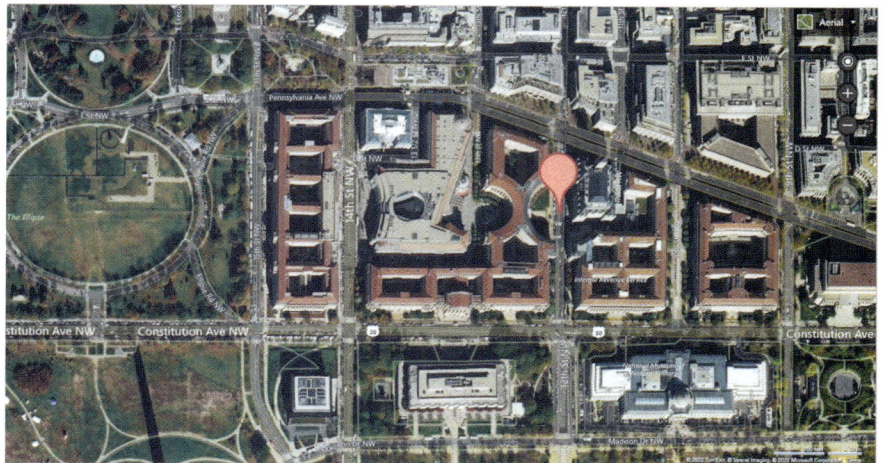

Microsoft Bing Maps

Family Tree Maker has partnered with Microsoft *Bing Maps* to let you access some of the most exciting technology available today. *Bing Maps* takes you beyond typical road maps by combining them with special satellite and aerial imagery to let you experience the world as it looks today.

As you visit different locations, you'll notice that the level of detail for each town, region, or country varies. In some areas you can zoom in close enough to see cars, rooftops, and street intersections; in other areas your view will disappear when you get within a mile of the location. Fortunately, *Bing Maps* is updated regularly and regions that may not have many images now will in the future. The most detailed views are of the United States, the United Kingdom, Canada, and Australia.

3   To get a 3D view of a location, click **Bird's eye**. Click the arrows on either side of the compass tool to change the direction of the view.

Note: Bird's-eye view is available only for certain parts of the world.

4   To turn the display of map labels such as street names on and off in Aerial and Bird's eye views, click the map view pop-up menu, choose **Aerial** or **Bird's eye**, and click the **Labels** switch control at the bottom of the list.

5   Choose **Streetside** to explore places as if you were there. This view is not available for all areas of the world. See "Using Streetside View" on page 126 for more information.

Moving Around a Map

You can quickly change the part of the map you're viewing by dragging it. Move the pointer over the map. When the pointer changes to a hand, click and drag the map in any direction you want.

Chapter 7: Using Maps   125

Zooming In and Out on a Map

You can use the zoom icons on the map tools to zoom in and out on the displayed map.

1 Click the plus ⊕ icon to zoom in one level at a time.

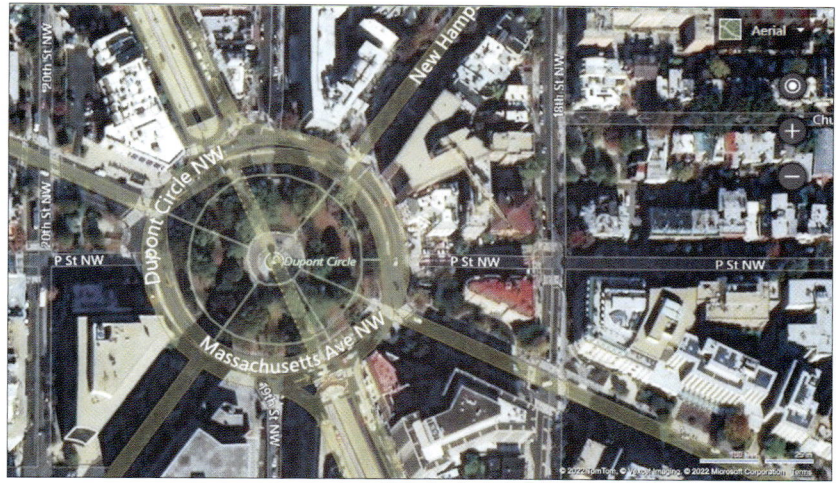

2 Click the minus ⊖ icon to zoom out one level at a time.

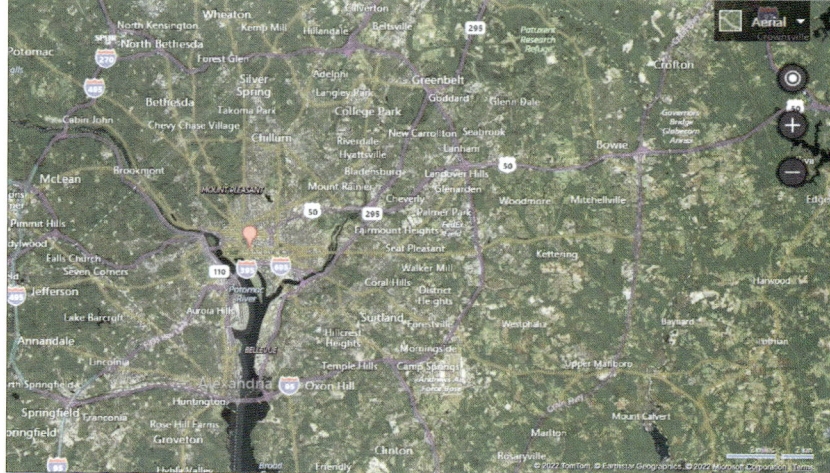

Using Streetside View

1 Look for Streetside locations by clicking the map view pop-up menu and choosing **Streetside**. The pointer changes to the blue man icon wherever Streetside views are available.

2 Streetside view is not available for all locations. On the map, locations that can be viewed from the Streetside perspective are shaded blue. If there are any such locations in the display area, the Streetside pointer icon is blue. Click the location for which you want to get the Streetside view.

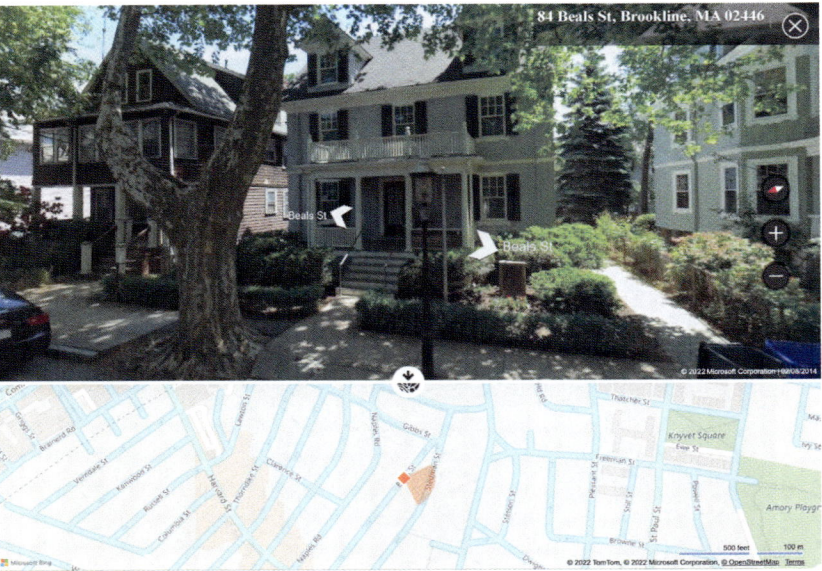

3 If there are no locations with Streetside view in the visible part of the map, the Streetside pointer icon turns red. Scroll the map until the pointer turns blue or click the Streetside item in the map view menu again to toggle off the Streetside pointer icon and blue street markings.

4 In Streetside view, use these means of navigation:
- Click the plus and minus buttons to zoom in and out.
- Click the arrows in the view to move along the streets.
- Drag the view to rotate the line of sight and look up or down.
- Click the compass icon to reset the view to looking due north.
- Click the **Show location on map** button to show the current Streetside location on a Road map. The location is marked by an orange diamond, and the field of vision is also shown. To jump to another location, drag the map so that the location you want comes under the orange diamond. To hide the Road map, click the **Hide map** button.

5 To leave Streetside view and return to the view you were in before entering Streetside (Road or Aerial), click the Close button in the top-right corner.

Finding Places of Interest

Family Tree Maker helps you search for places of interest such as libraries and cemeteries near important places in your family history. If you're planning a research trip, you can use the maps to view all the cemeteries and churches in your ancestor's hometown.

1 Click the **Places** button on the main toolbar.

2 If you've already entered the location in your tree, select it in the **Places** panel; otherwise, type the location's name in the blank field above the map on the right.

3 Choose a location type (such as libraries) from the pop-up menu and click **Go**. Blue pushpins appear for each location that matches your search.

128 Part 2: Building a Tree

4   Move the pointer over a pushpin to see a name and address for the location (if available).

Printing a Map

You can print maps directly from the software, whether it's an aerial shot of your ancestor's farm or the migration path your great-grandfather took across the country.

1   On the Places workspace, display the map you want to print. The display window shows what part of the map will be printed. You may need to resize the workspace to display more of the map.

2   Click the **Print** button below the main toolbar and choose **Print Map** from the pop-up menu. The Print dialog opens.

3   When prompted choose a printer, select the number of copies, and choose a page range.

4   Click **Print**.

Chapter 7: Using Maps   129

Viewing Locations in Groups

On the Places workspace, you can view locations in an alphabetical list or grouped together by country, county, city, and so on. If you have hundreds of places in your tree, groups make it easier to quickly find the one you're interested in. An added benefit is that you can see all people who are associated with a specific country or city with one click.

Note: To make sure locations are grouped together correctly, you'll need to resolve any place name errors. For help, see "Standardizing Locations" on page 315.

1   On the Places workspace, click the **Alphabetical/Groups** button to toggle between showing places in an alphabetical list or by groups.

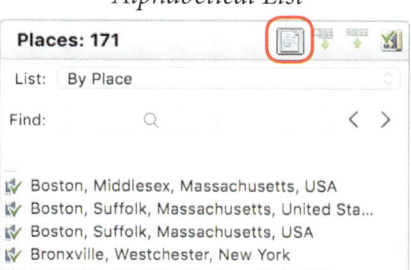
Alphabetical List

Groups List

2   To see all places within a group, click its disclosure triangle. To expand all groups, click the **Expand all nodes** button.

Viewing People and Facts Linked to a Location

Family Tree Maker lets you view all the events that took place at a certain location and the people associated with each event.

1. Click the **Places** button on the main toolbar.
2. Select a location in the **Places** panel. On the right side of the workspace, you'll see the selected location and the individuals who have life events associated with it.

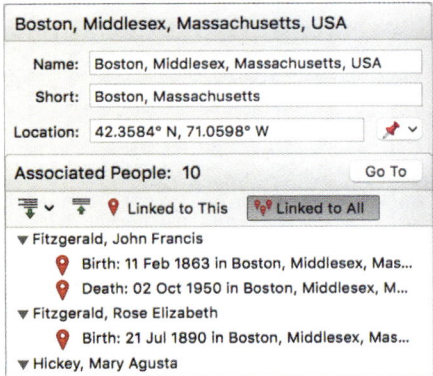

Tip: If you're viewing locations in groups, you can see all the people and events for a group by clicking the **Linked to All** button and then clicking a country, state, or county in the list of places. Or view people and events just for a particular selected location by clicking the **Linked to This** button.

3. Do one of the following:
   - To see the event that occurred at this location for a specific individual, click the disclosure triangle next to the individual.
   - To see the events that occurred at this location for all the individuals, click the **Expand all items in the tree** button and choose **Expand All**. (Click the **Collapse all items in the tree** button to close all the events.)
   - To always have all people and events related to the selected location showing, click the **Expand all items in the tree** button and choose **Expand All On Load**.

Creating Migration Maps

Maps can be extremely useful when tracing an ancestor. You can see at a glance all the locations that are connected with a specific individual or family, track migration patterns, and maybe discover where to locate more records.

Creating a Migration Map for an Individual

1 Click the **Places** button on the main toolbar. In the Places panel, choose "By Person" from the **List** pop-up menu.

2 Select the individual whose migration map you want to see. A map appears in the display area; the individual's birthplace is indicated by a green marker and death place by a dark red marker.

To the right of the map is every fact you've entered for the individual—and its location.

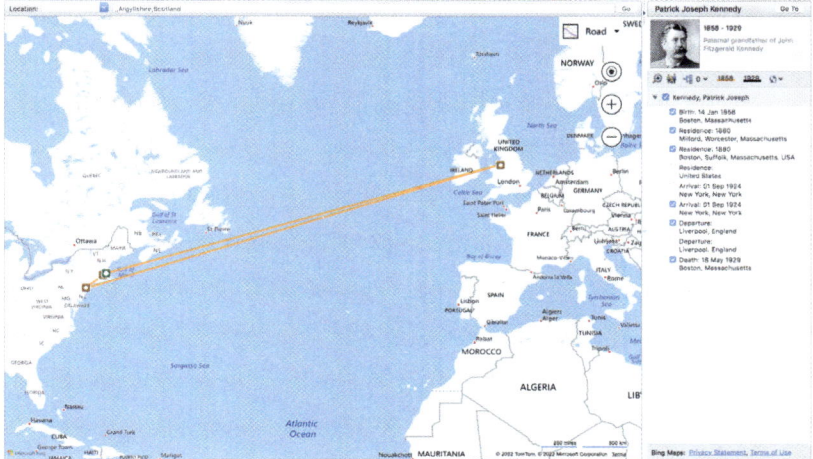

3 Select the checkbox next to a fact to include its location in the migration map.

4 Position the pointer over a marker to see the location's name and the fact associated with it.

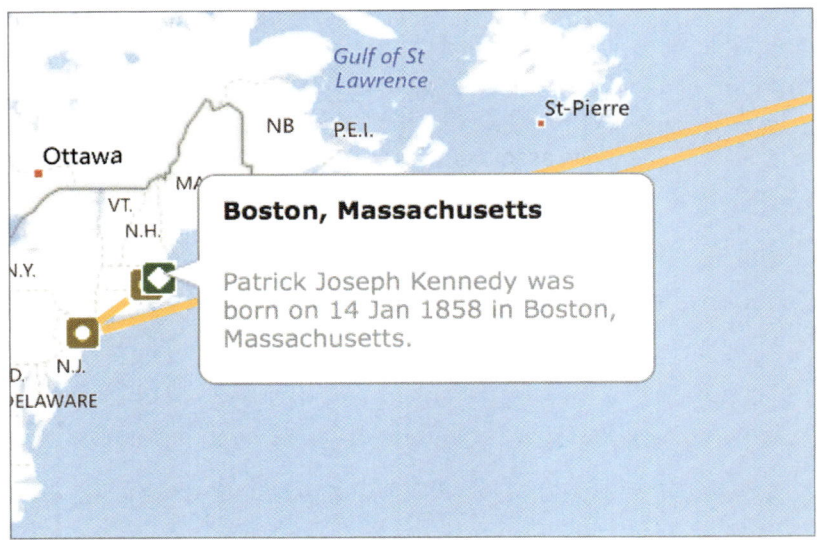

Creating a Migration Map for a Family

1 Click the **Places** button on the main toolbar. In the Places panel, choose "By Person" from the **List** pop-up menu and select an individual.

2 To view the locations associated with the individual's immediate family (parents, siblings, spouse, and children), click the **Include immediate family** button in the mapping toolbar.

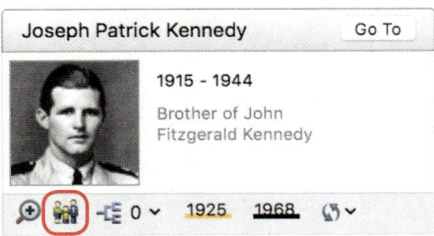

3 Select an individual on the right side of the map to highlight his or her life events on the map. The migration path for the individual is indicated by a thick line.

Tip: You can change the color of a migration path by clicking the line color buttons in the mapping toolbar.

4 To view locations associated with an individual's ancestors (up to four generations), click the **Ancestor generations** button in the mapping toolbar and choose the number of generations from the pop-up menu.

A map appears in the display area: birthplaces are indicated by green markers and death places by dark red markers; the migration path for each individual is indicated by a colored line.

Entering GPS Coordinates

Although the online maps are able to recognize most places, there are times when it won't be able to identify a location. Perhaps your grandmother is buried in a rural cemetery or census records show your family in a township that no longer exists. You can set a location's exact position using GPS (Global Positioning System) coordinates.

1 Click the **Places** button on the main toolbar, choose **By Place** from the **List** pop-up menu. In the **Places** panel, select the location you want to add GPS coordinates to.

2 Place the insertion point in the **Location** field and click the **Location calculator** button that appears.

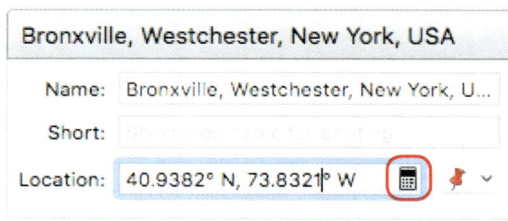

3 Type the coordinates for the location in degrees:minutes:seconds, degrees:decimal minutes, or decimal degrees. Then click OK.

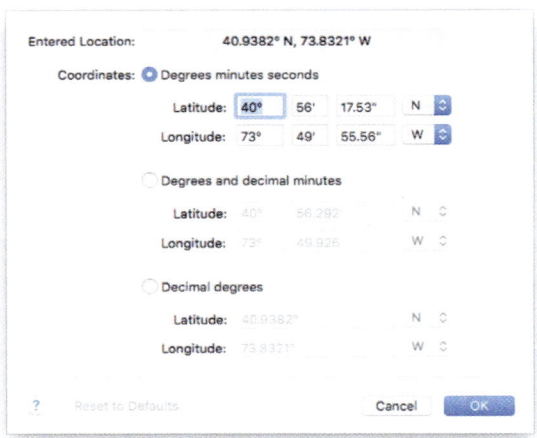

Entering a Display Name for a Location

Recording locations in a complete and consistent manner is an important part of creating a quality family history. Unfortunately, long location names can clutter your reports and charts. To avoid this problem, you can enter your own shortened or abbreviated display names. For example, instead of using Bronxville, Westchester, New York, USA, for a birthplace, you can enter Bronxville, NY, as the display name.

1 In the Places panel, select the location you want to change.
2 Type a display name in the **Short** field.

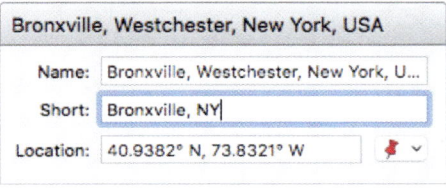

Chapter Eight
Researching Your Tree Online

As you enter stories and facts, you'll probably notice that more information about your family is waiting to be discovered—perhaps it's the burial location of your grandfather or the wedding certificate for your aunt and uncle. Family Tree Maker can help you fill in these gaps in your research with hints—behind-the-scenes searches of Ancestry and FamilySearch.

You can also search for information on RootsWeb.com or any of your favorite websites. If you find info that matches a family member, you can quickly add it to your tree—without leaving Family Tree Maker.

Ancestry Hints

Once your FTM tree is uploaded to Ancestry to create a linked Ancestry tree, Family Tree Maker automatically searches thousands of databases on Ancestry looking for information that matches people in your tree. When a possible match is found, a green leaf or "hint" appears next to an individual in the tree viewer, the editing panel, and the Index on the People workspace. You can view the results when it's convenient, and if the information is relevant, you can add it to your tree.

FamilySearch Hints

FamilySearch, the largest genealogy organization in the world, is operated by The Church of Jesus Christ of Latter-day Saints. Millions of people use FamilySearch records, resources, and services each year to learn more about their family history. FTM 2019 provides you with direct access to FamilySearch's Family Tree database of more than one billion names and hints linked to more than six billion online FamilySearch historical records. You can get automatic match suggestions (a blue square hint icon ▢), hints to historical records (a filled hint icon ■), search the database, and merge any person information you find into your own tree, just as you can with information you find on Ancestry's databases.

Note: If you don't want Family Tree Maker to automatically search Ancestry or FamilySearch when you're connected to the Internet, you can turn this feature off. To do this, choose **Family Tree Maker 2019>Settings** (**Preferences** on macOS 12 Monterey or earlier), click **General** and uncheck options for hints.

Viewing Ancestry and FamilySearch Hints

If Family Tree Maker finds records or trees on Ancestry or FamilySearch that might match an individual in your tree, you'll see a hint icon next to the person in the tree viewer, the editing panel, and the Index on the People workspace. Hold the pointer over the icon to see the number of records and trees that were found.

Note: To view Ancestry Hints you must have an Internet connection, log in to your Ancestry account, and have your FTM tree linked to your Ancestry tree. To get hints for new people you add to your tree, keep your FTM and Ancestry trees synced. To view the actual records and images, you must have an Ancestry subscription.

Chapter 8: Researching Your Tree Online   137

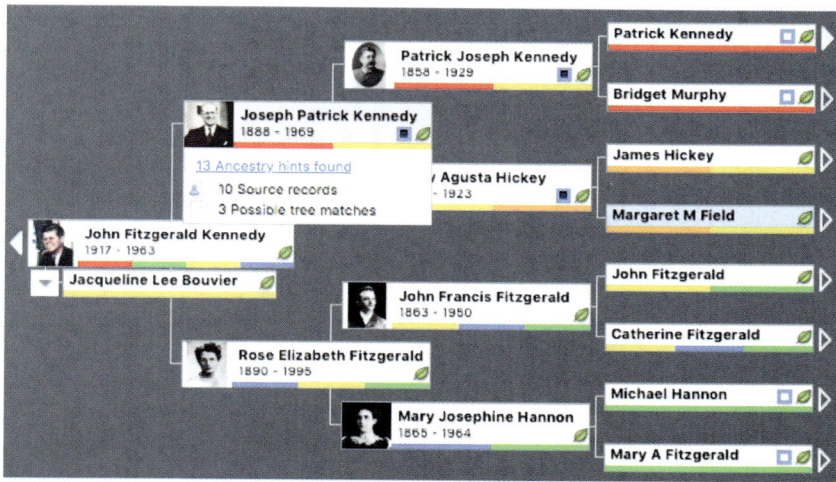

1   Go to the **Tree** tab on the People workspace. In the tree viewer or editing panel, click a hint icon.

2   Select a hint that interests you from the hint results list. If the record matches someone in your family, you can add it to your tree. (See "Adding Records to a Tree" on page 148.) If the record does not match anyone in your tree, you can ignore it. (See "Ignoring Hints" below.)

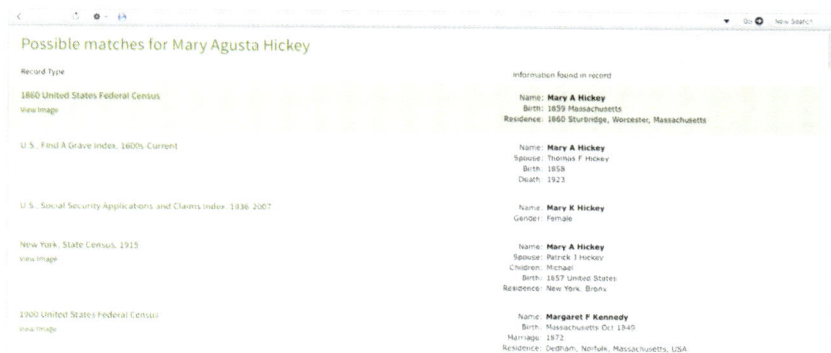

Ignoring Hints

If a hint is not relevant to someone in your tree, you can ignore it so it won't appear in your list of hints and matches again.

1 Access the hints for an individual.
2 On the Possible Matches page, click the item you want to ignore.
3 On the Search Results Detail toolbar, click the **Ignore record** icon (a circle with a diagonal line through it).

The **Ignore record** icon changes to a selected state when you click it to indicate the hint is being ignored.

Viewing Ignored Hints

If you've chosen to ignore specific hints for an individual, you can still view them at a later time.

1 Click the **Web Search** button on the main toolbar.
2 Using the mini pedigree tree or the **Index of Individuals** button, select the individual whose ignored hints you'd like to view.
3 Select Ancestry or FamilySearch in the Search Locations list.
4 Click the down arrow next to the **Web Search** button and choose **View Ignored Records** from the pop-up menu.
5 To take the hint off the Ignore list, click the **Ignore record** icon to deselect it.

Searching Ancestry

You don't have to wait for Ancestry hints to help you discover facts about your family, you can search the website any time you like.

Note: Although anyone can view Ancestry search results, you must have a subscription to view the actual records and images.

> **What Can I Find on Ancestry.com?**
> Ancestry.com is the world's largest online family history resource with more than 24 billion historical records—and more being added all the time. Here's a sample of the wealth of information available on Ancestry:
> - Over 6 billion historical records for the United States.
> - Records from over 80 countries worldwide.
> - Over 100 million family trees from all over the world—created by researchers just like you. Within these trees you'll find more than 13 billion ancestral profiles, more than 330 million photographs, scanned documents, and stories.
> - A complete U.S. census collection (1790–1940). You'll also find census records for the UK, Australia, Canada, and other countries.
> - Immigration records and passenger lists from 1820 to 1960.
> - Birth, marriage, and death records back as far as the 13th century.
> - More than 550 million military records from the 1600s to the Vietnam War and beyond.
> - More than 150 million pages from historical newspapers as far back as the 1700s.
> - More than 20,000 local histories, memoirs, journals, and biographies.
> - Thousands of photos from the Library of Congress, maps beginning in the 1500s, and photographs dating back to the mid-1800s.

1 Click the **Web Search** button on the main toolbar.

2 Select **Ancestry** in the Search Locations list. If you want to research someone other than the individual who is currently selected, use the mini pedigree tree or the **Index of Individuals** button to choose the appropriate person.

Notice that some fields have been filled in for you already.

By some fields you'll see an **Exact** checkbox. Use these to limit your searches to records that match your search terms exactly. Start by typing only one or two search terms, such as name and location.

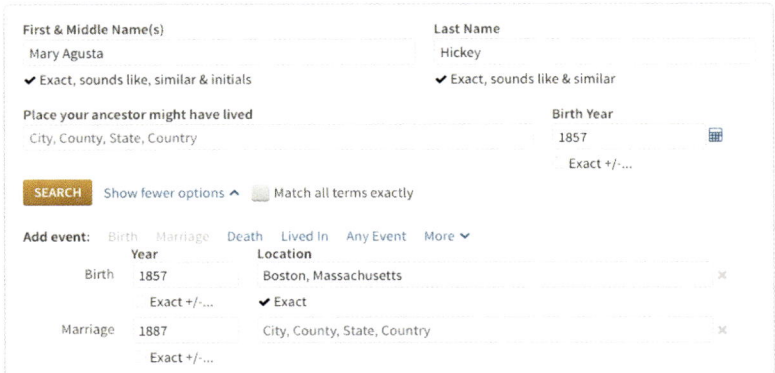

3 Add or delete names, dates, and places as necessary.

4 To display records for a specific country or ethnicity first in your search results, choose a command from the **Collection Focus** pop-up menu.

5 To limit your search results to a specific type of record:

- Select the **Historical Records** checkbox to search for birth records, censuses, military and immigration records, etc.
- Select the **Stories & Publications** checkbox to search for member-submitted stories, newspapers, and county histories.
- Select the **Family Trees** checkbox to search trees submitted by Ancestry members.
- Select the **Photos & Maps** checkbox to search maps, historical images, and member-submitted photos.

6 Click **Search**.

Chapter 8: Researching Your Tree Online   141

7 If you get a large number of search results or matches, click the **Edit Search** link to narrow your search. Try adding more dates, a gender, or a spouse's name. (You can also narrow your search by clicking a category link on the left.) If you get too few results or no matches, delete one or more of your search terms to broaden your search.

8 Select a search result to see the record or index. The tab at the bottom of the workspace lets you compare, side by side, the facts in your tree with the details found in the highlighted record.

9 If the information matches what you already know about the individual and his or her family, you can add the information to your tree. (See "Adding Records to a Tree" on page 148.)

Ancestry Search Tips

Ancestry automatically includes name variations, abbreviations, and nicknames when it searches for records. But if you're searching for an elusive ancestor, try these tips to get the most out of your searches:

- **Use wildcards.** Wildcards represent unknown letters in a name. Use an asterisk for up to six characters; a search for "fran*" will return results for Fran, Franny, Frank, Frannie, and Frankie. Use a question mark for a single character; a search for "Hans?n" will return matches such as Hansen and Hanson.
- **Search for similar-sounding names.** You can search for last names that "sound like" the one you're looking for. For example, a search for Smith would return Smithe, Smyth, and Smythe. To do so, click the "Exact..." link under the individual's surname. Then select the **Sounds like, Soundex,** and **Similar** checkboxes.
- **Estimate dates.** Not sure of the exact date of an event? Make an educated guess; you'll get better results than if you leave the field blank.
- **Add multiple locations.** If a family member lived in New York, Pennsylvania, and Illinois, add each of these residences to your search and you'll get results for all locations at once. To do this, click the "Show more options" link at the bottom of the search page. Then add additional locations in the event location fields.
- **Narrow your search by content.** Search for a specific type of content, such as a family trees, historical records, or maps. To do this, select the necessary checkboxes at the bottom of the search page.
- **Search in specific collections.** Ancestry has special collections focused on countries and ethnicities. If you're looking for an individual who lived in only one country, you can narrow your search to that location. Simply choose an option from the "Collection Focus" pop-up menu.

FamilySearch Search Tips

- **Search for name variations.** Try searching for variations in spelling or different variations of the same name. You can also try nicknames, different middle names and abbreviations.
- **Use wildcards.** Wildcards allow you to replace letters in a person's name and check for multiple spellings in a single search. A question mark (?) replaces a single character, and an asterisk (*) replaces multiple characters. For example, searching for Sm?th will return results for Smith, Smeth, or even Smythe. A search for Joh* will find matches such as John, Johnson, or Johnathon.
- **Estimate dates.** Not sure of the exact date of an event? Make an educated guess; you might get better results than if you leave the field blank.
- **Provide less information.** Adding too much information to your search may exclude results that don't have all that information, or where some of the information differs. For example, try entering just a name and one event, or use only the name if it's not very common.
- **Provide more or different information.** Adding more information may help to find a record that matches more closely.
- **Use exact searching carefully.** Keep in mind that using the "Match All Exactly" checkbox returns fewer results. On the other hand, exact searching might be very helpful, limiting the results to people who lived in a specific place and time.
- **Use other alphabets.** If the person was from a country with a different alphabet, try looking for the name written in the person's native language.

Important: You can use the Find feature to find only deceased people in the FamilySearch Family Tree; you cannot look up living people.

Searching FamilySearch

You can search the FamilySearch Family Tree database without waiting for FamilySearch hints to appear. This will produce a list of possible matches to people in your tree. You can then review the possible matches and merge any information that you find to be relevant into your Family Tree Maker tree.

1. Select a person in your tree.
2. Go to the **Web Search** workspace.
3. In the Search Locations list, select **FamilySearch.org**.
4. In the search form, enter information about an individual for whom you want to search.
5. Click **Find**. The search results appear.
6. Select a search result and look through the person's data in the Search Results Detail area. If this is the individual you were looking for, you can add the information you have found to your tree. (See "Adding Records to a Tree" on page 148.)

Matching a Person with FamilySearch

There's now a quick and convenient way to establish a link between a person in your FTM tree and the same person in the FamilySearch Family Tree which saves having to conduct a new search of the database each time. This is called "matching," and it has the major benefit of providing you with hints to historical records for matched people. Matching people is completely safe—it doesn't transfer any information from your computer or cause any changes to the data in your FTM tree other than adding a FamilySearch Person ID fact to the matched individual's record.

To match a person with FamilySearch, follow these steps:

1 On the People workspace, select the person you want to match to FamilySearch.

2 Do one of the following:

- Click the FamilySearch hint icon or hint link in the tree viewer or the editing panel.
- Control-click the person in the tree viewer, and then choose **Match Person to FamilySearch**.

The Web Search workspace opens with a list of search results.

3 Select a search result and look through the person's data in the Search Results Detail section. If this is the individual you were looking for, click the **Match** button.

4 A message appears with information about the Match People with FamilySearch feature. If you don't want to see this message again, select the **Don't show again** checkbox. Click **Match to FamilySearch**.

5 The Web Search workspace changes to display the person on FamilySearch who you have matched with the person in your FTM tree, together with a link that allows you to view hints to historical records for this person on FamilySearch (if there are any) and a list of possible alternate matches for the person in your FTM tree.

146   Part 2: Building a Tree

To see how matching works with FamilySearch hints, go to the **Tree** tab on the People workspace and find the matched person there. If there are hints to historical records for the matched person on FamilySearch, the center of the hint turns dark blue ■. Hold the pointer over the icon to see the ID of the matched person on FamilySearch, the number of hints found, and the number of hints to historical records that are available for the matched person on FamilySearch.

The FamilySearch ID fact is also added to the matched person in FTM 2019. It is shown in the list of facts on the Person tab and in the editing panel and can be displayed in the Index. This fact cannot be edited.

Merging FamilySearch Historical Records

Though you cannot merge FamilySearch historical records directly from within Family Tree Maker, you can review a record and attach it to a person using the FamilySearch website, and then merge the data in Family Tree Maker.

1 On the People workspace, select the person that is matched to FamilySearch.

2 Do one of the following:

   • Click the FamilySearch hint icon, then, in the WebSearch workspace that opens, click "Review historical records".

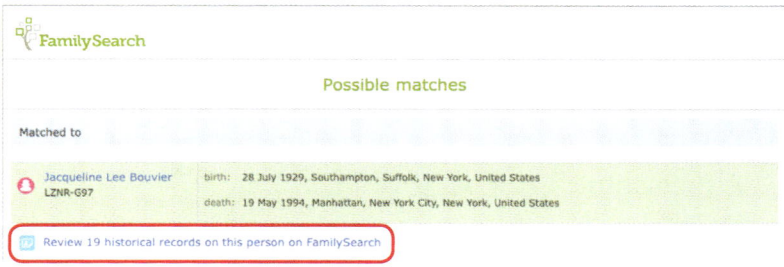

   • Click the "historical records" link from the FamilySearch tooltip in the tree viewer or the editing panel.

3 In the WebSearch workspace, log in to FamilySearch.org if needed.

4 Click **REVIEW & ATTACH** to select a historical record that you want to merge and attach to the person using FamilySearch.org.

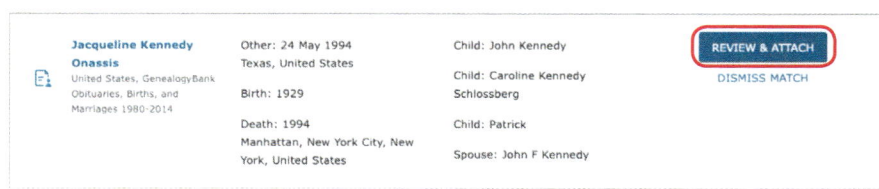

5   Click the person ID to return to the matched person in Family Tree Maker, and then merge the attached data for the individual. For more information, see "Adding Records to a Tree" below.

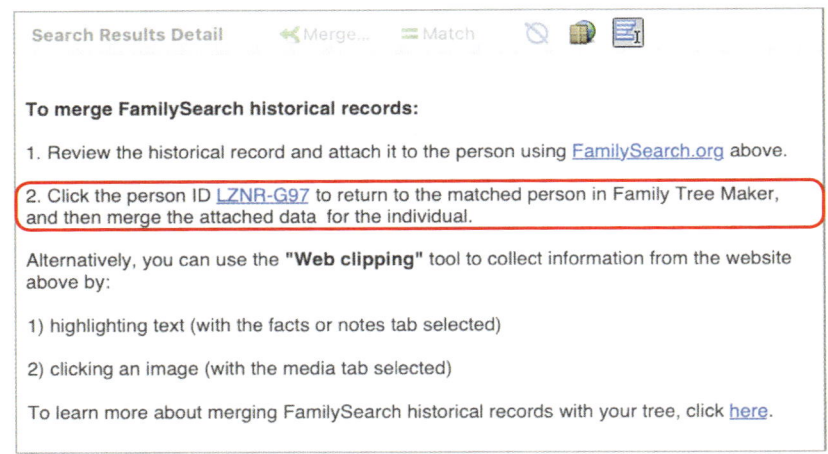

Alternatively, you can use the Web clipping tool to merge data. See "Copying Online Facts" on page 152.

Adding Records to a Tree

When you find a relevant record or family tree on Ancestry or FamilySearch, you can add the information directly to your tree using the Web Merge Wizard. You can choose the pieces of information you want to add and whether that information will be "preferred" or "alternate." The wizard can even include record images and sources for you automatically.

Note: It is always a good idea to save a backup of your tree file before making major changes using Web Merge.

1   In the Web Search workspace, select the record that you want to add to your tree.

2   Make sure the individual you want to add the record to is

selected in the **Person From Your Tree** section. If you need to add the record to a different person, click the **Select a different person** button (an index card) in the toolbar. Select an individual and click **OK**.

The bottom of the workspace displays the information in your tree compared side by side with the information found in the online record or tree.

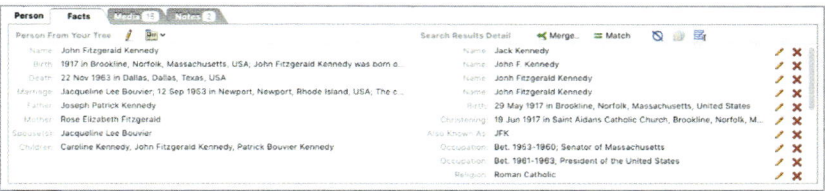

3   Click **Merge**. The Web Merge Wizard will open. Depending on the type of record you're accessing, the wizard may contain multiple pages.

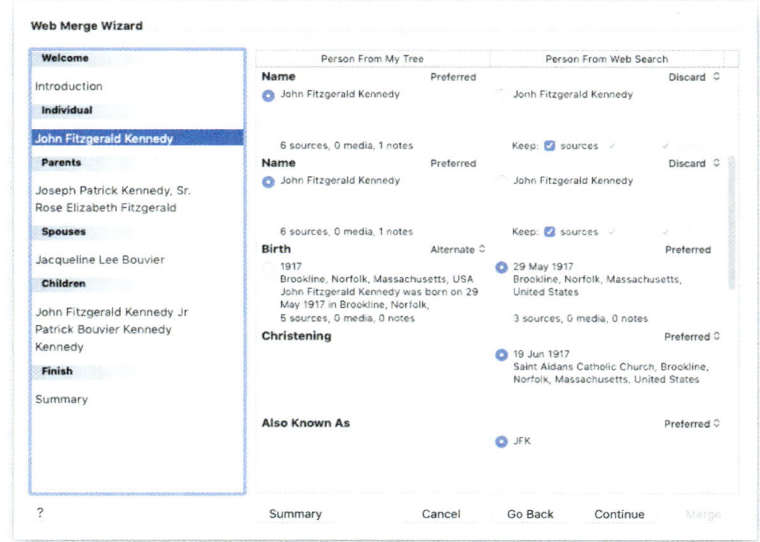

The left side of the dialog lists the names of the people included in the record you are adding. As you move through the wizard, each individual will be highlighted as you make decisions about his or her information. Next to the individuals' names, you'll see two columns: the **Person From My Tree** column shows the information you already have in your tree; the **Person From Web Search** column shows the information from the record.

4   Use the buttons next to the facts in the two columns to determine how each fact will be added:

- To keep a fact and mark it as "preferred," select the button next to the fact. The corresponding fact from the other source will be added as an alternate fact unless you choose to discard it.

- To remove a fact, click the arrow next to the **Alternate** heading and choose **Discard** from the pop-up menu. This fact will not be added to your tree. Though you may choose to discard some facts for a person, it is usually a good idea to keep all facts in case they turn out to be relevant.

If you discard a fact, you still have the option to add its source, media, and notes to your tree by clicking the corresponding checkboxes in the **Keep** group.

5   Click **Continue** and do one of the following:

- If the individual you want to add has parents, spouses, or children associated with the record, the wizard asks if you want to add the information found for the first additional family member. Go on to step 6.

- If the individual doesn't have relatives associated with the record, click the **Continue** button to go to the Summary dialog. Skip to step 8.

6   Choose what you want to do with each family member. You can ignore the person, add the person as a new individual in your tree, or merge the person with an existing individual in your tree.

The details about the additional family members appear in the **Person From Web Search** column, while the information you already have in your tree appears in the **Person From My Tree** column. You can compare the information you have with what Family Tree Maker has found. If more than one individual appears in the **Person From My Tree** column, you will need to select the individual with whom you want to merge the new information.

7   Click **Continue** and complete step 6 for every name in the record until all additional family members have been looked through. When you have made decisions for each family member, the Summary dialog opens.

8   Verify your selections in the Summary dialog. Click **Merge**. A message tells you when the information has been added successfully to your tree. Click **OK** to close the message.

Searching Online with Family Tree Maker

With Family Tree Maker, you have a convenient starting point for researching and expanding your family history—without interrupting your work. You can explore the Web using any of your favorite search engines or genealogy websites. Then use the "Web clipping" tool to select text and images you're interested in and add them to individuals in your tree.

152   Part 2: Building a Tree

1   Click the **Web Search** button on the main toolbar. Using the mini pedigree tree or Index of Individuals button, choose the individual whose information you want to search for.

2   In **Search Locations**, select the website you want to search, or type a website in the address field. The website opens.

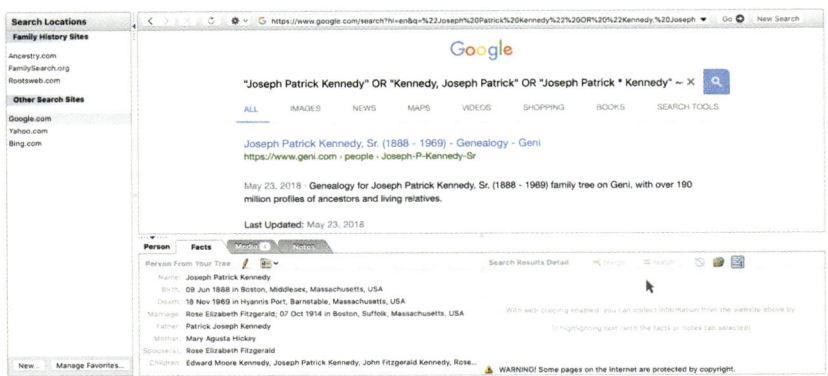

3   Look for information on your ancestors just as you would if you were performing any kind of online search.

Copying Online Facts

If you find details on a website that you'd like in your tree, you can use the "Web clipping" tool. In some cases, Family Tree Maker will recognize the type of information you're viewing and will give you relevant fields to choose from. For example, if you add info from the Social Security Death Index, you'll have the option to add the text to a name, Social Security Number, birth fact, or death fact.

1   Access the website you want to copy facts from.

2   If you want to link the facts to a different person, click the **Select a different person** button in the **Person From Your Tree** section which is located at the bottom of the window. Select an individual and click **OK**.

Chapter 8: Researching Your Tree Online   153

3   Click the **Facts** tab on the **Person From Your Tree** section's toolbar. On the Search Results Detail toolbar, click the **Enable web clipping** button.

4   Move the pointer over text on the website until the pointer turns into a cursor. Highlight the text you want to copy. A pop-up menu appears.

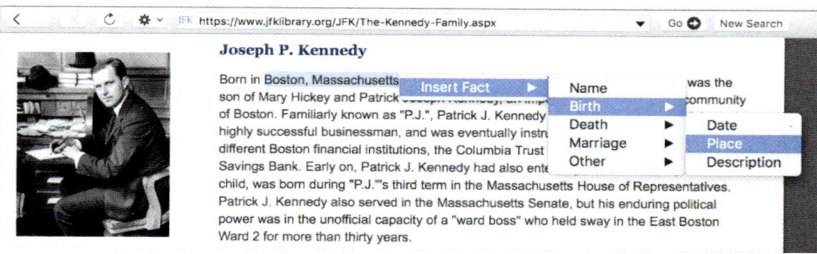

5   Choose a fact from the **Insert Fact** pop-up menu. For example, you can choose the birthplace fact. The highlighted information now appears in the Search Results Detail section.

Tip: You can copy multiple facts before adding the information to your tree; you don't need to add each fact individually.

6   When you have selected all the information you want, click **Merge**. The Web Merge Wizard will launch.

7   Choose how you want the information to be merged into your tree:

- To keep a fact and mark it as "preferred," select the button next to the fact. The corresponding fact for the other individual will be added as an alternate fact unless you choose to discard it.

- To remove a fact, click the arrow next to the **Alternate** heading and choose **Discard** from the pop-up menu. This fact will not be added to your tree. Though you may choose to discard some facts for a person, it is usually a good idea to keep all facts in case they turn out to be relevant.

If you discard a fact, you still have the option to add its source to your tree by clicking the **Keep sources** checkbox.

8   Click **Summary** to see how the information will be added to your tree. If necessary, click **Edit** to enter a source citation for the information. (The default source citation is the URL, or Web address, where the information was located.)

9   Click **Merge**. A message tells you when the information has been added successfully. Click **OK** to close the message.

Copying an Online Image

You may find family photos or historical documents that will enhance your family history. Family Tree Maker makes it easy to add these directly from a website to your tree.

Note: Before copying any images from the Web, make sure you aren't violating any copyrights and/or get permission from the owner.

1   Access the Web page with the image you want to copy.

2   If you want to link the image to a different person, click the **Select a different person** button in the **Person From Your Tree** section at the bottom of the window. Select an individual and click **OK**.

3   Click the **Media** tab on the **Person From Your Tree** section's toolbar. On the Search Results Detail toolbar, click the **Enable web clipping** button.

4 Move the pointer over the Web page until the image you want is highlighted by a green dotted line.

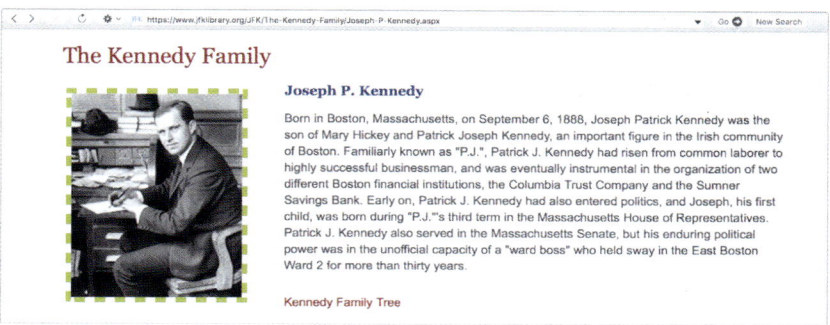

5 Click the highlighted image. A thumbnail of the image appears in the Search Results Detail section.

6 When you have selected all the images you want, click **Merge**. The Web Merge Wizard will open.

7 Click **Merge**. A message tells you when the image has been added successfully. Click **OK** to close the message.

Note: The image will be linked to the person in the **Person From Your Tree** section. You can also view it on the Media workspace.

Copying Online Text to a Note

While surfing the Web, you may come upon interesting stories about the founding of your grandfather's hometown or a description of the ship your great-grandparents sailed to America on. You can easily save this type of information using the "Web clipping" tool.

1 Access the website you want to copy information from.

156   Part 2: Building a Tree

2. If you want to link the notes to a different person, click the **Select a different person** button in the **Person From Your Tree** section. Select an individual and click **OK**.

3. Click the **Notes** tab on the **Person From Your Tree** section's toolbar. To add the text as a personal note, click the **Person note** button on the Search Results Detail toolbar; to add the text as a research note, click the **Research note** button.

4. On the Search Results Detail toolbar, click the **Enable web clipping** button.

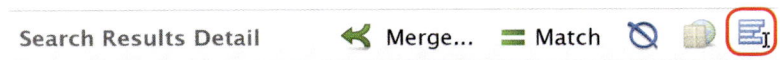

5. Move the pointer over text on the website until the pointer turns into a cursor. Highlight the text you want to copy. The **Insert Note** command appears.

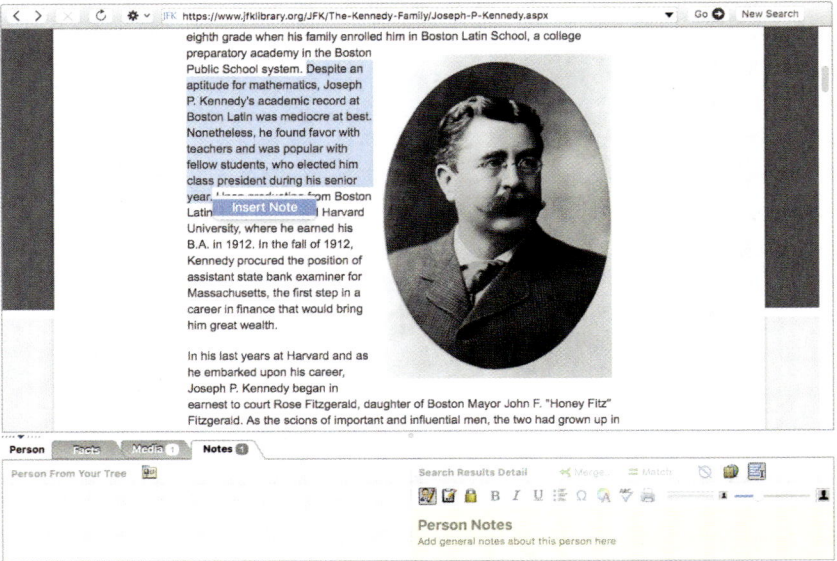

6 Click **Insert Note**. The information now appears in the **Search Results Detail** section.

7 Click **Merge**. The Web Merge Wizard will launch.

8 Click **Merge**. A message tells you when the text has been added successfully. Click **OK** to close the message.

Note: The notes will be linked to the person in the **Person From Your Tree** section. To view the notes later, go to the individual's Person tab on the People workspace and click the Notes tab at the bottom of the window.

Archiving a Web Page

Websites are constantly changing and even disappearing. If you find a website you want to refer to multiple times, or if you find a site that contains too much information to read in one sitting, you might want to archive the Web page. That way, you can read the page's contents and continue your research when it's convenient for you—without being connected to the Internet. When you archive a Web page, Family Tree Maker will save a "snapshot" of the page in HTML format that can be opened in any Web browser.

1 Access the Web page you want to archive.

2 If you want to link the archived page to a different person, click the **Select a different person** button in the **Person From Your Tree** section. Select an individual and click **OK**.

3 Click the **Facts**, **Media**, or **Notes** tab at the bottom of the workspace. On the **Search Results Detail** toolbar, click the **Create page archive** button.

A thumbnail of the page appears in the **Search Results Detail** section.

4. Click **Merge**. The Web Merge Wizard will launch.
5. Click **Merge**. A message tells you when the archived Web page has been added successfully. Click **OK** to close the message.

   Note: The archived page will be linked to the person in the **Person From Your Tree** section. To view the archived page later, go to the Media workspace.

Managing Research Websites

You can create a list of favorite family history websites so they're easy to visit.

Adding a Website to Your Favorites List

1. Click the **Web Search** button on the main toolbar. In **Search Locations**, click the **New** button.

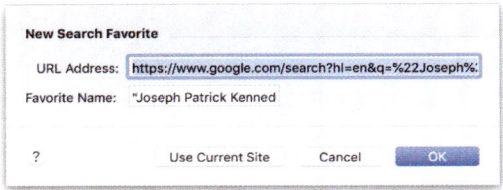

2. If you are currently viewing the website, click the **Use Current Site** button. If not, type the address for the website in the **URL Address** field.
3. Type a name for the website in the **Favorite Name** field. This can be any name that helps you identify the website.

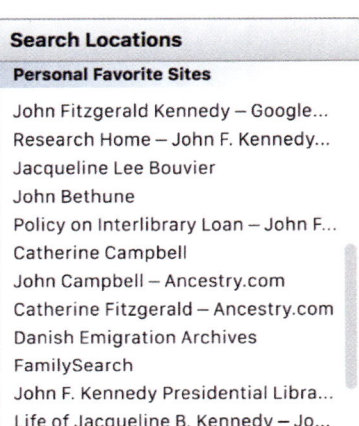

4 Click **OK**. The new website now appears in your list of favorites.

Sorting Your Website Favorites

If you've gathered quite a few favorite sites, you can sort the list so it appears in an order that's useful to you. For example, if you visit some websites daily, you can put them at the top of the list.

1 Click the **Web Search** button on the main toolbar. Click the **Manage Favorites** button at the bottom of the **Search Locations** area.

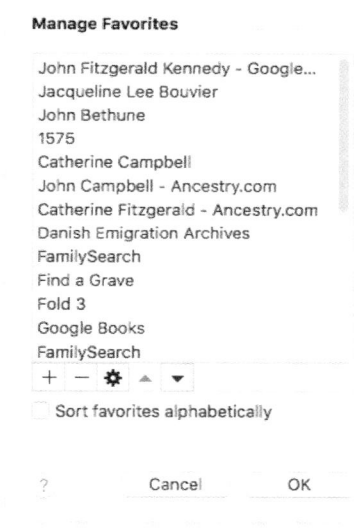

2 To display the websites in alphabetical order, select the **Sort favorites alphabetically** checkbox. To choose your own display order for the websites, deselect this checkbox, select a website and click the up and down arrows. When you're finished, click **OK**.

Part Three
Creating Charts, Reports, and Books

Chapter 9: Creating Family Tree Charts 163

Chapter 10: Running Reports 193

Chapter 11: Creating a Family History Book 221

Chapter Nine
Creating Family Tree Charts

After spending time gathering, compiling, and entering your family's history, it's time to show off your hard work. Family Tree Maker offers a wide variety of family tree charts to help you bring your family history to life. Add your own personal touch by customizing the charts with attractive backgrounds, colors, photos, fonts, and more. These charts help you quickly view the relationships between family members and are also a fun way to share your discoveries—hang a framed family tree in your home, print out multiple copies to share at a family reunion, or email charts to distant relatives.

As you begin creating your own charts, you might want to experiment with various formatting options, print out different versions, and see what you like best.

Pedigree Charts

The pedigree chart is a standard tool of genealogists and what most people think of when they hear the term "family tree." This chart shows the direct ancestors of one individual—parents, grandparents, great-grandparents, and so on.

Standard Pedigree Charts

In the standard pedigree chart (fig. 9-1), the primary individual is on the left side of the tree, with ancestors branching off to the right—paternal ancestors on top and maternal ancestors on bottom.

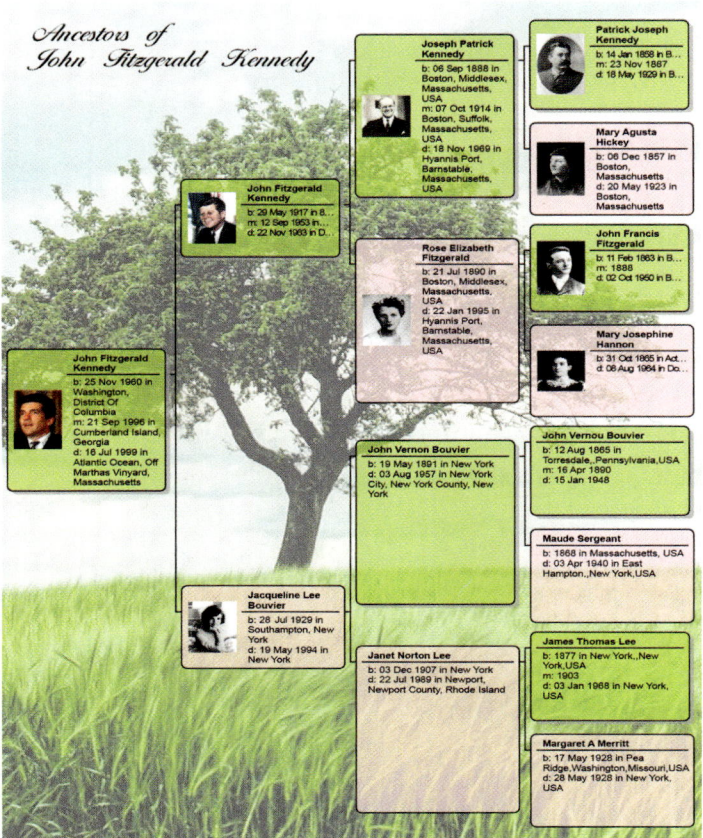

Figure 9-1. A pedigree chart using a custom template.

Vertical Pedigree Charts

In the vertical pedigree chart (fig. 9-2), the primary individual is shown at the bottom of the page, with his or her ancestors branching above the individual—paternal ancestors on the left and maternal ancestors on the right.

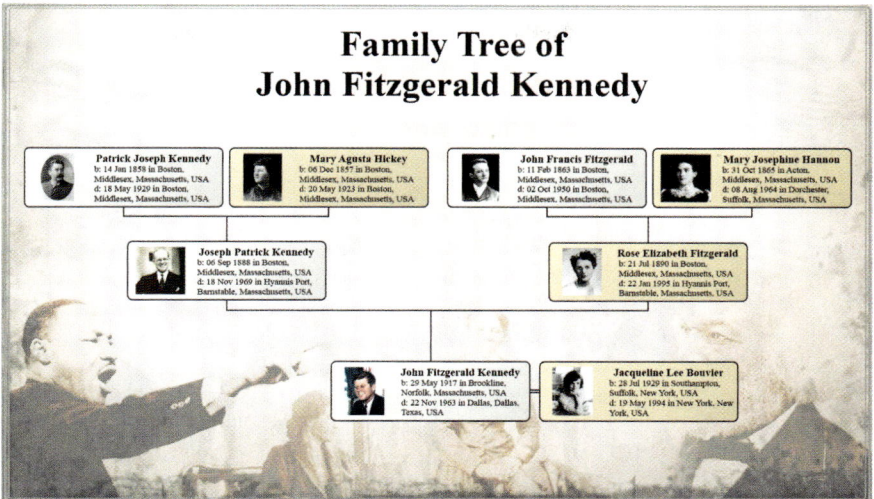

Figure 9-2. A customized vertical pedigree chart with images.

Hourglass Charts

An hourglass chart shows both the ancestors and descendants of an individual. The primary individual appears in the middle of the chart, with ancestors and descendants branching off in an hourglass shape.

Note: Because of its shape and the number of individuals included, most hourglass charts look best as posters.

Standard Hourglass Charts

In the standard hourglass chart, the primary individual appears in the middle of the chart, with ancestors branching above and descendants extending below the person.

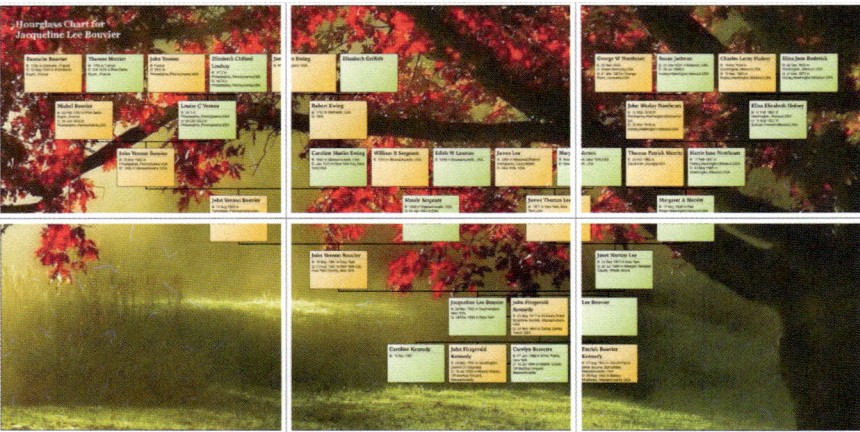

Figure 9-3. An hourglass poster spread over six pages.

The chart in figure 9-3 shows an hourglass chart laid out as a poster. Notice the white spaces running vertically and horizontally across the pages. These show the margins of a standard 8½" by 11" sheet of paper. If you want to print the tree at home, you can use these guides to tape the pages together.

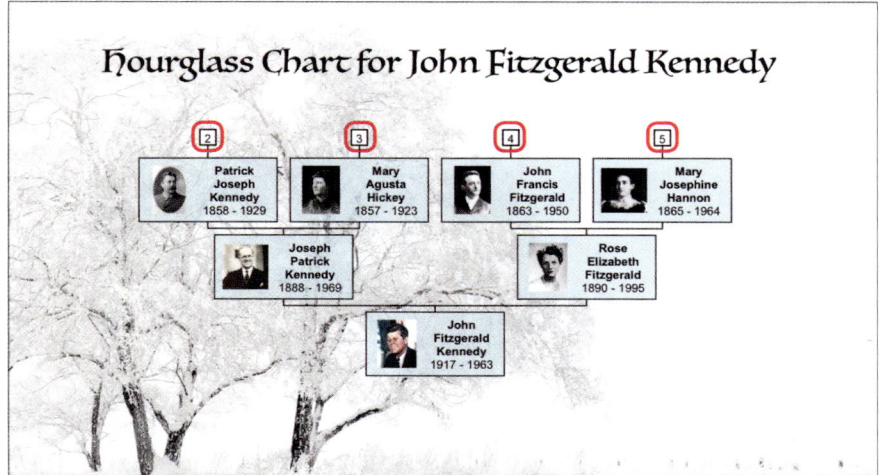

Figure 9-4. One page of a standard hourglass book chart.

You can also create standard hourglass charts that are useful for including in family history books. When you use the book layout, the chart is condensed into a series of individual family trees that appear on separate pages. The chart in figure 9-4 shows one page of a multi-page book chart. Notice the numbered boxes in the upper part of the chart. When you're viewing the chart in Family Tree Maker, you can click the box to access that page of the chart. And when your chart is printed, the numbered boxes help you navigate to related individuals found on other pages in the chart.

Horizontal Hourglass Charts

In the horizontal hourglass chart (fig. 9-5), the primary individual appears in the middle of the chart with ancestors branching to the right and descendants extending to the left of the person.

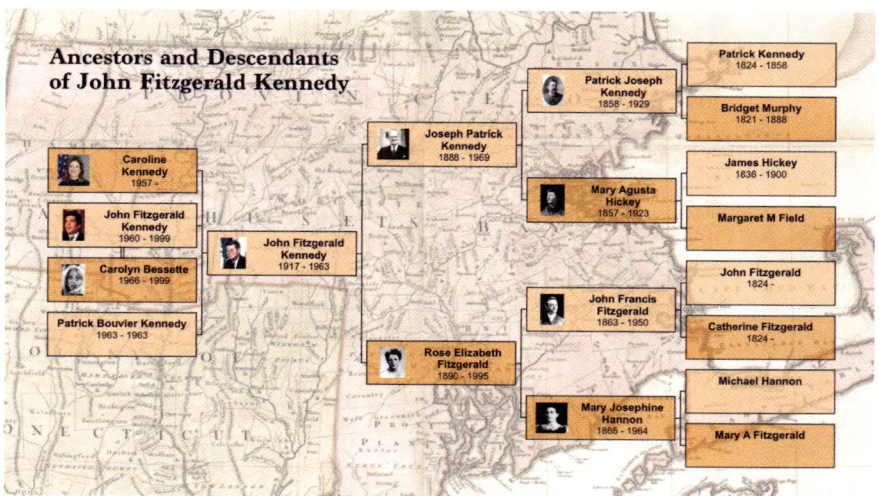

Figure 9-5. A horizontal hourglass chart.

Descendant Charts

The descendant chart shows the direct descendants of an individual—children, grandchildren, great-grandchildren, and so on. The primary individual is shown at the top of the chart, with descendants underneath in horizontal rows. You can also create a chart that shows the direct line between two selected individuals (fig. 9-6).

Figure 9-6. A direct-line descendant chart.

Bow Tie Charts

In the bow tie chart (fig. 9-7), the primary individual appears in the middle with paternal ancestors branching off to the left and maternal ancestors branching to the right.

Figure 9-7. A customized bow tie chart.

Note: Because of the shape and the number of individuals included, Bow Tie and Family Tree charts are available in poster layout only.

Family Tree Charts

In the family tree chart (fig. 9-8), the primary individual appears at the bottom of the chart, with ancestors branching above him or her in a tree shape.

Figure 9-8. A customized family tree chart with images.

Fan Charts

A fan chart displays an individual's ancestors in a circular shape, one generation per level. The primary individual is at the center or bottom of the chart. You can choose between a full circle, semi-circle (fig. 9-9), quarter-circle, and more.

Figure 9-9. A customized semi-circle fan chart.

Note: Because of its shape and the number of individuals included, this chart is available only in poster layout.

Extended Family Charts

The extended family chart (fig. 9-10) can display every individual you've entered in your tree or just the people you select. The chart is arranged so that each generation appears on a separate horizontal row: children, parents, and grandparents, etc.

Note: Because of its shape and the number of individuals included, this chart is available only in poster layout.

Chapter 9: Creating Family Tree Charts   171

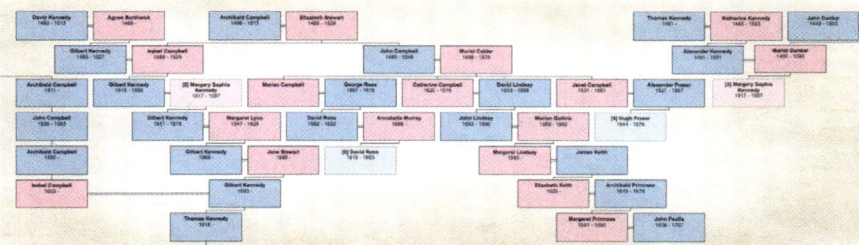

Figure 9-10. A section of an extended family chart.

Relationship Charts

The relationship chart (fig. 9-11) is a graphical representation of one person's relationship to another. The common relative is shown at the top of the chart, with direct-line ancestors and descendants shown vertically beneath the individual.

Figure 9-11. A relationship chart with a patterned background.

Creating a Chart

All charts are based on the last individual you were viewing in your tree. To change the primary individual in the chart, select an individual in the mini pedigree tree above the chart, or click the Index of Individuals button and select the person you want.

1. Go to the **Collection** tab on the Publish workspace. In **Publication Types**, select **Charts**.
2. Double-click the chart icon, or select its icon and click the **Detail** tab.
3. Use controls on the chart options panel to customize the chart.

Customizing a Chart

You can customize the contents and format of charts. For example, you can determine which facts are included and choose background images and fonts.

Note: You can save your custom changes as a template so you can use the same settings again. For instructions, see "Creating Your Own Template" on page 187.

Choosing Facts to Include in a Chart

In most charts you can choose which events or facts are included. Keep in mind, the more facts you add, the larger your chart will be.

1. Access the chart you want to change. In the editing toolbar, click the **Items to include** button.

The chart's default facts are shown in the Facts list. You can add and delete facts and change their display options.

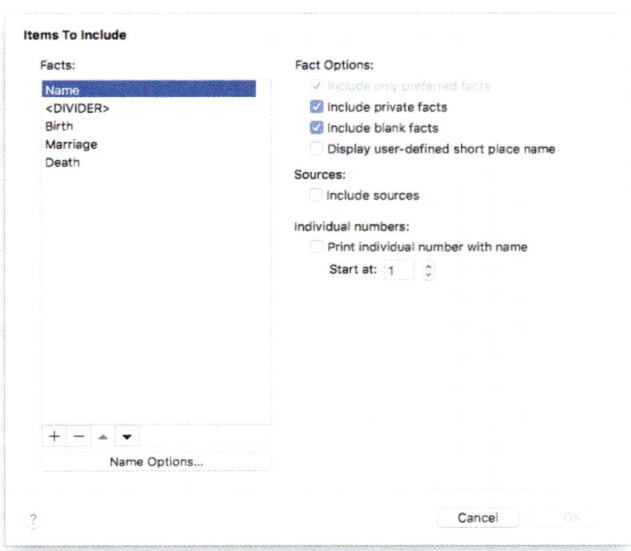

2 Do one of the following:

- To delete a fact, select the fact and click the **Delete** (-) button.
- To add a fact, click the **Add** (+) button. The Select Fact dialog opens. Select a fact and click **OK**.

3 Change the fact options as necessary:

- **Include only preferred facts.** Select this checkbox to include only preferred facts. If you have multiple facts for the same event, only the preferred one is included.
- **Include private facts.** Select this checkbox to include facts you've marked as private.

- **Include blank facts.** Select this checkbox to include a fact label even if the fact is empty.
- **Display user-defined short place name.** Select this checkbox to use shortened place names for locations.

4 To change a fact's format, select the fact in the Facts list and click the **Options** button. Select the options you want, click **OK**.

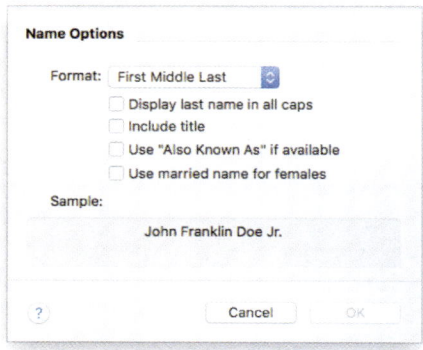

Note: Options vary by fact. For example, you can include dates and locations in births, marriages, and deaths.

5 Select the **Print individual number with name** checkbox to assign numbers to individuals in the chart.

6 Click **OK** again.

Changing a Chart's Title

You can change the title that appears at the top of a chart. Access the chart you want to change. In the editing panel, type a new name in the **Chart title** field.

To reset the original chart title, click the button with a blue arrow on it.

Including Source Information with a Chart

While you can't display sources in the actual chart, you can add a list of sources to the end of a chart (fig. 9-12).

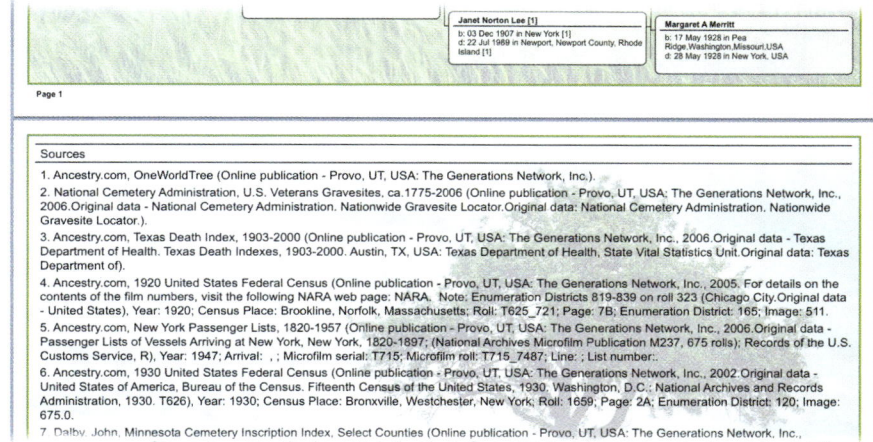

Figure 9-12. Sources on a pedigree chart.

1   Access the chart you want to change. In the editing toolbar, click the **Items to include** button.

2   Select the **Include sources** checkbox and click **OK**.

Adding Images to a Chart

You can personalize your charts and make them more appealing by adding backgrounds, family photographs, and portraits.

Adding a Background Image

Family Tree Maker comes with hundreds of attractive images you can use as chart backgrounds. Or you can create a background using an image on your computer or a photo in your tree.

1   Access the chart you want to change. In the editing panel, choose an image from the **Background** pop-up menu:

176 Part 3: Creating Charts, Reports, and Books

- To use an image on your computer, choose **Browse for an image**. Select an image and click **Open**.
- To use an image in your tree, choose **Select a media item**. Select an image and click **OK**.

2   Choose how the background will be displayed. To center the image on the page, choose **Center**. To stretch the image to fit the entire page, choose **Stretch**. To show a close-up of the image, choose **Zoom**. To show a series of the image, choose **Tile**.

3   Click the up and down arrows next to the **Transparent** percentage field to set the intensity of the image. You can also type an exact percentage directly in the field and press **Return**. At 0 percent, the image will look normal, while a higher percentage will fade the image so the chart is easier to read.

Adding Portraits to a Chart

You can include images of individuals in a chart. In order to do this, you must have already added the images to your tree and linked them to specific individuals. (For instructions see "Adding a Portrait for an Individual" on page 105.)

1   Access the chart you want to change. Choose an image type from the **Pictures** pop-up menu:

  - Choose **Thumbnail** to use low-resolution thumbnail images.
  - Choose **Photo** to use the photos at their actual resolution.

2   From the pop-up menu, choose how images are positioned next to fact boxes:

  - To align images with the middle of boxes, choose **Center**.
  - To align images with the top of boxes, choose **Top**.
  - To resize images to the same height as boxes, choose **Stretch**.
    Note: This option may cause your photos to look distorted.
  - To resize images to the same height as boxes (with cropped margins on the left and right side), choose **Zoom**.

3   To change the size of the photo or thumbnail, type a size in the **Inches wide** field.
    Note: The larger the image is, the less space available for facts.

4   Select the **Use silhouettes** checkbox to display a silhouette icon for individuals who don't have portraits.

Adding a Decorative Photo or Embellishment

You can add family photographs, borders, or embellishments to your charts.

1   Access the chart you want to change. In the editing toolbar, click the **Insert Image or Text Box** button.

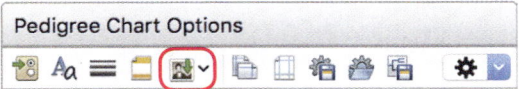

2   Choose an image type from the pop-up menu:

   - To use an image in your tree, choose **Insert Image from Media Collection**. Choose an image and click **OK**.
   - To use an image on your computer, choose **Insert Image from File**. Choose an image and click **Open**.
   - To use a graphic embellishment from the Family Tree Maker collection, choose **Insert Default Embellishment**. Choose an embellishment and click **Open**.

3   To resize an image, click it. Then move the pointer over the icon in the bottom-right corner. Click the corner and drag the image to the size you want.

4   To change the position of the image, move the pointer over the image, click it, and then drag the image to the location you want.

Adding Text

You can add text anywhere on a chart. For example, you could write a short biography of the main person in the chart (fig. 9-13).

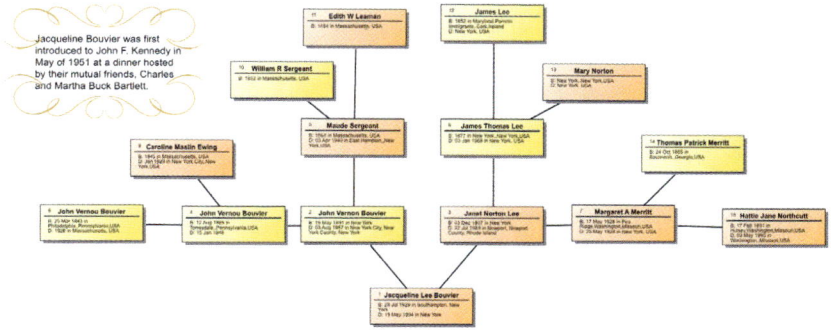

Figure 9-13. A family tree chart with a short biography.

1 Access the chart you want to add text to. In the editing toolbar, click the **Insert Image or Text Box** button.

2 Choose **Insert Text Box** from the pop-up menu.

3 To change the position of the text box, move the pointer over the text. When the pointer changes shape, click the box and drag it to the location you want.

4 To enter or edit text, double-click the box. Enter your text and click **OK**.

Tip: To change the text's size or color, click the **Fonts** button in the charts toolbar. In "Items Styles" select **Text Boxes**.

Changing the Header or Footer

You can define the headers and footers for each chart (the lines of text at the top and bottom of a chart).

Note: Not every option is available for every chart.

1 Access the chart you want to change. In the editing toolbar, click the **Header/Footer** button.

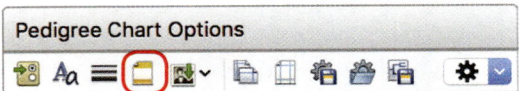

2 Change the header and footer options as necessary:
- **Chart Note.** Type the text you want to appear in the footer.
- **Draw box around footer.** Select this checkbox to enclose the footer in a box.
- **Print "Created with Family Tree Maker."** Select this checkbox to add this statement to the footer.
- **Include submitter info.** Select this checkbox to add your user information to the footer.
- **Include date of printing.** Select this checkbox to include the current date in the footer.
- **Include time of printing.** Select this checkbox to include the current time in the footer.
- **Include page/chart numbers.** Select this checkbox to include page numbers. From the pop-up menu, choose whether the number appears in the header or footer.

  In **Starting number** type the number of the chart's first page; in **Starting number for continuation charts**, type the number of the second page of the chart.

Chapter 9: Creating Family Tree Charts

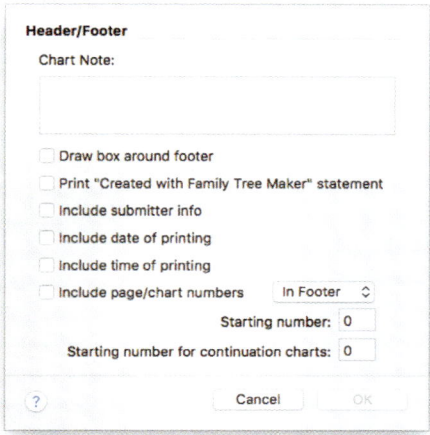

3 Click **OK**.

Changing Formatting for a Chart

You can change a chart's formatting such as its fonts, colors and borders, and box sizes.

Changing Layout Options

Depending on the number of individuals and facts in your chart, you may need to adjust the layout and spacing to best display each individual.

Note: Not every option is available for every chart.

1 Access the chart you want to change. The editing panel displays the options you can change.

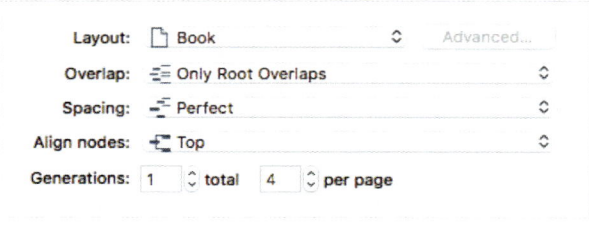

2 Change the chart's layout options as necessary:

- **Layout.** Choose **Book** to display the chart in pages suitable for using in a book; if a chart flows onto multiple pages, each page includes references to the generations continued on other pages. Choose **Poster** to display the chart in pages that can be linked together to form a poster (click the **Advanced** button to customize the poster format).

- **Overlap.** Determine the horizontal spacing of a chart. Choose **No Overlap** to space columns equally; choose **Columns Overlap** to overlap columns slightly; choose **Only Root Overlaps** to overlap the primary individual's column with the parents' column; choose **Fish Tail** to overlap all columns except for the last generation.

- **Spacing.** Change the vertical spacing. Choose **Perfect** to space rows evenly; choose **Collapsed** to space rows closer together; choose **Squished** to use minimal space between rows; choose **Custom** to adjust the spacing using the Advanced poster format.

  Tip: Collapse or squish columns if you want to fit many people on one page.

- **Align nodes.** Choose how lines connect individuals. Choose **Top** to use lines underneath names; choose **Center** to center lines next to each person; choose **Bezier** to use curved lines; choose **Straight** to use diagonal lines.

- **Center tree on page.** Select this checkbox to display the tree in the center of the page. If the chart is for a book, don't use this option. Instead, leave extra space in the left margin for binding.

- **Last descendant generation vertically.** Select this checkbox to show the last generation under their parents.

- **Boxes overlap page breaks.** Select this checkbox so boxes that fall on a page break will be split over two pages.
- **Include empty branches.** In the Book layout, displays all branches of the tree through the generations you have specified even if there is no person entered for them.

  Printing empty branches is useful when you want to collect more information about your family. You can fill out the boxes by hand and later transfer the information into Family Tree Maker.
- **Include duplicate ancestor lines.** If you have an instance of intermarriage in your family (for example, cousins marrying back into the family), you will have some duplicate individuals in your tree. Select this option if you want these individuals to print in your tree more than once.
- **Include siblings of primary individual.** Displays the brothers and sisters of the person selected for the chart. Siblings are displayed on the same level as the primary person. This option is not available in the Book layout.
- **Include spouses of primary individual.** Displays each husband or wife of the person selected for the chart.
- **Include all individuals.** Includes everyone entered in the tree file in the chart, even those individuals who may not be attached to the main tree. These unrelated people are displayed in a separate tree (or trees) at the bottom of the chart. When this option is not selected, unrelated people do not appear in the chart.
- **Display relationship label for each node.** Shows each person's relationship to the person in the **Relation from** field.
- **Show generation labels.** Displays the relationship of the generation (parent, grandparent, and so forth) to primary person

above each column of the chart (excluding the root). The font and box style can be configured for all generation labels by clicking the **Fonts** and the **Box and Line Styles** buttons.

Note: You cannot move the generation labels. If you manually change the location of the columns, the labels may no longer be aligned.

- **Show thumbnail.** Displays the picture you assigned to each person that appears on the chart. If a picture is not available, a silhouette is displayed instead.
- **Include civil/canon information.** Displays the civil and canon degrees of separation at the bottom of the chart. For more information, see "Civil Degree" and "Canon Degree" in the Relationship Calculator section of Chapter 14 (page 276).
- **Root Node at Fan Origin.** Orients the primary person's box so that it is square with the page. In charts of 90 degrees or less, the primary person's node is placed in the bottom-left corner of the chart. When not selected, the root node is placed closer to the other nodes and oriented with the chart.
- **Fan layout.** Specifies the number of degrees to use for the chart. The dark portion of each circle indicates how the chart will appear.

Adding Page Borders, Text Boxes, and Background Colors

You can enhance a chart by adding a border, background color, and text boxes.

1. Access the chart you want to change. In the editing toolbar, click the **Box and line styles** button.

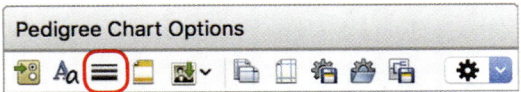

2 To change the format of text boxes, select a group in the Boxes list.

3 Change these options as necessary:
- Choose border, fill, and shadow colors from the pop-up menus.
- Select **Double line** to add two lines to box borders.
- Select **Rounded corners** to use round corners for box borders.
- Select **All boxes same size** to make all boxes on the chart the same size.
- Select **Semi-transparent** to make the background image or color partially visible through boxes.
- Select **Use gradient fill** to make a box's fill color go from light to dark.

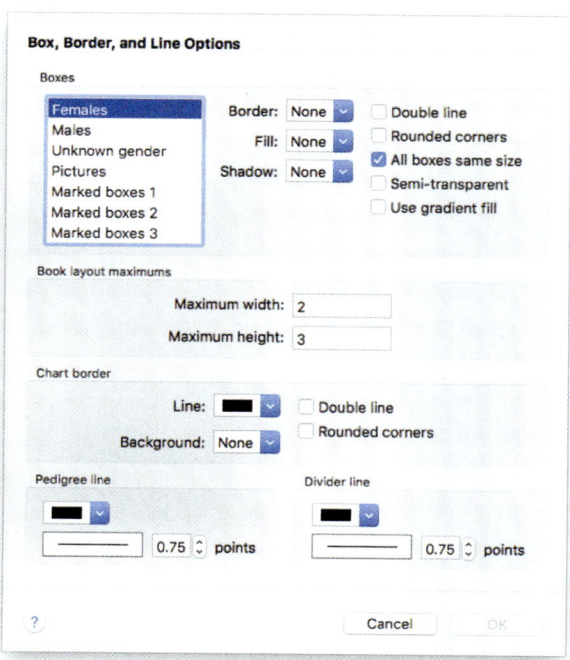

4 To change the size of boxes, type the maximum width and height (in inches) in "Poster layout initial box size."

5 To add a border to the entire chart, choose a color from the **Line** pop-up menu. Then select **Double line** to add two lines to the page border; select **Rounded corners** to use round corners.

6 To add a colored background, choose the color from the **Background** pop-up menu. (Choose "None" for a blank background.)

7 To change the format of pedigree and divider lines, choose colors from the pop-up menus. Then choose the line thickness.

8 Click **OK**.

Changing Fonts

You can change the appearance of the text in charts to make it more formal, more fun, or maybe just more readable.

1 Access the chart you want to change. In the editing toolbar, click the **Fonts** ![Aa] button.

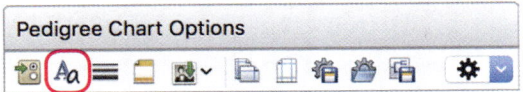

2 Select the text element, such as the chart title, you would like to change.

3 Choose a font from the **Font** pop-up menu. You can also change the size of the text, its style, color, and alignment.

4 Click **OK**.

Using Chart Templates

Family Tree Maker comes with several templates you can use to quickly dress up your family tree charts. You can also turn your own chart designs into templates.

Creating Your Own Template

After you've customized a chart with your favorite fonts and colors and changed the spacing and layout to make everyone fit perfectly on the page, you don't want to lose your settings. You can save your modifications as a template, and you won't have to recreate your changes if you want to use them on another chart.

1   After you've modified a chart, click the **Save settings** button in the editing toolbar.

2   Select one of these options:
    - **Save as preferred template.** This option saves the current settings as the preferred template for all charts. However, this template isn't permanent; if you modify the preferred template, the old settings will be written over.
    - **Create new template.** This option lets you name the template and add it to the list of custom chart templates.

3   Click **Save**. To apply the template to a chart, see the next section.

Using a Custom Template

Family Tree Maker lets you use attractive templates to instantly change the look of your chart.

You can apply custom templates to any chart. And if the results aren't exactly what you want, you can modify it.

1   Access the chart you want to apply a template to. In the editing toolbar, click the **Use saved settings** button .

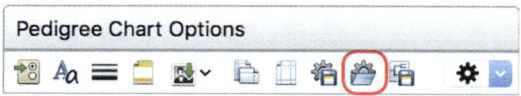

2   Select one of these template options:
    - **Default.** This is the default chart template.
    - **Preferred.** This is a template you have created and saved as your preferred template.
    - **Custom.** These are the custom templates found in Family Tree Maker (or templates you have created).

3   Click **Use**.

Saving Charts

You can save a specific chart in Family Tree Maker, or you can save a chart in different file formats to export.

Saving a Specific Chart

If you like a chart you've created, you'll probably want to save it. That way you can view it again without having to recreate it.

Tip: Your saved charts are added to your TreeVault Antenna tree.

1   Click the **Save chart** button in the editing toolbar.

2   Type a unique name for the chart. For example, don't use generic terms like "Pedigree Chart" or "Relationship Chart."

3   Click **Save**.

Tip: To open a saved chart, go to the Collection tab on the Publish workspace. In Publication Types, select **Saved Charts**. Then double-click the chart you want to open.

Saving a Chart as a File

You may want to save a chart as an image or PDF so you can share it easily with family or post it online.

1. Access the chart you want to save.
2. Click the **Share** button above the editing panel. From the pop-up menu, choose one of these commands:
    - **Export to PDF.** An Adobe PDF (Portable Document Format) is useful because it keeps the formatting you select. If you print a chart or send it to a relative, the chart will look exactly as you see it on your monitor. You cannot make changes to the PDF within Family Tree Maker.
    - **Export to One Page PDF.** This option exports the chart as one page (regardless of size). Use this option if you're creating a poster-sized chart or printing a chart at a copy store.
    - **Export to Image.** This option lets you create an image of the chart as a bitmap or JPEG, or in another image format.
3. Select the location where you want to save the chart; then type a name for the chart and click **Save**.

Printing a Chart

1. Access the chart you want to print.
2. Click the **Print** button above the editing panel.
3. When prompted choose a printer, select the number of copies, and choose a page range.
4. Click **Print**.

Large Chart Printing

With Family Tree Maker, you can order a large, high-quality, professional print of your chart from the Family ChartMasters website in just a few clicks.

1   Access the chart you want to print.
2   Click the **Share** button above the editing panel, and then choose **Order Large Print at Family ChartMasters** from the pop-up menu.
3   In the message that appears, click **Export Chart to PDF**.
4   Change any options as necessary and click **Save**.
5   When the export process is complete, a new message appears. Click the **Go to Family ChartMasters Website** button.
6   The Family ChartMasters website opens in your default web browser. Follow the onscreen instructions to upload the exported file and order a large format print of your family tree.

Sharing a Chart

You can share your charts with others by emailing them as PDFs.

Note: You must be connected to the Internet and have a desktop email application to use this feature.

1   Access the chart you want to email.
2   Click the **Share** button above the editing panel. From the pop-up menu, choose **Send as PDF**.
3   Change any options as necessary and click **Save**. Family Tree Maker opens a new email (with the file attached) in your default email application.
4   Send the email as you would any other.

Charting Companion Plug-In

If you like making charts with Family Tree Maker, you'll love the amazing array of additional chart types and settings you get with Progeny Genealogy's Charting Companion.

You can access the plug-in from the Tools menu and it will work directly with your charts as though it were part of Family Tree Maker.

Charting Companion provides more than a dozen unique chart types not found in Family Tree Maker, including the DNA Matrix, DNA Simulation, Descendant Fan (a combination of descendant and family tree fan charts), plus a great collection of embellishments, and lots of special options for printing.

To get the plug-in, please visit www.familytreemaker.com and follow the **GIFT Collection** link.

Tip: For more information, visit ftm.support/cc.

Chapter Ten
Running Reports

Family Tree Maker includes a number of reports to help you organize and understand the information you've entered in your tree. You can create detailed reports about a single family, such as the family group sheet, relationship reports that show marriage events, bibliographies and source reports that help you keep track of your research.

Each report can be customized—options differ by report. You can change fonts, add background images, and add headers and footers.

Genealogy Reports

Genealogy reports are a staple of serious family historians. These narrative reports contain biographical details about individuals. Relationships between people are shown using numbering systems that are unique to each report. You can choose from ancestor-ordered reports (Ahnentafels) or descendant-ordered reports.

Ahnentafel Report

The Ahnentafel (a German word meaning "ancestor table") is a numbered list of individuals (fig. 10-1). Its format is ancestor-ordered, meaning that it starts with one individual and moves backward in time to that individual's ancestors. This type of report isn't used frequently because it shows two family lines at the same time.

Ancestors of John Vernon Bouvier

Generation 1

1. **John Vernon Bouvier**, son of John Vernou Bouvier and Maude Sergeant was born on 19 May 1891 in New York, New York, USA. He died on 03 Aug 1957 in New York, New York, New York, USA. He married **Janet Norton Lee**. She was born on 03 Dec 1907 in New York, New York, USA. She died on 22 Jul 1989 in Newport, Newport County, Rhode Island, USA.

Generation 2

2. **John Vernou Bouvier**, son of John Vernou Bouvier and Caroline Maslin Ewing was born on 12 Aug 1865 in Torresdale, Philadelphia, Pennsylvania, USA. He died on 15 Jan 1948. He married **Maude Sergeant**, daughter of William R Sergeant and Edith W Leaman on 16 Apr 1890.

3. **Maude Sergeant**, daughter of William R Sergeant and Edith W Leaman was born in 1868 in Massachusetts, USA. She died on 03 Apr 1940 in East Hampton, Suffolk, New York, USA.

Maude Sergeant and John Vernou Bouvier had the following child:

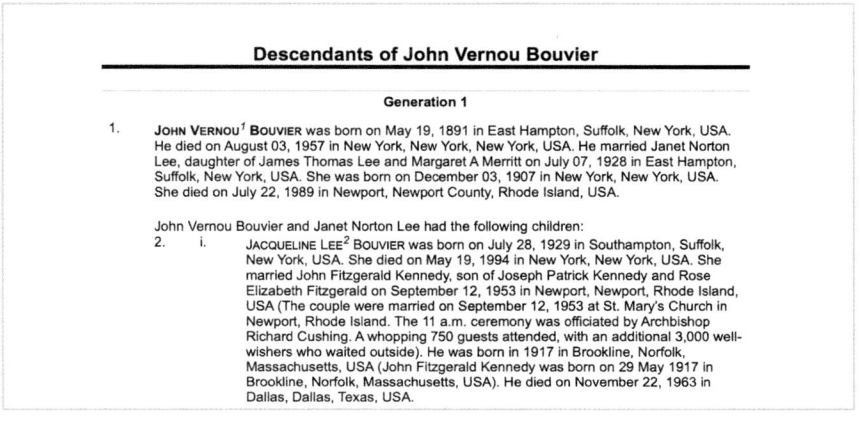

Figure 10-1. An Ahnentafel (ancestor report).

Descendant Report

A descendant report (fig. 10-2) is a narrative report that includes biographical information about each individual. It is descendant-ordered, meaning it starts with an individual and moves forward in time through that individual's children and grandchildren. You have four numbering system options: Register, NGSQ, Modified Henry, and d'Aboville.

Descendants of John Vernou Bouvier

Generation 1

1. JOHN VERNOU[1] BOUVIER was born on May 19, 1891 in East Hampton, Suffolk, New York, USA. He died on August 03, 1957 in New York, New York, New York, USA. He married Janet Norton Lee, daughter of James Thomas Lee and Margaret A Merritt on July 07, 1928 in East Hampton, Suffolk, New York, USA. She was born on December 03, 1907 in New York, New York, USA. She died on July 22, 1989 in Newport, Newport County, Rhode Island, USA.

John Vernou Bouvier and Janet Norton Lee had the following children:

2. i. JACQUELINE LEE[2] BOUVIER was born on July 28, 1929 in Southampton, Suffolk, New York, USA. She died on May 19, 1994 in New York, New York, USA. She married John Fitzgerald Kennedy, son of Joseph Patrick Kennedy and Rose Elizabeth Fitzgerald on September 12, 1953 in Newport, Newport, Rhode Island, USA (The couple were married on September 12, 1953 at St. Mary's Church in Newport, Rhode Island. The 11 a.m. ceremony was officiated by Archbishop Richard Cushing. A whopping 750 guests attended, with an additional 3,000 well-wishers who waited outside). He was born in 1917 in Brookline, Norfolk, Massachusetts, USA (John Fitzgerald Kennedy was born on 29 May 1917 in Brookline, Norfolk, Massachusetts, USA). He died on November 22, 1963 in Dallas, Dallas, Texas, USA.

Figure 10-2. A Register descendant report.

Person Reports

Person reports give you an overview of your tree and help you focus on specific individuals.

Custom Report

Custom reports (fig. 10-3) let you explore your tree in ways that are interesting to you. For example, you can create a custom report of birthplaces or causes of death.

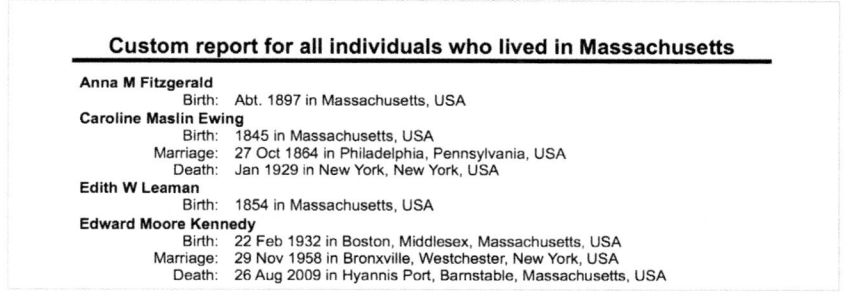

Figure 10-3. A custom report of all individuals who lived in Massachusetts.

Data Errors Report

The Data Errors Report (fig. 10-4) lists all instances where data is missing or may be incorrect. This includes nonsensical dates (e.g., an individual being born before his or her parents were born), missing dates, and duplicate individuals. (For more information see "Running the Data Errors Report" on page 314.)

Name	Birth Date	Potential Error
Lee Bouvier		The birth date is missing.
Muriel Calder	13 Feb 1498	The marriage date is missing.
Catherine Fitzgerald	Abt. 1824	The marriage date is missing. The individual has the same last name as his/her spouse, John Fitzgerald.
John Fitzgerald	Abt. 1824	The individual has the same last

Figure 10-4. A Data Errors Report.

Individual Report

The Individual Report (fig. 10-5) lists every fact and source you have recorded for a specific individual.

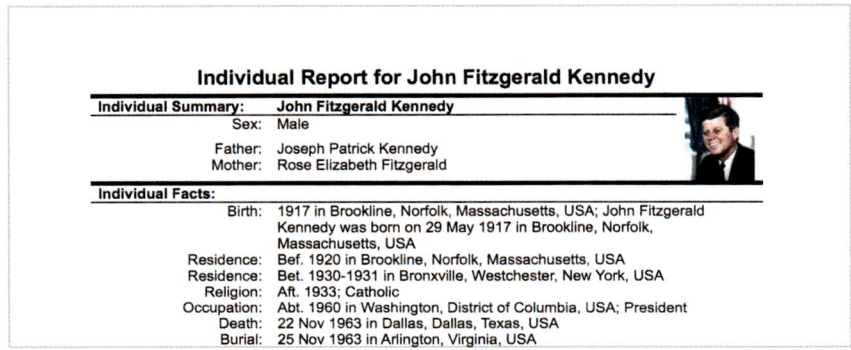

Figure 10-5. An Individual Report.

LDS Ordinances Report

The LDS Ordinances Report (fig. 10-6) is useful for members of The Church of Jesus Christ of Latter-day Saints and displays LDS-specific ordinances such as baptisms and sealings.

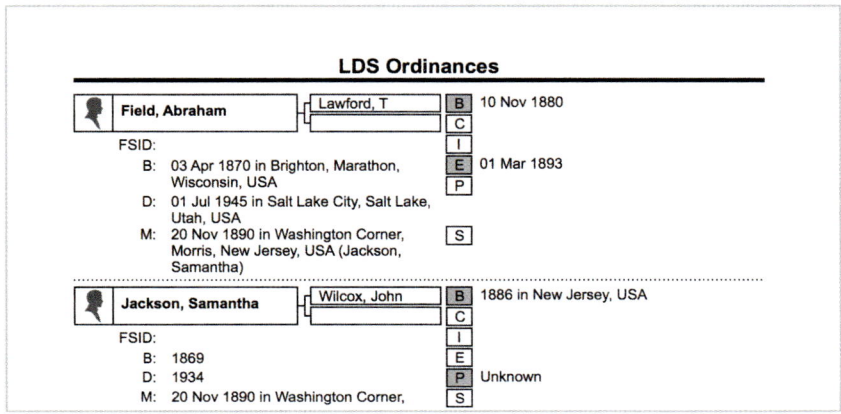

Figure 10-6. An LDS Ordinances Report.

LDS Ordinance Summary Report

The LDS Ordinance Summary Report (fig. 10-7) lists all people in the tree and their LDS ordinances status. You can restrict the report to selected individuals.

LDS Ordinance Summary

Name	Lifespan	Spouse	B	C	I	E	P	S
Field, Abraham	1870 - 1945	Jackson, Samantha	X			X		
Jackson, Samantha	1869 - 1934	Field, Abraham	X					X
Lawford, Thomas	1851 - Unknown				X			
Smith, Herbert	Unknown - Unknown	Steward, Phoebe Jackson	X					
Steward, Phoebe Jackson	1900 - 1948	Smith, Herbert					X	

Figure 10-7. An LDS Ordinance Summary Report.

Note: Choose **Family Tree Maker 2019>Settings** (**Preferences** on macOS 12 Monterey or earlier) and then select the **Show LDS information** checkbox to access the LDS Ordinances Report and the LDS Ordinance Summary Report.

List of Individuals Report

The List of Individuals Report has five options: all individuals in your tree, all individuals and their ID numbers, a list of anniversaries, a list of birthdays (fig. 10-8), and a contact list.

Birthday List

Name	Birth	Birthday	Death	Age
Bessette, Carolyn	07 Jan 1966	53	16 Jul 1999	33
Kennedy, Patrick Joseph	14 Jan 1858	161	18 May 1929	71
Bouvier, Michel	02 Feb 1792	227	09 Jun 1874	82
Fitzgerald, John Francis	11 Feb 1863	155	02 Oct 1950	87
Calder, Muriel	13 Feb 1498	520	1575	76

Figure 10-8. A list of birthdays.

Notes Report

The Notes Report (fig. 10-9) lets you view the person, research, relationship, or fact notes you've entered in your tree.

Notes Report

Kennedy, John Fitzgerald	**1917 - 22 Nov 1963**
Person Note:	In September 1935, Kennedy made his first trip abroad when he traveled to London with his parents and his sister Kathleen. He intended to study under Harold Laski at the London School of Economics (LSE), as his older brother had done. Ill-health forced his return to America in October of that year, when he enrolled late and spent six weeks at Princeton University. He was then hospitalized for observation at Peter Bent Brigham Hospital in Boston.
NameFact Note:	John Fitzgerald Kennedy was named in honor of Rose's father, John Francis Fitzgerald, the Boston Mayor popularly known as Honey Fitz. Before long, family and friends called this small blue-eyed baby, Jack.
Kennedy, Joseph Patrick	**06 Sep 1888 - 18 Nov 1969**
Research Note:	The couple had nine children. As Kennedy's business expanded, he

Figure 10-9. A report of several notes.

Surname Report

The Surname Report (fig. 10-10) lists the total number of individuals with a specific surname, the number of males and females with that surname, and the birth year of the earliest and the most recent person with that surname who appears in your tree.

Surname Report

Surname	Count	Male	Female	Earliest	Most recent
Kennedy	36	26	10	1461	1963
Campbell	14	8	6	1400	1603
Fraser	14	10	4	1527	1635
Stewart	14	4	10	1400	1650
Fitzgerald	9	3	6	1824	1899
Bethune	7	5	2	1491	1633
Bouvier	7	5	2	1758	1933
Ross	7	6	1	1557	1679
Lindsay	6	3	3	1503	1772
Shriver	6	5	1	1916	1916
Lawford	5	2	3	1923	1923

Figure 10-10. A Surname Report sorted by name count.

Task List

A task list (fig. 10-11) displays all research tasks on your to-do list. You can see each task's priority, category, and creation and due dates. To learn more about creating and managing tasks, see "Research To-Do List" on page 281

Task List

Status	Task Information	Date Due
☐ ❗	Scan photos for mom's personal history Task for: General Task Categories: Created: 2/10/18	2/16/18
☐ ⬤	Write to Berks County Historical Society for Reed/Rieth church records Task for: General Task Categories: Reed Created: 2/10/18	2/13/18

Figure 10-11. A research to-do list.

Timeline Report

A timeline (fig. 10-12) lists an individual's life events with the date and location of the event and the person's age at the time. You can also include events for an individual's immediate family (such as birth, marriage, and death) and historical events.

Timeline Report for Joseph Patrick Kennedy

Yr/Age	Event	Date/Place/Description
1888	Birth	06 Sep 1888 Boston, Middlesex, Massachusetts, USA
1890	Birth (spouse) Rose Elizabeth Fitzgerald	21 Jul 1890 Boston, Middlesex, Massachusetts, USA
1891 2	Birth (brother) Francis Kennedy	11 Mar 1891
1892 3	Death (brother) Francis Kennedy	14 Jan 1892
1892 3	Birth (sister) Loretta Kennedy	06 Aug 1892
1898 10	Birth (sister) Margaret Kennedy	22 Oct 1898

Figure 10-12. A timeline for an individual and his family.

Relationship Reports

Relationship reports are just what they sound like. They show the relationships between different individuals and families in your tree.

Family Group Sheet

A family group sheet (fig. 10-13) is one of the most commonly used reports in family history. It is a detailed report about a single family (primarily the parents and children of a family, although it also includes the names of the couple's parents), including names, birth, death, and marriage information; notes; and sources. If the individual has more than one spouse, additional family group sheets will be created for each family.

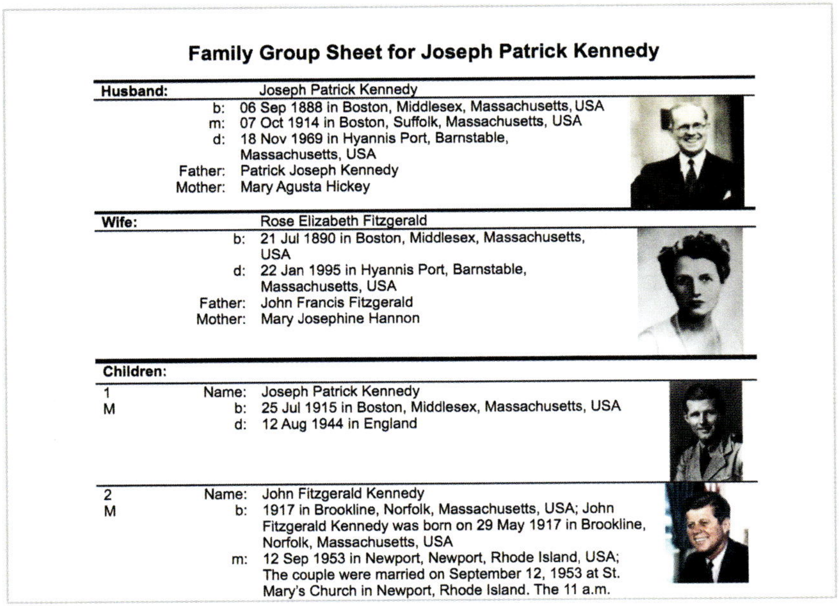

Figure 10-13. A family group sheet.

Kinship Report

The Kinship Report (fig. 10-14) helps you determine how individuals in your tree are related to a specific person.

```
                    Kinship Report for Joseph Patrick Kennedy
Name:                           Birth Date:        Relationship:
Kennedy, Joseph Patrick         06 Sep 1888        Self
Kennedy, John                   1715               3rd great grandfather
Kennedy, Kathleen "Kick" Agnes  20 Feb 1920        Daughter
Kennedy, Patricia               06 May 1924        Daughter
Kennedy, Rosemary               13 Sep 1918        Daughter
Kennedy, Patrick Joseph         14 Jan 1858        Father
Kennedy, Kara Anne              27 Feb 1960        Granddaughter
Kennedy, John Fitzgerald        25 Nov 1960        Grandson
Kennedy, Michael LeMoyne        27 Feb 1958        Grandson
Kennedy, Patrick Bouvier        07 Aug 1963        Grandson
Kennedy, Patrick Joseph Francis 1760               Great grandfather
Fitzgerald Henry Jones
```

Figure 10-14. A Kinship Report.

Marriage Report

The Marriage Report (fig. 10-15) shows husbands and wives, their marriage dates, and relationship statuses.

```
                           Marriage Report
Husband:            Wife:                   Marriage Date:    Relation:
Bouvier, Eustache   Mercier, Therese        03 Feb 1789       Spouse - Ongoing
Bouvier, John Vernon Lee, Janet Norton                        Spouse - Ongoing
Bouvier, John Vernou Sergeant, Maude        16 Apr 1890       Spouse - Ongoing
Bouvier, John Vernou Ewing, Caroline Maslin 27 Oct 1864       Spouse - Ongoing
Bouvier, Michel     Vernou, Louise C        29 May 1828       Spouse - Ongoing
Fitzgerald, John    Fitzgerald, Catherine                     Spouse - Ongoing
Fitzgerald, John    Hannon, Mary            1888              Spouse - Ongoing
Francis             Josephine
Hulsey, Charles Leroy Roderick, Eliza Jane  31 Jul 1856       Spouse - Ongoing
Kennedy, John       Bouvier, Jacqueline     12 Sep 1953       Spouse - Ongoing
Fitzgerald          Lee
Kennedy, John       Bessette, Carolyn       21 Sep 1996       Spouse - Ongoing
Fitzgerald
Kennedy, Joseph     Fitzgerald, Rose        07 Oct 1914       Spouse - Ongoing
Patrick             Elizabeth
```

Figure 10-15. A Marriage Report.

Outline Ancestor Report

The Outline Ancestor Report (fig. 10-16) shows where everyone fits in the family. Starting with a relative, it moves to the past, showing the primary individual's parents, grandparents, great-grandparents, and so on, generation by generation in outline format, with each individual on a separate line.

```
       Outline Ancestor Report for Joseph Patrick Kennedy
  1  Joseph Patrick Kennedy b: 06 Sep 1888 in Boston, Middlesex, Massachusetts, USA, d: 18 Nov
     1969 in Hyannis Port, Barnstable, Massachusetts, USA
     +  Rose Elizabeth Fitzgerald b: 21 Jul 1890 in Boston, Middlesex, Massachusetts, USA, m: 07
        Oct 1914 in Boston, Suffolk, Massachusetts, USA, d: 22 Jan 1995 in Hyannis Port,
        Barnstable, Massachusetts, USA
  ..2  Patrick Joseph Kennedy b: 14 Jan 1858 in Boston, Middlesex, Massachusetts, USA, d: 18
       May 1929 in Boston, Middlesex, Massachusetts, USA
       +  Mary Agusta Hickey b: 06 Dec 1857 in Boston, Middlesex, Massachusetts, USA, m: 23 Nov
          1887, d: 20 May 1923 in Boston, Middlesex, Massachusetts, USA
    ......3  Patrick Kennedy b: 1824 in Ireland, d: 22 Nov 1858 in Boston, Middlesex, Massachusetts,
             USA
```

Figure 10-16. An Outline Ancestor Report.

Outline Descendant Report

The Outline Descendant Report (fig. 10-17) starts with an ancestor and outlines each generation of descendants; you can choose the number of generations to show in the report.

```
          Outline Descendant Report for Patrick Kennedy
 ..... 1  Patrick Kennedy b: 1824 in Ireland, d: 22 Nov 1858 in Boston, Middlesex, Massachusetts,
          USA
  .....    +Bridget Murphy b: 1821 in Wexford, Ireland, d: 20 Dec 1888 in Boston, Middlesex,
           Massachusetts, United States, m: 26 Sep 1849 in Boston, Middlesex, Massachusetts, USA
  ..........  2  Patrick Joseph Kennedy b: 14 Jan 1858 in Boston, Middlesex, Massachusetts, USA, d:
                 18 May 1929 in Boston, Middlesex, Massachusetts, USA
  ..........    +Mary Agusta Hickey b: 06 Dec 1857 in Boston, Middlesex, Massachusetts, USA, d: 20
                May 1923 in Boston, Middlesex, Massachusetts, USA, m: 23 Nov 1887
  ...............  3  Francis Kennedy b: 11 Mar 1891, d: 14 Jan 1892
  ...............  3  Loretta Kennedy b: 06 Aug 1892, d: 1972
  ...............  3  Margaret Kennedy b: 22 Oct 1898, d: 15 Nov 1974
  ...............  3  Joseph Patrick Kennedy b: 06 Sep 1888 in Boston, Middlesex, Massachusetts,
                      USA, d: 18 Nov 1969 in Hyannis Port, Barnstable, Massachusetts, USA
  ...............    +Rose Elizabeth Fitzgerald b: 21 Jul 1890 in Boston, Middlesex, Massachusetts,
                     USA, d: 22 Jan 1995 in Hyannis Port, Barnstable, Massachusetts, USA, m: 07 Oct
                     1914 in Boston, Suffolk, Massachusetts, USA
  ....................  4  Joseph Patrick Kennedy b: 25 Jul 1915 in Boston, Middlesex, Massachusetts,
```

Figure 10-17. An Outline Descendant Report.

Parentage Report

The Parentage Report (fig. 10-18) lists each individual, his or her parents, and their relationship (e.g., biological, adopted, foster).

Parentage Report

Name	Parents	Relationship
Kennedy, Loretta	Kennedy, Patrick Joseph	Biological
	Hickey, Mary Agusta	Biological
Kennedy, Margaret	Kennedy, Patrick Joseph	Biological
	Hickey, Mary Agusta	Biological
Kennedy, Francis	Kennedy, Patrick Joseph	Biological
	Hickey, Mary Agusta	Biological
Hickey, Mary Agusta	Hickey, James	Biological
	Field, Margaret M	Biological

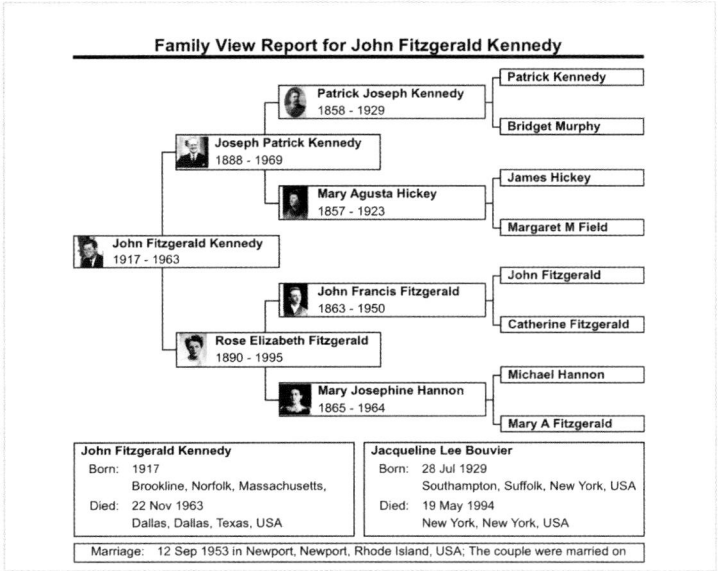

Figure 10-18. A Parentage Report.

Family View Report

The Family View Report (fig. 10-19) shows three generations of ancestors for an individual and his or her parents and children.

Figure 10-19. A Family View Report.

Place Usage Report

The Place Usage Report (fig. 10-20) lists the locations in your tree and each person associated with them. You can also include specific events, such as birth or marriage, that occurred at that location.

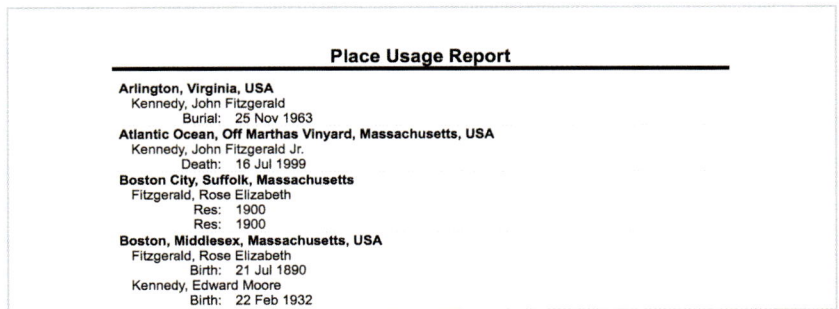

Figure 10-20. A Place Usage Report.

Media Reports

Media reports let you view media items individually or in groups.

Photo Album

A photo album (fig. 10-21) shows a person's birth and death dates, the names of their parents, and all photos linked to them.

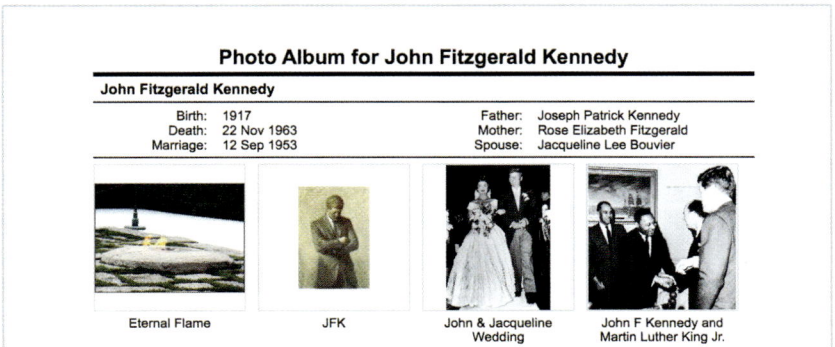

Figure 10-21. A photo album for an individual.

Media Item Report

A Media Item Report (fig. 10-22) shows an item or its icon, its caption, date of origin, description, and the people the item is linked to.

Figure 10-22. A Media Item Report.

Media Usage Report

The Media Usage Report (fig. 10-23) lists your media items. For each item you'll see a thumbnail, name, location on your computer, and people it is linked to.

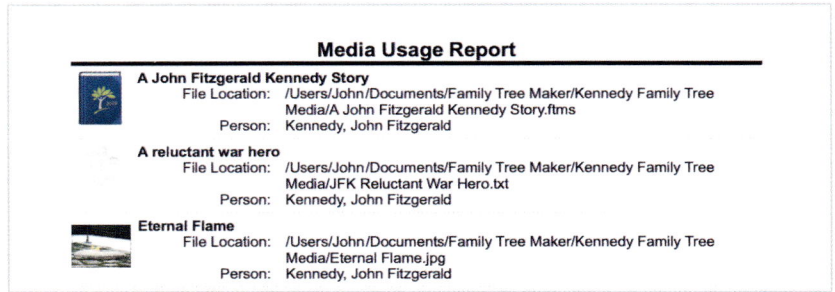

Figure 10-23. A Media Usage Report.

Source Reports

Family Tree Maker includes several reports that help you see how you've sourced facts in your tree.

Source Bibliography

A bibliography (fig. 10-24) is a detailed list of all the sources used in your research.

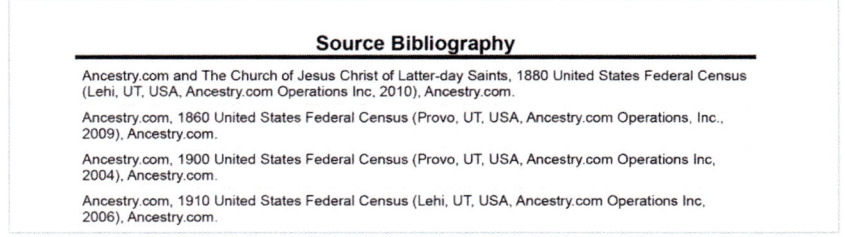

Figure 10-24. An annotated bibliography.

Documented Facts Report

The Documented Facts Report (fig. 10-25) shows an individual and the events you've entered source information for.

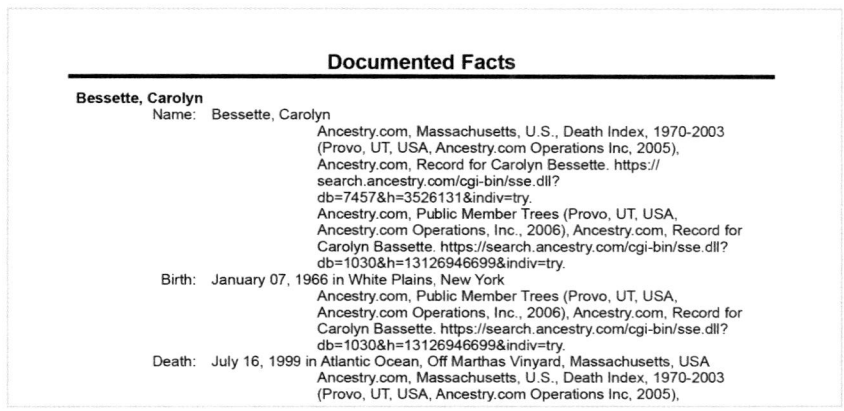

Figure 10-25. A Documented Facts Report.

Undocumented Facts Report

The Undocumented Facts Report (fig. 10-26) shows individuals and events that don't have sources associated with them.

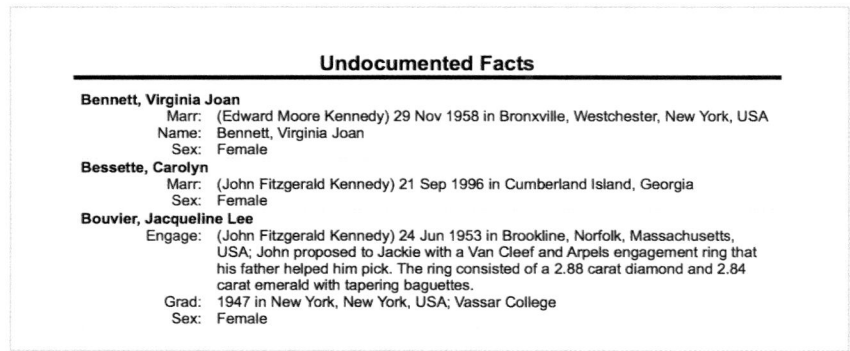

Figure 10-26. An Undocumented Facts Report.

Source Usage Report

The Source Usage Report (fig. 10-27) shows each source and the individuals and facts associated with it.

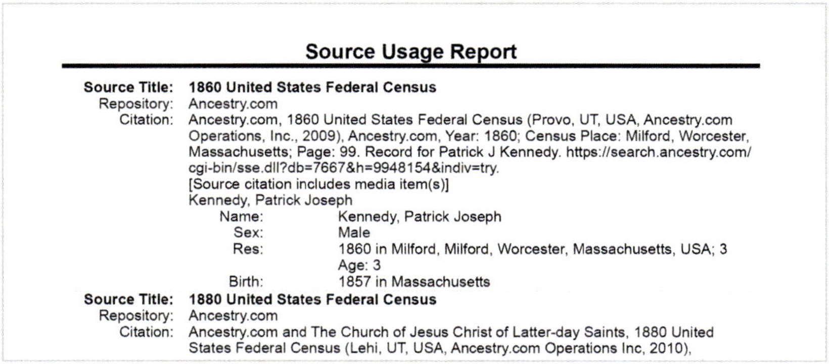

Source Usage Report

Source Title: **1860 United States Federal Census**
Repository: Ancestry.com
Citation: Ancestry.com, 1860 United States Federal Census (Provo, UT, USA, Ancestry.com Operations, Inc., 2009), Ancestry.com, Year: 1860; Census Place: Milford, Worcester, Massachusetts; Page: 99. Record for Patrick J Kennedy. https://search.ancestry.com/cgi-bin/sse.dll?db=7667&h=9948154&indiv=try.
[Source citation includes media item(s)]
Kennedy, Patrick Joseph
Name: Kennedy, Patrick Joseph
Sex: Male
Res: 1860 in Milford, Milford, Worcester, Massachusetts, USA; 3 Age: 3
Birth: 1857 in Massachusetts

Source Title: **1880 United States Federal Census**
Repository: Ancestry.com
Citation: Ancestry.com and The Church of Jesus Christ of Latter-day Saints, 1880 United States Federal Census (Lehi, UT, USA, Ancestry.com Operations Inc, 2010),

Figure 10-27. A Source Usage Report.

Calendars

You can make calendars (fig. 10-28) that display birthdays, death dates, and anniversaries for your immediate family or ancestors.

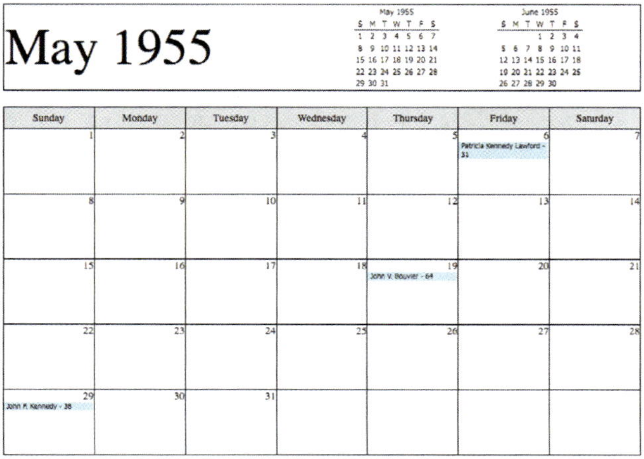

Figure 10-28. A calendar showing birth dates for all individuals.

Creating a Report

All reports are based on the last individual you were viewing in your tree. To change the primary individual in the report, select an individual in the mini pedigree tree above the report, or click the Index of Individuals button and select the person you want.

1   Go to the **Collection** tab on the Publish workspace. In **Publication Types**, select the report type you want.
2   Double-click the report icon, or select its icon and click the **Detail** tab.
3   Use controls on the report options panel to customize the report.

Customizing a Report

You can customize the contents and format of reports. For example, you can determine which individuals and facts are included in the report and choose background images and fonts.

Choosing Facts to Include in a Report

In some reports you can choose which events or facts you'd like to include.

1   Access the report you want to change. In the editing toolbar, click the **Items to include** button.

The Items to Include dialog opens. The report's default facts are shown in the Facts list. You can add and delete facts and also change their display options.

210   Part 3: Creating Charts, Reports, and Books

2 Do one of the following:

- To add a fact, click the **Add** (+) button. The **Select Fact** dialog opens. Select a fact and click **OK**.
- To delete a fact, select the fact and click the **Delete** (-) button.
- To change the order facts are listed in for a person, select the fact and click the up ▲ or down ▼ arrow buttons under the list of facts.

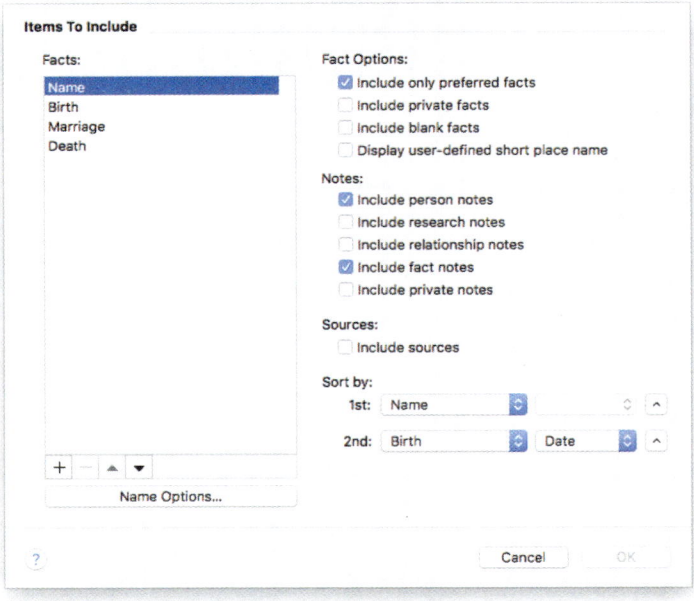

3 Change settings by selecting the appropriate checkbox:

- **Include only preferred facts.** If you have multiple facts for the same event, only the preferred one is included.
- **Include private facts.** Facts you have marked as private will be included.

- **Include blank facts.** All fact labels will be included even if the fact is empty.
- **Display user-defined short place name.** The shortened place names you have created for locations will be used.

4 To change a fact's format, select the fact in the Facts list and click the **Name Options** button. Select the options you want and click **OK**.

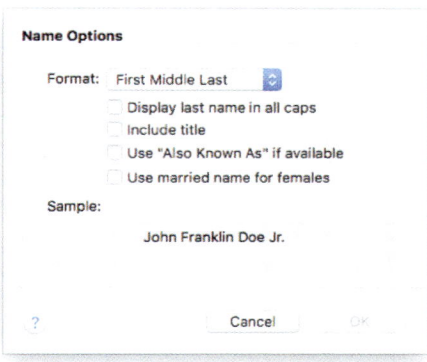

Note: The options vary by fact. For example, you can include dates and locations in births, marriages, and deaths.

5 Choose notes to include in the report:
- Select **Include person notes** to show person notes linked to individuals.
- Select **Include research notes** to show research notes linked to individuals.
- Select **Include relationship notes** to show person notes linked to relationships.
- Select **Include fact notes** to show notes linked to facts.
- Select **Include private notes** to show a note even if it has been marked as private.

6   To show sources in the report, select the **Include sources** checkbox.

7   Click **OK**.

Choosing Individuals to Include in a Report

In many reports, you can choose which individuals will be included. For example, you can choose a specific ancestor and his or her descendants. You can also choose individuals by picking specific criteria (for example, you may want to create a report that shows all individuals who were born in a particular city).

1   Access the report you want to change. You can select individuals for the report in the editing panel.

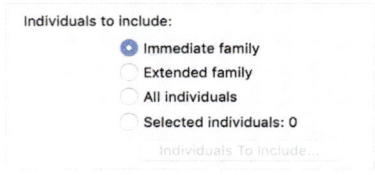

2   Do one of the following:

- To include the individual's children, spouses, and parents, select **Immediate family**.
- To include the individual's immediate family, grandchildren, and in-laws, select **Extended family**.
- To include everyone in your tree, select **All individuals**.
- To choose specific individuals, select **Selected individuals**. The Filter Individuals dialog opens. Select a name and then click **Include** to add the person. You can also click **Retrieve Filter** and add a specific group of people by choosing a Smart Filter that you have created earlier. See "Smart Filters" on page 14 for more information. When you're finished adding individuals, click **Apply**.

Note: Lists of individuals in reports will remain static even when Smart Filters (which produce lists that change dynamically) are used to create them. To refresh the list of individuals in a report based on a Smart Filter, you will need to retrieve the filter again.

Changing a Report's Title

You can change the title that appears at the top of a report. Access the report you want to change. In the editing panel, type a new name in the **Report title** field.

Adding a Background Image

Family Tree Maker comes with hundreds of attractive images you can use as report backgrounds. Or you can create a background using an image on your computer or a photo in your tree.

1. Access the report you want to change. In the editing panel, choose an image from the **Background** pop-up menu:

   - To use an image on your computer, choose **Browse for an image**. Select an image and click **Open**.

   - To use an image in your tree, choose **Select a media item**. Select an image and click **OK**.

2   Determine how the background will be displayed. To center the image on the page, choose **Center**. To stretch the image to fit the entire page, choose **Stretch**. To show a close-up of the image, choose **Zoom**. To show a series of the image, choose **Tile**.

3   Click the up and down arrows next to the **Transparent** percentage field to set the intensity of the image. You can also type an exact percentage directly in the field and press Return. At 0 percent, the image will look normal, while a higher percentage will fade the image so the report is easier to read.

Changing the Header or Footer

You can define a report's headers and footers (the lines of text at the top and bottom of the page).

1   Access the report you want to change. In the editing toolbar, click the **Header/Footer** button.

2   Change the header and footer options as necessary:

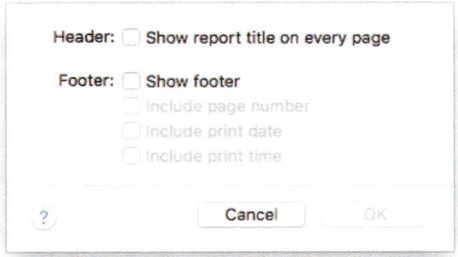

- **Show report title on every page.** Select this checkbox to display a header (the title) on each page of the report.
- **Show footer.** Select this checkbox to display a footer on each

page of the report. Select **Include page number** to display a page number on the left side of the footer; select **Include print date** to display the current date on the right side of the footer; select **Include print time** to display the current time next to the current date.

3 Click **OK**.

Changing Fonts

You can change the appearance of the text in reports to make it more formal, more fun, or maybe just more readable.

1 Access the report you want to change. In the editing toolbar, click the **Fonts**  button.

2 Select the text element, such as the report title, you want to change.

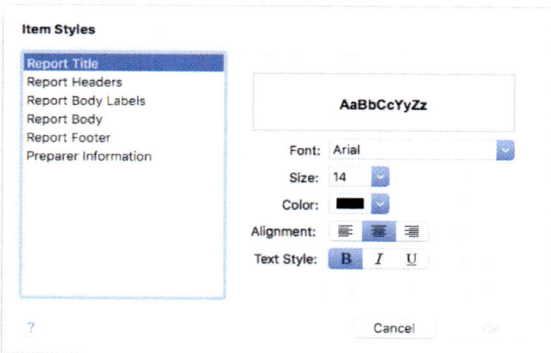

3 Choose a font from the **Font** pop-up menu. You can also change the size of the font, its style, color, and alignment.

4 Click **OK**.

Saving Reports

You can save a specific report in Family Tree Maker, or you can save a report in different file formats to export.

Saving the Settings for a Report

After you've customized a report, you can save your settings so you won't have to recreate these changes the next time you view the report. The settings you can save depend on the report, but generally include fact options, fonts, headers and footers, page layouts, and background images.

Note: You cannot save settings in one report and use them in another. For example, if you save settings in the Parentage Report, you cannot use these settings in the Kinship Report.

1   After you've modified a report, click the **Save settings** button in the editing toolbar.

2   A message asks if you want to use the current settings as the preferred settings for this report type. Click **OK**.

Tip: To change back to the report's default settings, click the **Use report settings** button in the editing toolbar. Then select **Default settings** and click **OK**.

Saving a Specific Report

If you like a report you've created, you'll probably want to save it. That way you can view it again without having to recreate it.

Tip: Your saved reports are added to your TreeVault Antenna tree.

Chapter 10: Running Reports 217

1 After you've modified a report, click the **Save report** button in the editing toolbar.

2 Type a unique name for the report. For example, don't use generic terms like "Family Group Sheet" or "Custom Report".

3 Click **Save**.

Tip: To open a saved report, go to the Collection tab on the Publish workspace. In Publication Types, select **Saved Reports**. Then double-click the report you want to open.

Saving a Report as a File

You may want to save a report as a document or spreadsheet so you can share it easily with family or post it online.

1 Access the report you want to save.
2 Click the **Share** button above the editing panel. From the pop-up menu, choose one of these commands:
   - **Export to PDF.** An Adobe PDF (Portable Document Format) is useful because it keeps the formatting you select. If you print your report or send it to a relative, the report will look exactly as you see it on your monitor. You can't change a PDF within Family Tree Maker.
   - **Export to CSV.** This spreadsheet format organizes information into fields (comma-separated values). Although you can export any report to a CSV file, it is most useful for statistical reports that use columns, such as the Marriage report.
   - **Export to RTF.** This creates a basic text file but can include information such as font style, size, and color. This universal format can be read by nearly all text editing applications.
   - **Export to HTML.** Hypertext Markup Language is the standard language for creating and formatting Web pages.

   Each format has its own export options. After you choose a format type, you may be able to choose options such as page borders and text separators.

3 Select the location where you want to save the report and type a name for it. Then click **Save**.

Printing a Report

When you are done creating and customizing a report, you may want to print it out. Family Tree Maker makes it easy to choose setup options and print a report.

1 Access the report you want to print.
2 Click the **Print** button above the editing panel.
3 When prompted choose a printer, select the number of copies, and choose a page range.
4 Click **Print**.

Sharing a Report

You can share reports with others—via email—in a variety of formats.

Note: You must be connected to the Internet and have a desktop email application to use this feature.

1 Access the report you want to email.
2 Click the **Share** button above the editing panel. From the pop-up menu, choose one of these commands:
  - **Send as PDF.** A PDF retains printer formatting and graphical elements so that when it is opened it looks as it would on the printed page.
  - **Send as CSV.** This format organizes information into fields (comma-separated values) and is meant to be imported into spreadsheet applications.
  - **Send as RTF.** This creates a basic text file but can include information such as font style, size, and color. This universal format can be read by nearly all text editing applications.

- **Send as Image.** This option lets you create an image of the report as a bitmap, JPEG, and other image formats.

Each format has its own export options. After you choose a format type, you may be able to choose options such as page borders and text separators.

3 Change any options as necessary and click **Save**. Family Tree Maker opens a new email (with the file attached) in your default email application.

4 Send the email as you would any other.

Chapter Eleven
Creating a Family History Book

Wouldn't you love to have a printed family history to share your family stories, photographs, maps, and research? And what could be more convenient than using the same software to organize your family history *and* create a book to tell your ancestral story?

Family Tree Maker has a publishing tool to help you create a quality family history book that you and your family will enjoy for years to come. The tool is a desktop book-building feature built into the Family Tree Maker software. It's a great way to assemble a traditional genealogy using images, facts, charts, and reports from your tree.

The Desktop Book-Building Tool

Getting started with the book-building tool is easy because you can use the facts, charts, reports, and timelines already in your tree. Add some personal stories and photos and you've created a book you can email to family members or get printed at a copy shop.

Starting a Family History Book

1 Go to the **Collection** tab on the Publish workspace. In **Publication Types**, select **Books**.

2 Double-click **Genealogy Book**. The Save Book dialog opens.

3 Type a title for the book in the **Book Name** field and click **Save**. The book opens in the text editor.

Tip: Saved books are added to your TreeVault Antenna tree.

Accessing a Saved Book

1 Go to the **Collection** tab on the Publish workspace. In **Publication Types**, select **Saved Books**.

2 Double-click the book you want to open, or select its icon and click the **Detail** tab. The book opens in the text editor.

Setting Up a Book

When you create a book you can enter the name of the author and title and add headers and footers.

1 Access the book you want to set up.

2 In the book outline toolbar, click the **Book Properties** button.

3 Change the book's properties as necessary:
- **Book Title.** Type the name of the book. This is the title that will appear in the book's headers and footers; it is not added to the title page automatically.
- **Author.** Type the author of the book.
- **Header.** Choose a header type from the pop-up menu. Headers are typically the title of a book, but you can have no header, or a combination of the book title, chapter name,

and page number. To change the header's font, click **Change Font** and select a style and size.

Note: You can change the header for a specific page using Item Properties. For instructions see "Changing an Item's Settings" on page 231.

- **Footer.** Choose a footer type from the pop-up menu. Footers are typically page numbers, but you can have no footer, or a combination of the book title, chapter name, and page number. To change the footer's font, click **Change Font** and select a style and size.

    Note: You can add or remove the footer from a specific page using Item Properties. For instructions see "Changing an Item's Settings" on page 231.

- **Page Numbers Use Roman Numerals.** Select this checkbox to use standard Roman numerals (i, ii, iii, iv) for the book's front matter—title page, table of contents, dedication, etc.

- **Starting number.** Choose what page you want the body of the book to start on (the front matter—title page, table of contents, dedication, etc.—will be numbered separately).

4 Click **OK**.

Adding Content to a Book

You can add any number of items to your family history book, including stories, photos, reports, charts, and even an automatically generated table of contents and index.

Adding Text

Don't let your family history book become a dry recitation of facts. Add interest by including family stories and memories. If your grandfather immigrated to America when he was young, don't just list this fact in an individual report. Include an excerpt from his journal that tells how he felt when he saw the Statue of Liberty, for example.

Family Tree Maker has two options for entering text: you can manually type text or import text from another text file or document.

Adding a Smart Story (Text Item)

Before you can add text, you'll need to add a text item to the book. A text item is basically a blank sheet of paper in the book's text editor. Creating one is much like opening a new document in a word-processing program. You can use it to create everything from an entire chapter to a simple page with a photo and a caption.

1   Access the book you want to add a text item to. In the book outline toolbar, click the **Add Book Item** button.

2   Select **Other**. Then double-click **Smart Story (Text Item)**, or select its icon and click **Add**. A blank page opens.

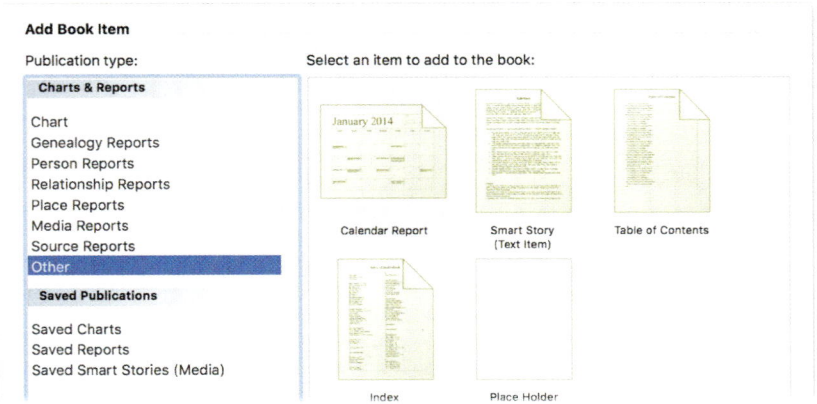

Entering Text Manually

You can use the text editor to write your own family narratives.

1   Select a text item in the book outline.

2   Place the insertion point where you want the text and begin typing.

Importing Text from Another Document

If you've already written part of your book in another text editing application, you don't have to re-type your text or copy and paste sections into Family Tree Maker. You can import the entire .doc/.docx, .rtf/.rtfd, or .txt document at once—without losing formatting.

1   Select a text item in the book outline.

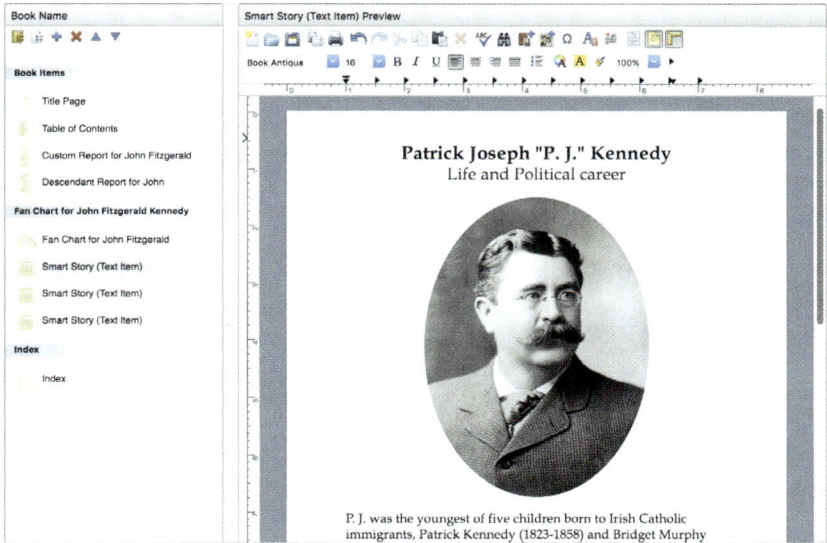

2   Place the cursor where you want the text; then click the Open Document button in the text editor toolbar.

3   Navigate to the document you want to import and click **Open**.

Formatting Text

The text formatting options available in Family Tree Maker are similar to most word processing applications. You can change fonts, text size, and spacing.

1   Select a text item in the book outline.
2   Format the text using these options:
    - **Change the font color, size, or style.** Select the text you want to change. Control-click and choose **Character** from the shortcut menu. The Font dialog opens. Make any necessary changes and close the dialog.
    - **Change the amount of space between lines of text.** Select a paragraph. Control-click and choose **Paragraph** from the shortcut menu. Click the arrows next to **Inter-line spacing** to change the spacing. Click **OK**.
    - **Change the amount of space between paragraphs.** Select the paragraphs. Control-click and choose **Paragraph** from the shortcut menu. Click the arrows next to **Paragraph spacing** to change the spacing. Click **OK**.

Adding Images

What family history book would be complete without photos, letters, historical records, and maps? Family Tree Maker lets you add images from your family tree or images you've stored on your computer that you don't necessarily want to keep in your family tree—for example, clip art or embellishments.

1   Select a text item in the book outline.
2   Place the insertion point where you want the image to appear.

3 Do one of the following:

- To use an image in your tree, click the **Insert image from media collection** button in the text editor toolbar. Select the image and click **OK**.

- To use an image on your computer, click the **Insert image from file** button in the text editor toolbar. Navigate to the image you want and click **Open**.

4 To define how the image interacts with text, Control-click it and choose "In Line," "Top and Bottom," "Square," "Behind Text," or "In Front of Text" from the **Text Wrapping** shortcut menu. You can also move the image by dragging it to a new location.

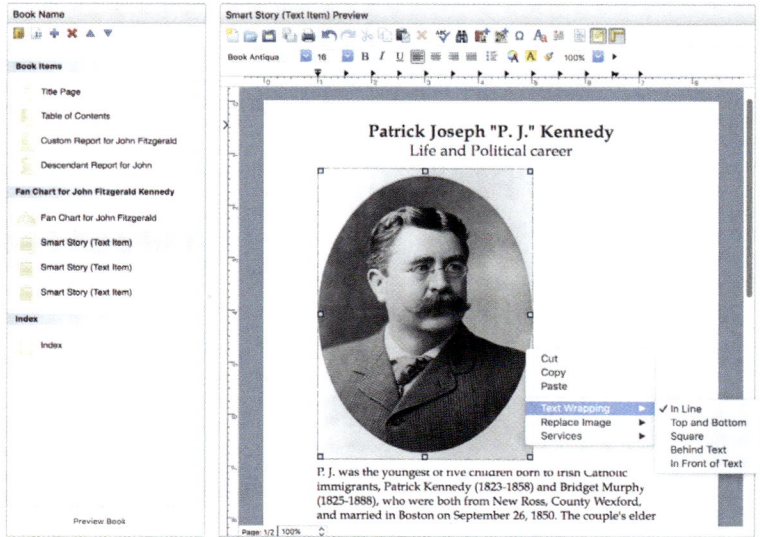

5 To resize an image, select it. Then drag a selection handle to change the size. To maintain the image's proportions, drag the image from a corner.

Adding a Chart or Report

You can add as many charts and reports to a book as you'd like. Make sure you choose ones that are appropriate for your audience. For example, you may want to share more personal and informal reports in a book meant for your children, but you'll want to remove facts about living relatives if you are sharing the book with other genealogists.

1   Access the book you want to add a chart or report to. In the book outline toolbar, click the **Add Book Item** button.

2   In the Add Book Item dialog, select the category for the chart or report you want to use. Then double-click the chart/report, or select its icon and click **Add**.

    Tip: You can also select **Saved Charts** or **Saved Reports** to use documents you've already created.

3   Use the editing panel to customize the chart or report (for instructions see chapters 9 and 10).

Adding a Placeholder

If you want to incorporate a story, chart, or photo from outside Family Tree Maker, you can use a placeholder to reserve a specific number of pages until you're ready to add the information.

1   Access the book you want to add a placeholder to. In the book outline toolbar, click the **Add Book Item** button.

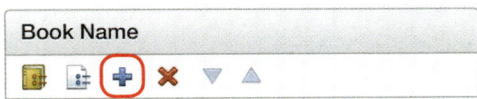

2 In the Add Book Item dialog, select **Other**. Then double-click **Place Holder**, or select its icon and click **Add**.

3 Choose the number of pages you want to reserve using the **Number of pages** arrows.

Tip: Give the placeholder a descriptive name so you don't forget what you were going to use it for. You can change its name by clicking the Book Item Properties button in the book outline toolbar.

Creating a Table of Contents

Family Tree Maker can generate a table of contents for a book automatically. If you make changes to a book (such as adding a chart or moving a chapter), the table of contents and its page numbers will be updated to reflect the changes.

Note: The table of contents is added after the title page. You can change the order of the front matter—table of contents, dedication, preface, etc.—but you cannot move the table of contents out of the front matter.

1 Access the book you want to add a table of contents to. In the book outline toolbar, click the **Add Book Item**  button.

2 In the Add Book Item dialog, select **Other**. Then double-click **Table of Contents**, or select its icon and click **Add**. The table of contents opens.

Although you cannot edit the table of contents, you can customize its font, size, and color by clicking the **Fonts** button under the "Table of Contents Options" heading.

Creating an Index of Individuals

Family Tree Maker can automatically generate a list of all individuals in the book's reports and charts (names mentioned in text items will *not* be included). If you make changes to the book (such as adding a new chart) Family Tree Maker will update the index to reflect the change.

Note: The index cannot be moved; it must be the last item in your book.

1   Access the book you want to add an index to. In the book outline toolbar, click the **Add Book Item** button.

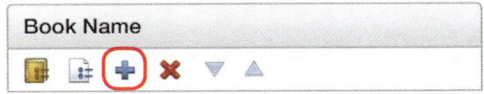

2   In the Add Book Item dialog, select **Other**. Then double-click **Index**, or select its icon and click **Add**. The index opens.

Although you cannot edit the index, you can customize its font, size, and color by clicking the **Fonts** button under the "Index Options" heading.

Organizing a Book

As your book grows, you may find that it has changed from the project you originally envisioned and that you need to make some adjustments. Perhaps you've uncovered additional records and photos and you want to rearrange a couple of chapters to include them. Family Tree Maker makes it easy to change titles, move chapters, or even delete sections you don't need.

Changing an Item's Settings

A Family Tree Maker book is made up of a variety of different book items: text items, charts, reports, etc. You can change settings for each book item.

1 Select an item in the book outline.

2 In the book outline toolbar, click the **Book Item Properties** button.

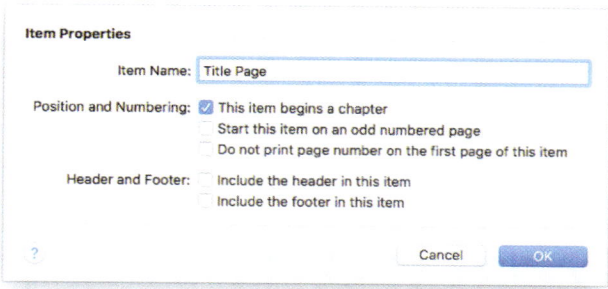

The Item Properties dialog opens.

3 Change the item's settings using these options:

- **Change the item's title.** Type a title in the **Item Name** field. This is the title that will appear in the book's table of contents and this item's headers and footers.

- **Make this item start a new chapter.** Select the **This item begins a chapter** checkbox.

- **Make the first page of this item start on an odd-numbered (right-facing) page.** Select the **Start this item on an odd numbered page** checkbox. Typically each chapter starts on an odd-numbered page.

- **Prevent a page number from appearing on the first page of an item.** Select the **Do not print page number on the first page of this item** checkbox. Typically chapter openers do not include a page number. You may also want to use this option for reports, charts, and full-page images.
- **Display headers in the item.** Select the **Include the header in this item** checkbox.
- **Display footers in the item.** Select the **Include the footer in this item** checkbox.

4 Click **OK**.

Rearranging Book Items

The book panel shows all the items in a book. The order in which they're displayed in this outline is the order in which they'll print. You can change this order at any time.

1 Select an item in the book outline.
2 To change an item's order in the outline, select the item. Then click the **Move Up** ▲ and **Move Down** ▼ arrows in the book outline toolbar. (You can also drag items to the desired location.)

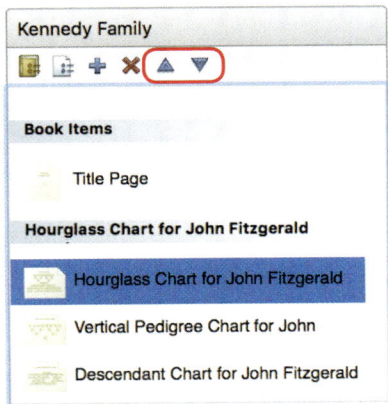

Deleting a Book Item

If you don't want a text item, report, or chart in your book, you can delete it.

1. Select an item in the book outline.
2. Click the **Delete Book Item**  button.

Printing a Book at Home

When you are done creating your book, you can make copies on your home printer.

Tip: If you want to see what your book will look like when it is printed, click the **Preview Book** button below the book outline.

1. Access the book you want to print.
2. Click the **Print** button below the main toolbar.
3. When prompted choose a printer, select the number of copies, and choose a page range.
4. Click **Print**.

Exporting a Book

You can export your book as a PDF or text file and take it to a copy shop to be printed and professionally bound or email it to family members.

1. Access the book you want to export; then click the **Share** button below the main toolbar.
2. Choose an export option from the pop-up menu.
3. Change any options as necessary and click **Save**.

Family Book Creator Plug-In

Family Book Creator by Stefan Harms is a plug-in for Family Tree Maker which turns your research into a detailed personalized book with just a few clicks.

Different book types and languages are supported. You may create your book documents directly in word processor file formats (DOCX, DOC, RTF, ODT) or platform independent file formats (PDF, EPUB, JPEG, PNG) without the need of having Microsoft Word or any other word processor or PDF application installed.

Family Book Creator is able to create the following types of books:

- Alphabetical family register
- Ancestors of the selected individual
- Descendants of the selected individual and preferred spouse
- Relatives of the selected individual

To get the plug-in, please visit www.familytreemaker.com and follow the GIFT Collection link.

Tip: For more information, visit ftm.support/fbc.

Part Four
Managing Your Trees

Chapter 12: Working with Trees 237

Chapter 13: Using TreeVault Cloud Services 267

Chapter 14: Tools and Preferences 275

Chapter 15: Family Tree Problem Solver 303

Chapter Twelve
Working with Trees

In Chapter 3 you learned how to create and import new trees. This chapter explains the many tools Family Tree Maker has to help you manage, share, and protect your trees.

Managing Your Trees

This section explains how to manage your trees effectively, whether you're working on one comprehensive tree or multiple trees.

Using the Tree Browser

The Tree Browser makes it easy to locate, view, and manage all of your trees, all in one place. Whether it's an FTM, Ancestry, or TreeVault tree, a backup file, or a GEDCOM, you can quickly find what you're looking for and see everything you need to know about it. The Tree Browser also enables you to track down tree files you have misplaced, even in the most obscure corners of your computer's hard disk.

1 Choose **View > Tree Browser**, or click the **Select Tree** pop-up menu on the main toolbar and then click **Tree Browser**. The Tree Browser window appears.

2 In the left part of the window, select the group of trees you want to work with:
- **Recent**. The trees that you have recently had open in Family Tree Maker.

- **All Trees**. All of the tree files on your computer that you can open in Family Tree Maker. The tree files are sorted by category: files from the current version of Family Tree Maker, files from previous versions of the application, backup files, and GEDCOMs.
- **FTM Folder**. The tree files in the folder that Family Tree Maker uses to store your FTM trees. By default this is the Family Tree Maker folder located in the Documents folder on your hard disk. The tree files in this group are also sorted by category.
- **Ancestry**. Your online Ancestry trees.
- **TreeVault**. Displays the status of the tree in your TreeVault account.

A list of the trees in the selected group appears in the middle column of the window.

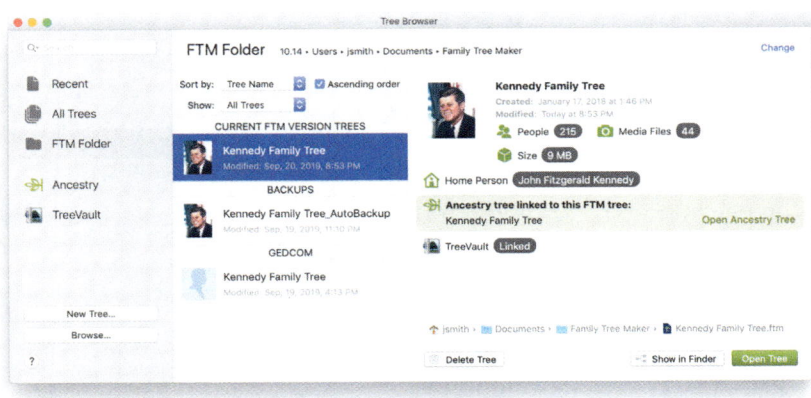

3 Use the **Sort by** and **Show** pop-up menus to narrow your search for a particular tree.

4 Select a tree in the list to view information about it in the right part of the Tree Browser window.

5 Do one of the following:

- Click **Open Tree** to open the selected tree in Family Tree Maker.
- Click **Show in Finder** to open the folder where the selected tree file is located in the Finder.
- Click **Delete Tree** to delete the selected tree file from your computer.
- Click **Browse** in the bottom-left corner of the **Tree Browser** to try to locate the tree you want manually.

Note: The buttons available may vary depending on the kind of tree you have selected.

To create a new tree from the Tree Browser, click the **New Tree** button in the bottom-left corner of the window.

To find a tree by name:

1 Open the Tree Browser.

2 Click in the search field.

3 Enter the name or a part of the name of the tree that you want to find, then press **Return**. A list of trees that match what you've entered appears in the right part of the window.

4 Select a tree to view information about it. If this is the tree you were looking for, use the available buttons to perform the actions you want. See step 5 above for information about using the buttons.

Opening a Tree

When you launch Family Tree Maker, it automatically opens on the New Tree tab of the Plan workspace. You can open the last tree you were working on or switch to any other tree at any time. To do that, click the **Select Tree** pop-up menu on the main toolbar, and choose the tree you want.

If the tree you want isn't in the list, choose **Tree Browser**, and then click **All Trees**. Select the tree you want and click **Open Tree**.

Note: If you try to open a GEDCOM, or a file from another genealogy program, the software automatically opens the **New Tree** tab so you can import it (for instructions see "Importing a Tree File" on page 30). If you try to open a tree file from a previous version of Family Tree Maker, the software automatically opens the **New Tree** tab so you can import the tree or an alert will prompt to convert the tree file.

Viewing Information About a Tree

You can view a summary of your tree file, such as its size and the last day you created a backup. You can also see information about the people in your tree, for example, the number of marriages, individuals, and surnames.

1   Go to the **Current Tree** tab on the Plan workspace. A basic summary of your tree file appears at the top of the workspace.

2   To see additional statistics, click the **More** button. The Statistical Information dialog opens.

Renaming a Tree

You can change the name of a tree at any time.

1   On the main toolbar, click the **Select Tree** pop-up menu, move the pointer over the tree name, and then choose **Rename Tree**.

2   Type a name for the tree and click **OK**.

    Note: If this is your Source tree, the name of your Antenna tree will change too. Any linked Ancestry trees will not be renamed.

Deleting a Tree

To delete a tree, use the Tree Browser or follow these steps:

1   On the main toolbar, click the **Select Tree** pop-up menu, move the pointer over the tree name, and then choose **Delete Tree**.

2   If you want to delete the media files that are linked to the tree, select **Move selected attachments to the Trash as well** and select the files you'd like to delete. Then click **Move To Trash**.

Using Privacy Mode

If your tree contains personal information about living family members, you might want to "privatize" your tree before exporting a family history book or printing a family tree chart. In privacy mode information about living individuals, such birth dates, will not be displayed. Be aware that you cannot edit the tree until you turn off privacy mode.

1   Choose **File>Privatize File**. "Privatized" appears in the title bar and a checkmark appears next to the **Privatize File** command in the **File** menu.

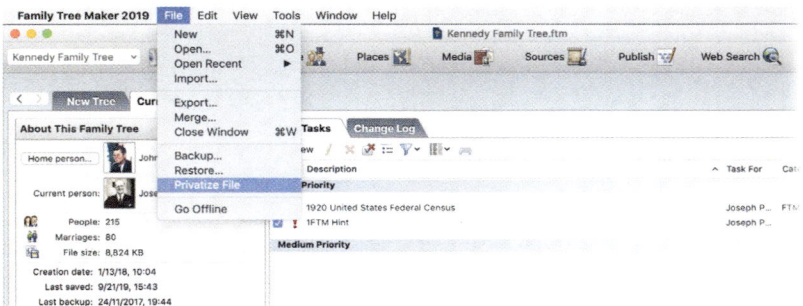

2   To continue working in your tree, turn off privacy mode by choosing **File>Privatize File** again.

Exporting a Tree File

If you want to share your family tree with someone, you can export all or part of a tree as a GEDCOM, the standard file format used to transfer data between different genealogy software. (Be aware that images, audio files, and videos cannot be included in GEDCOMs.) You can also export your tree as a Family Tree Maker file.

Tip: To export a specific branch of your family tree, go to the People workspace. Select the person whose family you want to export. Control-click and choose **Export Branch**.

1 Choose **File**>**Export**. If an information message appears, click **OK**. The Export dialog opens.

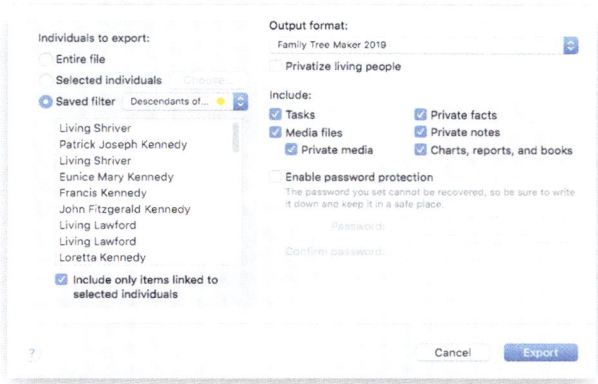

2 Do one of the following:
- To export the entire tree, select **Entire file**.
- To select specific individuals to include in the file, select **Selected individuals**. A dialog opens. Select an individual then click **Include** to add the person. When you're finished selecting individuals, click **Apply**.
- To export a list of individuals produced by a Smart Filter, click **Saved filter**. Then choose the Smart Filter you want to apply. See "Smart Filters" on page 14.

3 Choose a GEDCOM or Family Tree Maker option from the **Output format** pop-up menu.

4 Choose the information you want included in the export file:
- **Privatize living people.** Select this checkbox to exclude information about living individuals. Names and relationships will be exported but facts and shared facts will not.
- **Private facts.** Select this checkbox to export facts marked as private.

> **GEDCOM**
> Because your great-aunt may not use the same software you do, you'll need to share your family history with her in the GEDCOM format. GEDCOM stands for GEnealogical Data COMmunications; it allows genealogy files to be opened in any genealogy software program—on Macs or PCs.

- **Private notes.** Select this checkbox to export notes marked as private.
- **Media files.** Select this checkbox to include all media files in your tree except for media marked as private.
- **Private media.** Select this checkbox to include media files marked as private.
- **Tasks.** Select this checkbox to include your research to-do list. This option is not available for GEDCOMs.
- **Charts, reports, and books.** Select this checkbox to include charts, reports, and books you've saved. This option is not available for GEDCOMs.
- **Include only items linked to selected individuals.** Click this checkbox to include only tasks, notes, and media items that are linked to the individuals you're exporting.

5 Depending on the output format you have chosen, you can select the **Enable password protection** checkbox or the **Export as password-protected ZIP file** checkbox. The **Password** and **Confirm password** fields become available. Enter the password you want to use for protection of your exported tree. Make sure your password is not easy to guess. It should be at least eight characters long and contain digits as well as letters. You, or

anyone you give the file to, will have to enter exactly the same password when opening or unpacking your exported tree. Passwords cannot be recovered, so it's a good idea to write the password down and keep it in a safe place.

6 Click **Export**.

7 Navigate to the location where you want to save the tree file.

Note: Family Tree Maker automatically gives the exported file the same name as the original tree, with current date at the end. If you want to use a different name, you can change it.

8 Click **Save**. A message tells you when your tree file has been exported successfully.

Backing Up Tree Files

Your family trees are important; not only do they contain your family's history, they represent hours of hard work. Unfortunately, computer files can be corrupted by viruses or accidentally deleted. You can preserve your family history through regular backups. Then, if your original tree is damaged or you want to revert to a previous copy, you can restore it from the backup.

It's also good practice to have Family Tree Maker back up trees automatically every time you quit the application (see "General Preferences" on page 285).

Tip: Apart from traditional backups, there are two new features in FTM 2019 that provide additional protection for your tree data. Consider creating a continuously updated TreeVault Antenna tree that can restore all the data from your FTM tree in an emergency; and use Turn Back Time to roll back up to 1000 recent changes to your tree.

Backing Up a Tree File

1   Open the tree you want to back up and compact it. See "Compressing a Tree File" on page 251 for more information.

2   Choose **File>Backup**. The **Backup the Tree** dialog opens.

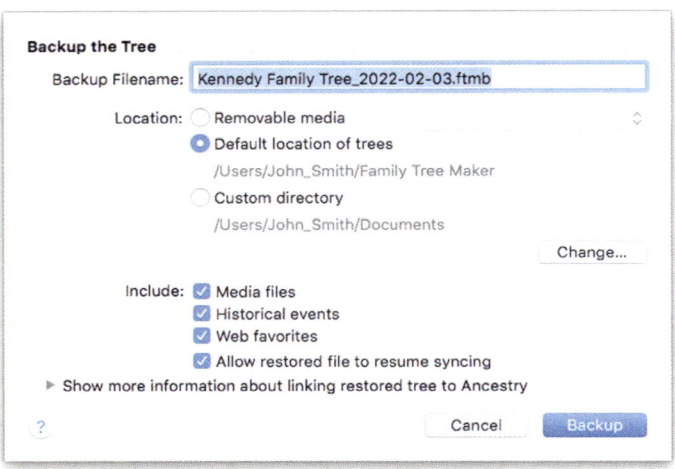

3   If you want a new name to distinguish your backup file from your original tree, type a new name in the **Backup Filename** field. For example, if you back up your trees to the same USB flash drive every time, and this backup file has the same name as the tree file that is already on the drive, then this backup will write over the original file.

4   Select one of these backup types:

- **DVD or flash drive.** Select **Removable media**. In the pop-up menu, choose your DVD drive or flash drive.

- **Hard disk.** Select **Default location of trees** to save the backup to the folder where your current tree is saved; click **Change** to select a new location on your hard disk.

5 Choose the information you want to include in the backup:
- **Media files.** Click this checkbox to include all media items from the tree's media folder.
- **Historical events.** Click this checkbox to include historical events you've created or edited for timelines.
- **Web favorites.** Click this checkbox to include your favorites list on the Web Search workspace.

6 If the tree is linked to an Ancestry tree, select the **Allow restored file to resume syncing** checkbox so the backup file can be synced with the Ancestry tree if necessary.

7 Click **Backup**. A message tells you when the tree file has been backed up successfully.

Note: Backup files cannot be opened in other genealogy applications like GEDCOMs can. They can only be opened with the version of Family Tree Maker in which they were created or later.

Restoring a Tree from a Backup

If you need to use your backup file as your working tree, you can restore it when necessary.

1 If your backup file has been copied to a removable media, copy it back to your hard disk.

2 Choose **File>Restore**. A file management dialog opens.

3 Navigate to the backup file you want to restore and click **Open**.

Note: You can identify a backup file by its file extension (the letters after the file name). Family Tree Maker backups use .ftmb.

The tree will open. Any info you entered in the original tree since you created this backup will not be included.

Tip: For more information, visit ftm.support/backup.

Turn Back Time

From time to time you will probably make a change in your tree that in hindsight turns out to have been a mistake. And that one false step might have led to a string of unwanted changes. With the Turn Back Time feature you can easily return your tree to the exact state it was in just before the original mistake was made without having to undo all of your actions one by one. That's because the Turn Back Time change log keeps track of your last thousand changes, including Web Merge changes and operations that affect multiple objects, such as syncing or merging trees. And, unlike the Undo command in the Edit menu, Turn Back Time works even if you've closed and reopened the tree after the changes were made.

Tip: When used with TreeVault cloud services (see page 267), Turn Back Time lets you cut way back on backups. Not only will you have an up-to-the-minute complete backup copy of your tree in the Family Tree Maker cloud at all times, you'll also have a matching Turn Back Time change log — because it's also backed up automatically when using TreeVault. So if disaster should strike, and, for example, your hard drive crashes a few days after you accidentally delete your spouse's favorite cousin, you'll not only be able to get your complete tree back instantly with TreeVault's Emergency Tree restore service, you'll be able to get that cousin back too. Actually, with your backed up Turn Back Time change log, it will still be possible to roll back any of the last thousand changes you made before the crash. Which, for all practical purposes, means that without lifting a finger, you'll be automatically safe-keeping the equivalent of a thousand backups.

Here's how to roll back the changes:

1. Go to the **Current Tree** tab on the Plan workspace.
2. Click the **Change Log** tab to see an ordered list of up to 1000 of

Chapter 12: Working with Trees 249

the most recent changes that you have made to your tree. You can print the list by clicking the **Print Change Log** button at the top of the tab.

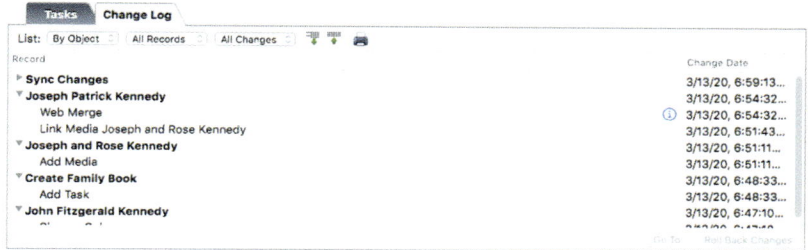

3 A blue information icon next to a change indicates that this is a "multiple objects change," like a tree sync or a tree merge, so many objects in your tree may have been modified. To view a full list of the affected objects, click the information icon. To print the list, click **Print** in the pop-up window that appears.

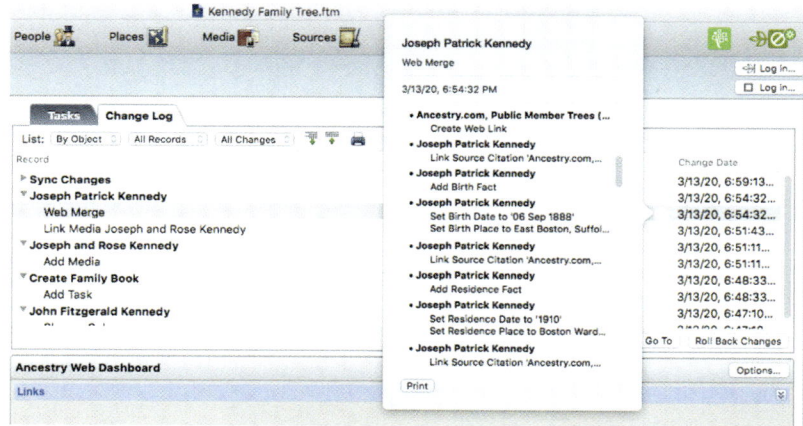

4 Use the **first** pop-up menu in the **List** bar to order the list of changes by the date they were made or by the object (person record, media item, Smart Filter, etc.) that was changed. If you choose to view the changes sorted by object, click the disclosure triangle next to the name of an object to see a list of the changes that were made to it. You can click the **Expand all nodes** button to view all lists of changes sorted by object and the **Collapse all nodes** button to show only the names of the objects again.

5. To display changes made only to people, media, or sources, choose the corresponding option from the **second** pop-up menu in the **List** bar. To display all changes, choose **All Records**.

6. To display changes according to the type of change that was made (addition, change, or deletion), choose an option from the **third** pop-up menu in the **List** bar.

7. To sort changes from the earliest to the latest or the other way around, click the **Change Date** column header.

8. Select a change in the list.

9. Do one of the following:
    - If you want to locate the person, media item, or source to which the selected change was made, click **Go To**. You will be taken to the place in Family Tree Maker where you can review the record and its associated information and make any necessary corrections or changes.
    - To reverse the selected change and all the changes that were made after it, click **Roll Back Changes**. (If you have reviewed the record, you will need to go back to the **Change Log** tab and select the change again.)

10. If you decided to roll back the changes, review the list of everything that will be undone in the dialog that appears. To print out the list of changes, click **Print**. Make sure the **Backup your tree before rolling back changes** checkbox is selected so that your tree is securely backed up before proceeding. Then click **Roll Back Changes** to confirm the rollback.

Compressing a Tree File

As you work in a tree you will add and delete quite a bit of information. However, even when you delete info, the tree file size may not change. You should compress a tree periodically to remove unnecessary bits of data and optimize performance.

1   Choose **Tools>Compact File**.
2   To back up your tree file before you compress it, select the **Back up file before compacting** checkbox (recommended).
3   To have the tree file analyzed more deeply prior to compacting, select the **Perform extended analysis** option. This may significantly increase the duration of the compacting process.
4   Click **Compact**. If you chose to back up your tree file, the Backup dialog opens. Change any options and click **Backup**.
5   When Family Tree Maker is finished, a message shows how much the file size was reduced by. Click **OK**.

Because file compression happens behind the scenes, you won't see changes in your tree, but you should notice better performance and a smaller overall tree file size.

Uploading a Tree to Ancestry

Chapter 3 explains how to start a new tree by downloading an existing tree from Ancestry. Family Tree Maker also lets you upload a tree to Ancestry. It's easy, free, and because your tree will be online, it can be shared with family around the world.

Note: To upload a tree to Ancestry, you do not need a subscription, but you must log in to your Ancestry account and have Internet access.

Uploading and Linking a Tree to Ancestry

When you upload a tree to Ancestry, you create a link between your desktop Family Tree Maker tree and its corresponding tree on Ancestry. This means that additions, deletions, or edits you make in your Family Tree Maker tree will be duplicated in your Ancestry tree (and vice versa). (For more information see "Working with Linked Trees" on page 256.)

Be aware that the time it takes to upload your tree is determined by tree size (including the size of the media collection) and the speed of your Internet connection. Your tree will be transmitted in the background in two stages. Media items are processed first and data is uploaded during the final stage. The tree will appear online when both media and tree data are uploaded.

Note: When you upload and link a tree to Ancestry, you must upload your entire tree; you can't choose which part of your tree is uploaded.

1. Open the tree you want to upload to Ancestry. Then go to the Plan workspace and click the **Current Tree** tab.
2. Click the **Upload and Link to Ancestry** button. Click **Continue** in the **Sync Weather Report** dialog.
3. Enter a name in the **Ancestry tree name** field.
4. Choose whether you want to make your Ancestry tree public or private. See "Privacy Options for Ancestry Trees" below for more information.
5. If you don't want your private tree to appear in search results on Ancestry or third-party search engines such as Google, select the **Exclude this tree from Ancestry search index** checkbox.
6. Choose whether your Ancestry and FTM trees will be synced manually or automatically. (For more information on synchronization options, see "Setting Up Syncing" on page 257.)

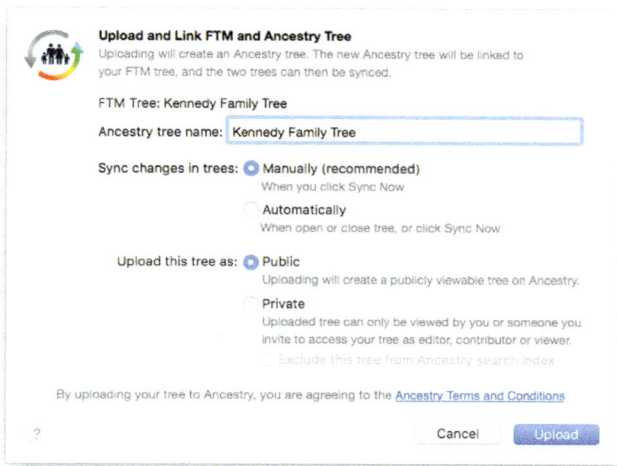

7   Click **Upload**. A message lets you know when the tree has been uploaded successfully.

8   To view your tree on Ancestry, select the **View Ancestry tree** checkbox and click **OK**.

Privacy Options for Ancestry Trees

When you upload your tree to Ancestry, you can choose between two levels of privacy:

- **Public.** If your tree is public, Ancestry subscribers can view your entire tree (except information about living individuals and private notes), and your tree will appear in search engines such as Google.

- **Private.** If your tree is private, limited information about individuals in your tree (name, birth year, birthplace) will still appear in Ancestry search results. No one will be able to view your entire tree or any attached photos and records unless he or she asks your permission and you grant it. You can also invite other people to view your tree.

Differences Between FTM and Ancestry Trees

Most content in your tree is uploaded and/or synced seamlessly between Family Tree Maker and Ancestry. However, because Ancestry and FTM trees are in different formats, there are a few differences you should be aware of.

Content	Differences
Facts	In general fact dates, names, places, and descriptions (including alternate facts) are the same in Family Tree Maker and Ancestry trees. However, some fact types have different labels. For example, the Physical Description fact in Family Tree Maker is the Description fact in Ancestry trees. The Ancestral File Number, User Reference Number (Person), Relationship ID facts are not uploaded to Ancestry.
Media items	• The caption of a media item in Family Tree Maker is the same as the **Title** field on Ancestry. • Video items, audio records, and AlbumWALK talking photos are not transferred between Family Tree Maker and Ancestry. • Media categories are not uploaded to Ancestry. • Media items attached to relationships in Family Tree Maker are uploaded to Ancestry as linked to each person individually, but not to the relationship. • Ancestry citation media you've merged into Family Tree Maker won't be re-uploaded to Ancestry. • Documents in these formats can't be uploaded to Ancestry tree: .exe, .dll, .bat, .htm/.html, and .mht. • Photos that exceed 15MB will be resized when uploaded to Ancestry—your original file will not be affected. Images need to be in one of these formats: .bmp, .gif, .jpeg, .jpg, .png, .tif, .tiff, .ico, .j2k, .jp2. • Documents in .doc, .docx, .pdf, .rtf, .txt, .ftms formats will be uploaded unless they exceed 15MB.

Content	Differences
Places	Shortened place names and GPS coordinates in Family Tree Maker are not uploaded to Ancestry trees.
Publications	Saved reports, charts, and books cannot be transferred from Family Tree Maker to Ancestry.
Privacy	In Family Tree Maker, in the privatized tree only you can view information you have entered for a living individual. In your Ancestry tree, only people you give permission to can view information about living individuals.
Sources	• Sources created with templates will transfer to Ancestry. Some fields cannot be uploaded online. • Media items attached to citations are uploaded; attached to sources are uploaded but not linked. • Citation linked to facts for several individuals is uploaded as a separate citation for each individual.
Stories	• A story created on Ancestry will become an .htm file in Family Tree Maker, which can be viewed in a Web browser. You can edit the text in a word-processing program. • Smart Stories created in Family Tree Maker will become text files (.rtf) in Ancestry. The story can't be viewed in your Ancestry tree but the document can be downloaded.
Notes and tasks	In Family Tree Maker you can create a variety of notes: person, research, fact, relationship, media, and source citation note. Only person notes can be uploaded to Ancestry trees. Tasks are not uploaded.
Web links	Web links are not uploaded, downloaded, or synced.

Note: Unlike an Ancestry tree, a TreeVault Antenna tree stores all data, including publications, exactly as they are in your FTM tree, without any differences.

Working with Linked Trees

Family Tree Maker makes entering information into your tree fast and easy. It also contains powerful tools to help you organize your media items, cite sources, and create charts and reports. But because the program is on your desktop, sharing your tree with others can be time-consuming, and, if you don't have a laptop, you won't have access to your tree on the go.

Fortunately, FamilySync® gives you the freedom to view and update your tree no matter where you are. First, create your tree in Family Tree Maker. Then upload and link it to Ancestry. When you go to the library or a family member's home—anywhere with Internet access—make changes to your tree online. Then sync the changes to your FTM tree when you get home. (You can also download and link a tree you've already created on Ancestry. For information see "Downloading a Tree from Ancestry" on page 32.)

Each Ancestry tree can link to multiple FTM trees. It's not necessary to break an old link to download a tree to a new computer. To link the trees on multiple computers to a single Ancestry tree, follow these steps:

1 Back up your FTM tree manually, including media and sync information. (See "Backing Up a Tree File", page 246).

2 Copy the backup file to the other computer with a flash drive.

3 On the other computer, restore your tree from the backup.

The changes made in any of the trees can be applied to other trees automatically or manually. The core data in your linked trees is synchronized in all directions. But some types of data will not sync, remaining only on the computer they were created on.

Note: For more information on what does and doesn't sync, open Family Tree Maker Help from the **Help** menu and search for the "Syncing FTM and Ancestry Trees" topic or visit ftm.support/sync.

Setting Up Syncing

When you link your FTM and Ancestry trees together, you can choose how your trees will be synchronized. You have two options:

- **Manually.** You can synchronize your trees by clicking the **Sync Now** button on the **Current Tree** tab or clicking the Ancestry Sync icon and choosing "Sync Now" from the pop-up menu.
- **Automatically.** Family Tree Maker checks for changes when you open a tree or close the program. If it detects differences between the trees, it synchronizes the changes automatically. You can also sync your trees any time by clicking the **Sync Now** button on the **Current Tree** tab.

You can also choose whether or not Family Tree Maker will display a list of changes you've made to your Ancestry and FTM trees that you can review before syncing.

Changing Your Current Sync Setting

When you upload or download a linked tree, you will choose how your trees will be synced. You can change this setting at any time.

1 Go to the **Current Tree** tab on the Plan workspace.

2 Click the down arrow next to the **Sync Now** button and choose "Sync Options" to open the Sync Options dialog.

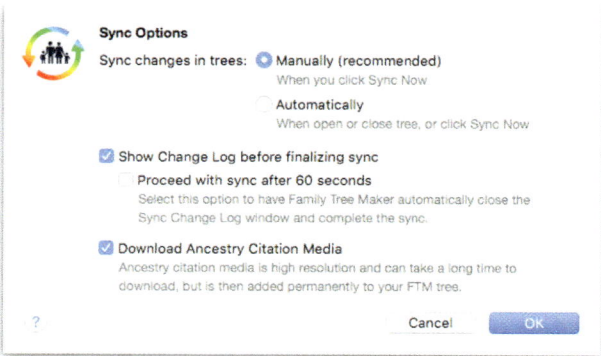

3 Select **Automatically** or **Manually**.

4 To download images of historical records from Ancestry when your trees sync, select the **Download Ancestry Citation Media** checkbox.

5 Click **OK**.

Creating a Log of Recent Sync Activity

You can set up FamilySync so that every time you sync your Ancestry and FTM trees you can view a list of changes—the number of people, sources, and media items that have been added, updated, or deleted from your tree since the last sync.

1 Go to the **Current Tree** tab on the Plan workspace.

2 Click the down arrow next to the **Sync Now** button and choose "Sync Options" to open the Sync Options dialog.

3 Select the **Show Change Log before finalizing sync** checkbox.

4 Select the **Proceed with sync after 60 seconds** checkbox to have Family Tree Maker automatically close the Sync Change Log dialog and complete the sync.

5 Click **OK**. The next time your trees are synced, you'll see the Sync Change Log (fig. 12-1).

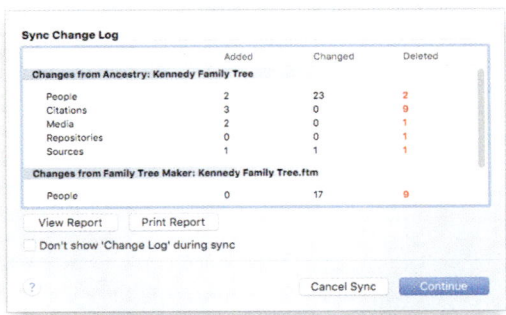

Figure 12-1. The Sync Change Log.

The number of items deleted from the trees, if there are any, is displayed in red. You will be asked to confirm deletion if you proceed.

To proceed with the sync, click the **Continue** button. To reject the changes, click the **Cancel Sync** button. Click the **View Report** button to see specific details about what changes will be included in the sync.

Viewing a Tree's Sync Status

The Ancestry Sync icon in the upper-right corner lets you see at a glance whether your FTM and Ancestry trees are synced. A check mark icon means that the trees are up-to-date; an icon with two vertical arrows means that you have changes waiting to be synced (fig. 12-2).

Figure 12-2. Left, trees are in sync; right, trees need to be synced.

The Ancestry Sync icon also displays the sync weather report status. See "Getting a Sync Weather Report" below for more information.

You can also see the date and time when your tree was last synced on the Current Tree tab on the Plan workspace (fig. 12-3).

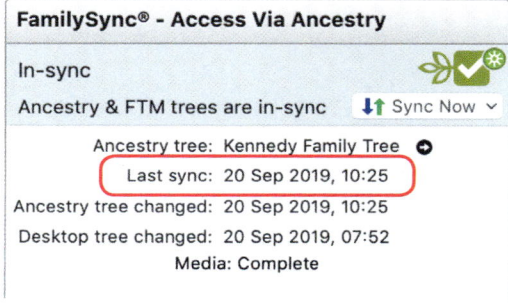

Figure 12-3. Date and time of last sync.

Syncing Trees Manually

You can sync your tree manually at any time. However, be aware that you can't work in your Ancestry or FTM tree until synchronization is complete. This may take a few seconds to a few minutes.

On the Plan workspace, click the **Current Tree** tab; then click the **Sync Now** button. On other workspaces, click the Ancestry Sync icon and choose "Sync Now" from the pop-up menu.

Note: You can't sync your trees from Ancestry; you must use Family Tree Maker. To see the changes in your Ancestry tree, you'll need to reload the Ancestry website in your Web browser.

Getting a Sync Weather Report

Wouldn't it be great if you could know when there was a problem with syncing so you could just stay away for a time and come back when it was safe? Now each time you go to sync, if there's a reason you should maybe think twice, a dialog pops up to say so. The red dialog appears if the sync system is down, or if syncing is for some reason downright dangerous. This status is actually a kind of "kill switch" and syncing is temporarily disabled. The orange dialog appears when caution is in order. You can still sync but the Weather Report message system lets us tell you what's up.

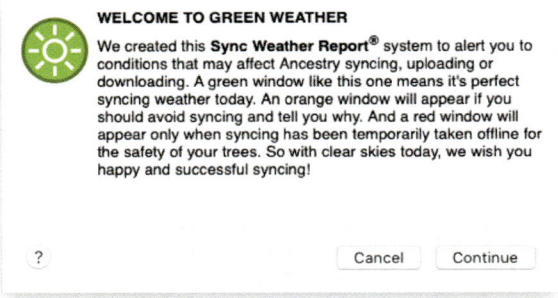

Figure 12-4. *Sync Weather Report.*

In fact, you don't even have to try syncing a tree to find out what the sync weather is like. Just take a look at the Ancestry Sync icon, which can be found in the top-right corner of the application window and in the FamilySync panel in the bottom-left part of the Current Tree tab on the Plan workspace. It not only displays the sync status, it lets you instantly see the latest weather report as well:

 No problems found, safe to sync.

 Problems may occur, syncing is not recommended.

 Serious connection problems, syncing is impossible.

Resolving Conflicts Between Linked Trees

When you change the same fact in your FTM and Ancestry trees, you'll need to choose which information to keep (fig. 12-5). For example, if you change a deathplace in Family Tree Maker and a family member changes the same deathplace in your Ancestry tree, when you try to sync your trees, you'll be prompted to fix the issue.

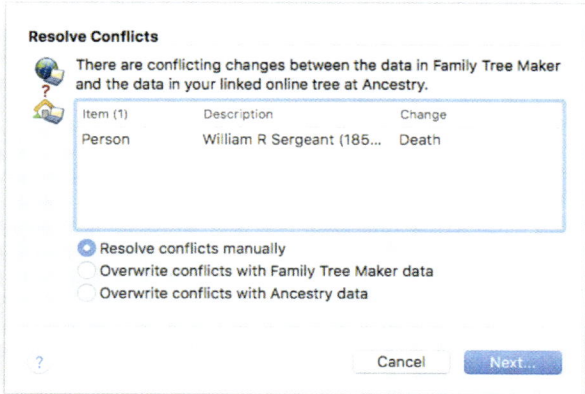

Figure 12-5. A message showing conflicts between linked trees.

1 Do one of the following:

- To keep the information entered in Family Tree Maker, select **Overwrite conflicts with Family Tree Maker data**.
- To keep the information entered in the Ancestry tree, select **Overwrite conflicts with Ancestry data**.
- To manually choose which information to keep, select **Resolve conflicts manually**.

2 Click **Next**. If you are overwriting data, the sync continues. If you are resolving the conflict manually, choose the facts you want to keep and click **Continue**.

Important: Deletions always take priority over other changes. For example, if you delete an individual in your Ancestry tree and change the same individual's birthplace in your FTM tree, when you sync the trees together the individual will be deleted.

Unlinking Trees

If you no longer want your FTM and Ancestry trees linked together, you can remove the connection between them.

Warning: If you unlink your FTM and Ancestry trees, changes will no longer be synchronized, and you cannot relink the trees, but you can upload or download the tree again to create a new link. Also note that Ancestry hints will not appear in an unlinked tree.

1 Go to the **Current Tree** tab on the Plan workspace.

2 Click the down arrow next to the **Sync Now** button and choose "Unlink Tree" from the pop-up menu.

Changing Privacy Settings

When you upload a tree to Ancestry, you choose whether your Ancestry tree will be public (the default) or private. However, you can change its privacy settings at any time. (For more information on the differences between public and private trees, see page 253.)

1. Go to the **Current Tree** tab on the Plan workspace.
2. Click the down arrow next to the **Sync Now** button and choose **Manage Ancestry Tree Privacy** from the pop-up menu. The **Tree settings** page opens in the default web browser.

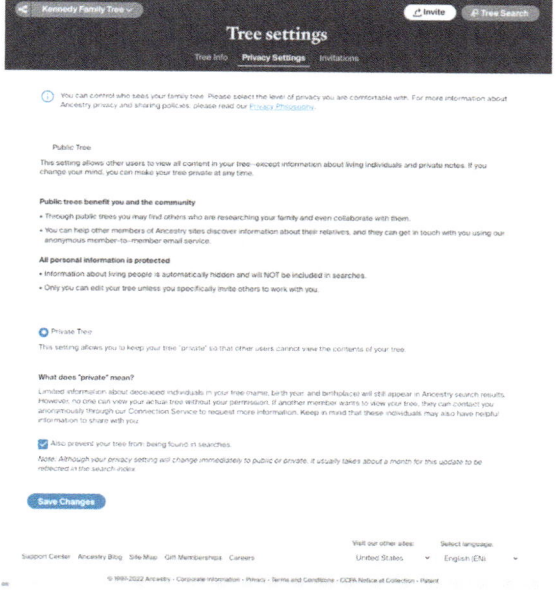

3. Select **Public Tree** to let other Ancestry subscribers view your tree; select **Private Tree** to prevent others from viewing your tree.

   Note: If your tree is private, Ancestry subscribers can still see names, birth dates, and birthplaces from your tree in search results. However, to see your full tree or any attached photos and records, they'll have to ask you for permission. If you don't want your tree to appear in search results either, select the **Also prevent your tree from being found in searches** checkbox.

4. Click **Save Changes**.

Inviting Others to View Your Ancestry Tree

You can invite friends and family to view your Ancestry tree. You can even let them add new information or photos.

Warning: Anyone assigned the role of "editor" can add, edit, or delete information in your Ancestry tree. These changes will be made to your FTM tree when the trees are synced together.

1. Go to the **Current Tree** tab on the Plan workspace.
2. Click the **Invite to Ancestry Tree** button. The **Tree settings** page opens in the default web browser.

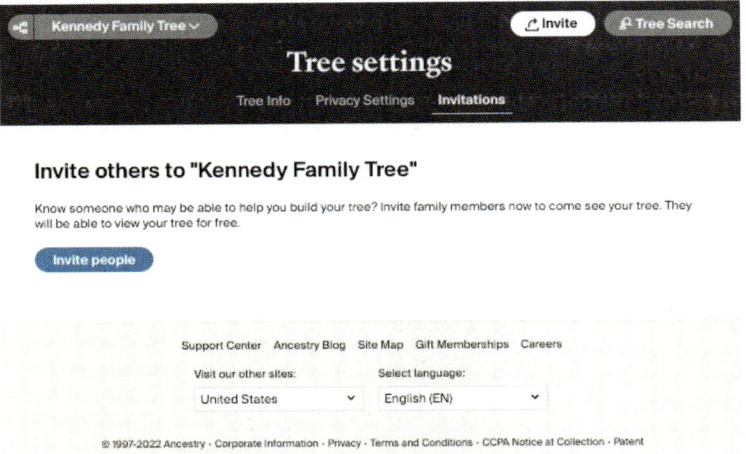

Note: If you've already invited people to your tree, you'll need to click the **Sync Now** button and choose **Manage Ancestry Tree Invitees** to invite more people to your tree.

3. Click the **Invite People** button.
4. Do one of the following:
   - Click **Email** or **Username**, and then enter the person's email or Ancestry username respectively to address the invitation.
   - Click **Invite Link**, which allows you to create a unique personal link for the person you want to invite.

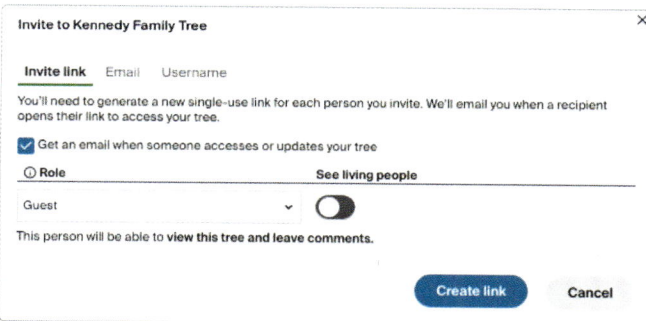

5 Assign the person one of these roles: editor, contributor, guest (see below).

6 If you have entered an email address or Ancestry username, you can include a personal message to the invitee. Then click **Send Invites**.

7 If you have chosen the **Invite Link** option, click **Create link**, and then click **Copy link**. The link will be copied to the Clipboard. You can then share the link with the invitee by email, instant message, or any way you prefer.

Roles in Ancestry Trees

When you invite people to view your tree, they can participate in different ways, depending on the role you assign them:

- **Editor.** Editors can add, edit, or delete anyone in your tree, add stories and photos, and leave comments. They can also see living individuals. Editors cannot delete or rename the tree, change tree settings, or invite others to the tree.

- **Contributor.** Contributors can add photos or stories to your tree, but they cannot add or edit people. You can choose whether or not they see living individuals.

- **Guest.** Guests can only view your tree and leave comments. You can choose whether or not they see living individuals.

Chapter Thirteen
Using TreeVault Cloud Services

🌿 Welcome to TreeVault

Think of TreeVault cloud services as the digital hub for your genealogy research. You start by uploading your tree from Family Tree Maker to TreeVault. That creates a private Antenna tree which is updated automatically each time you make a change in your FTM Source tree.

We'll be adding new services with each update, but here's the starting lineup:
- Emergency Tree restore service
- Next of Kin service
- Family Tree Maker Connect mobile app
- Historical Weather service
- AlbumWALK connection

To get started with TreeVault cloud services, you just need to create a TreeVault account and then log into it to activate the services in Family Tree Maker.

🌿 Creating a TreeVault Account

There are two ways to go about creating a TreeVault account. The first is to click the **Create Account** button on step 2 of the Family Tree Maker registration wizard, which appears when you open the application for the first time after installation.

268 Part 4: Managing Your Trees

If you don't do it then, you can set up an account at any time by choosing **Connect to TreeVault Cloud Services** from the **Family Tree Maker 2019** menu and clicking the "**Create Account**" link in the dialog that appears. In both cases the Create Your TreeVault Account webpage will open in your default web browser.

1 Enter your information in the fields. All fields are required.

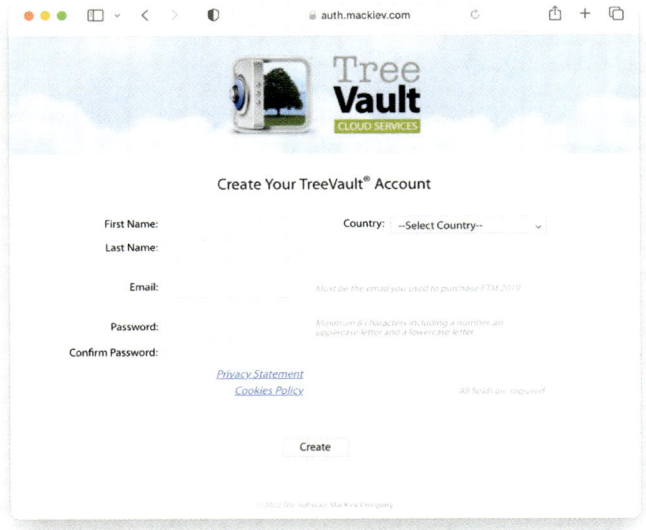

Note: If you obtained a TreeVault subscription when purchasing FTM 2019, make sure the email address you enter is the same one you used to make the purchase. (You can always change the address you use for the account later in TreeVault Account Manager.)

2 Click **Create**.

3 In FTM 2019, click the **TreeVault** icon on the main toolbar or in the **TreeVault Cloud Services** panel on the **Current Tree** tab on the Plan workspace, and then click **Log in**.

4 In the **TreeVault Login** window, enter the email address and password that you provided in step 1, and then click **Log In**. After completing these steps, your TreeVault account will be active and you will be logged in and ready to create your Antenna tree.

Tip: For more information, visit ftm.support/TreeVault.

🌱 Emergency Tree Restore Service

You start by choosing one of your trees—usually your most complete tree—to be your FTM Source tree, and then upload its data to create a TreeVault Antenna tree. The Antenna tree is updated automatically each time you make a change in your Source tree in Family Tree Maker. This means you have an up-to-date copy of your family history ready to be recovered if your hard disk crashes or some other catastrophe strikes. For more information, choose **TreeVault User Guide** from the **Help** menu.

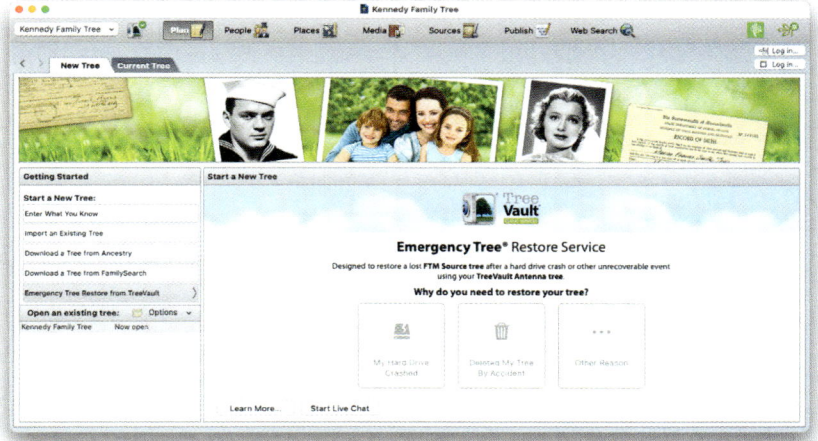

Next of Kin

The Next of Kin service was designed to provide Family Tree Maker users the peace of mind that comes with knowing that your years of family history research will be passed along to a designated successor—a person of your choice who will inherit the family tree data in your TreeVault account.

The legally valid Next of Kin certificate can be passed on to a family member who can use it to take over ownership of your TreeVault account and Family Tree Maker license when you are no longer able to work on your family's history. The certificate will allow your designated successor to receive a copy of Family Tree Maker, a unique passcode generated by TreeVault, and instructions on how to gain access to the account in order to retrieve and preserve your family tree.

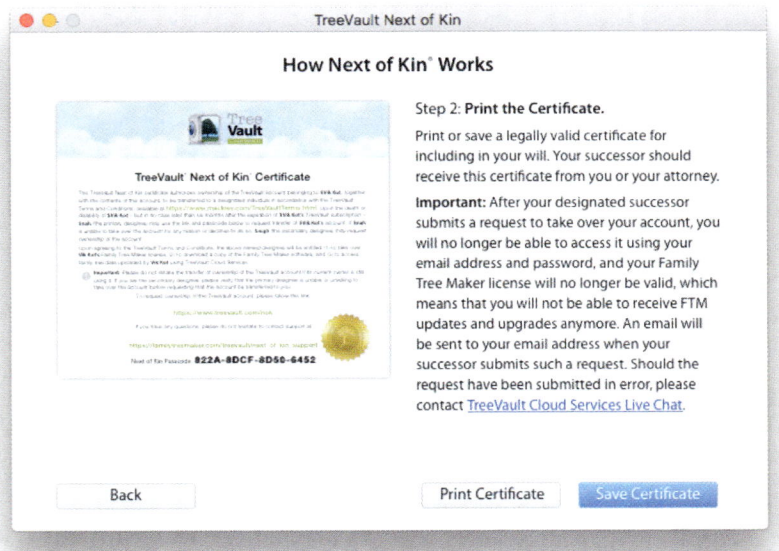

🌿 Family Tree Maker Connect

The free Family Tree Maker Connect mobile app from Software MacKiev provides a real-time view of your TreeVault Antenna tree. Since the Antenna tree is automatically updated when you make changes in your Source tree, Family Tree Maker Connect is ideal for using your mobile device as a continuous tree view monitor placed next to your computer.

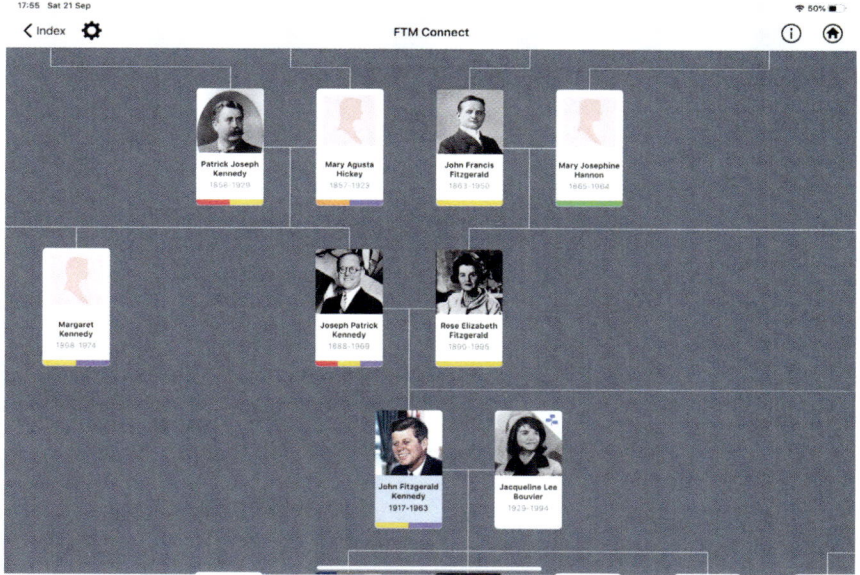

For more information, choose **TreeVault User Guide** from the **Help** menu or visit ftm.support/connect.

Historical Weather

When you log in to TreeVault, you instantly get access to more than a billion historical weather records from more than 100,000 weather stations in 180 countries and their territories. With the oldest records from as far back as the 18th century, historical weather reports add color and context to your family's story. You can, for example, discover whether it was rainy or fine on your grandparents' wedding day, get to know just how much snow fell on that magical white Christmas your mother remembers from her childhood, or find out how cold it was and how hard the wind was blowing on the winter's day when your great-grandfather first stepped ashore onto North American soil.

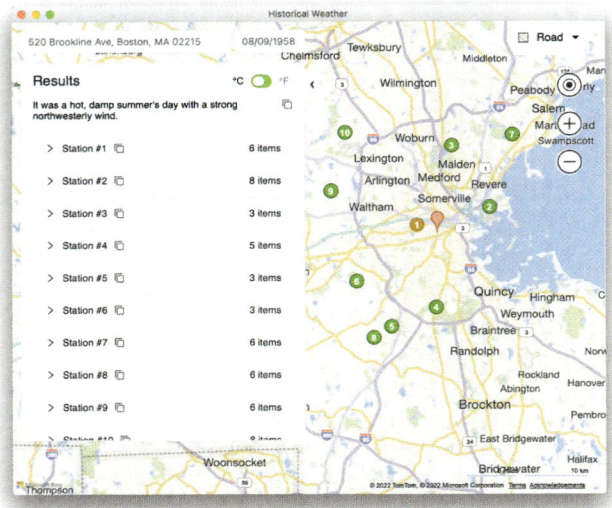

The Historical Weather service automatically converts the weather data to short text summaries displayed with the records from weather stations. You can copy these summaries to paste wherever you need or include them automatically in the Smart Stories you create. See "Creating Smart Stories" on page 69.

🌿 AlbumWALK Connection

When creating talking photos with the AlbumWALK app for iOS and Android, you can take advantage of the powerful versatility of TreeVault cloud services. Just log in to your TreeVault account from the app and import the names of the people in your Antenna tree to benefit from these convenient features:

- When you enter names for the people in your talking photos, the app suggests matching names from your Antenna tree.
- Using a suggested name for a person in a photo links them with the individual in your Antenna tree. So if you change a linked name in your FTM Source tree, it will automatically be updated in AlbumWALK too.
- When an AlbumWALK talking photo with linked names is added into your FTM Source tree, the media will be automatically linked to the corresponding people in the tree.
- A handy mini-tree view appears in AlbumWALK showing the parents and children of any person in the Index (People List) so you can make sure you are linking to the right "John Smith".

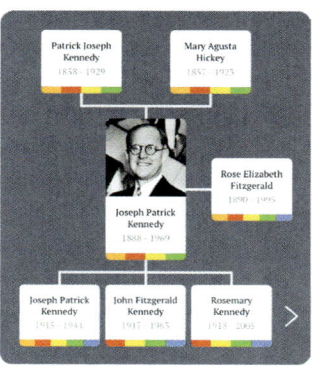

For more information, choose **TreeVault User Guide** from the **Help** menu.

Note: Visit www.albumwalk.com for availability and pricing.

Chapter Fourteen
Tools and Preferences

Using Family Tree Maker Tools

If you need some extra help calculating approximate birth dates, understanding how individuals are related to each other, or creating a to-do list, Family Tree Maker has several tools that can help.

Soundex Calculator

Soundex is a term familiar to serious family historians. It's a coding system used by the government to create indexes of U.S. census records (and passenger lists) based on how a surname sounds rather than how it is spelled. This was done to compensate for potential spelling and transcription errors. For example, "Smith" may be spelled "Smythe," "Smithe," or "Smyth." Using Soundex, these "Smiths" are all identified by the same code (S530). You can use Soundex to find surnames that use the same code and then search for ancestors using all these surname variations.

Choose **Tools>Soundex Calculator**. Type a surname in the **Name** field, or click **Index** to select someone in your tree.

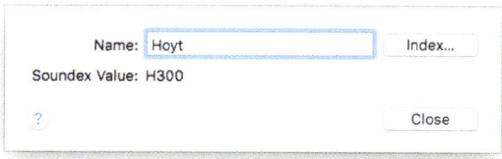

Relationship Calculator

The relationship calculator helps you identify how two people in your tree are related, shows an individual's nearest common relative, and gives his or her canon and civil numbers.

Note: Canon and civil numbers indicate the degree of relationship between individuals. Canon laws (used in the United States) measure the number of steps back to a common ancestor. Civil degree measures the total number of steps from one family member to another.

1. Choose **Tools**>**Relationship Calculator**. In the first field you'll see the home person. In the second field you'll see the individual who is the current focus of the tree.

2. To change the individuals whose relationship you're calculating, click the **Person from people index** button (the index card) next to a name. In Index of Individuals select a new person and click **OK**.

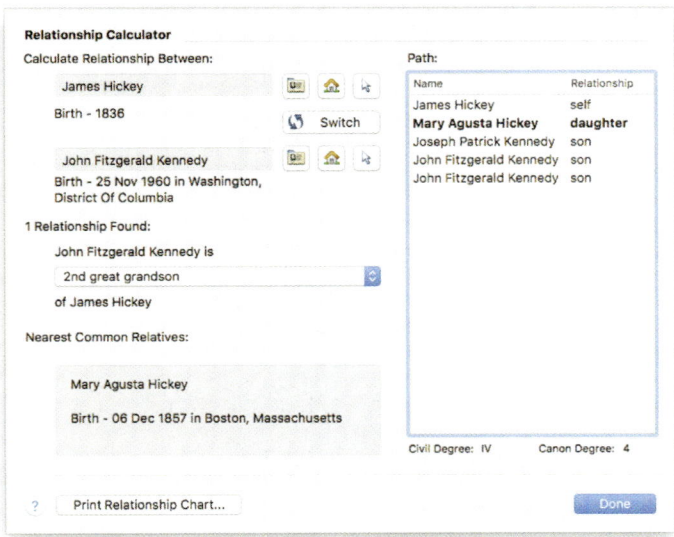

The individuals' relationship is listed underneath their names. If they have multiple connections (for example if they are cousins who married), use the pop-up menu to see each relationship. You can also see how the individuals are related in the Path section.

Date Calculator

You can use the date calculator to figure out an individual's birth year, age at the time of a specific event, or the date of an event. For example, if you know the date your grandmother was married and you know how old she was when she got married, you can determine the approximate year she was born.

1 Choose **Tools>Date Calculator**. The date calculator opens.

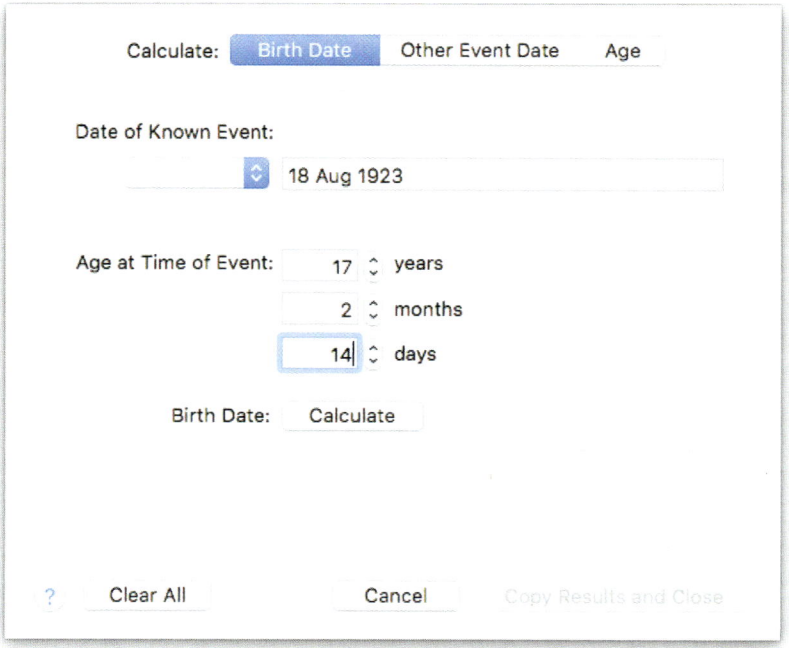

2 Use this chart to help you enter dates into the calculator:

To calculate this	Do this
A birth date	• Click **Birth Date**. • Enter a date in the **Date of Known Event** field. • Enter the individual's age in the **Age at Time of Event** fields.
The date of a specific event	• Click **Other Event Date**. • Enter a date in the **Birth Date** field. • Enter the individual's age in the **Age at Time of Event** fields.
An individual's age on a specific date	• Click **Age**. • Enter a date in the **Birth Date** field. • Enter a date in the **Date of Known Event** field.

3 Click **Calculate**. The calculated event date or age appears.

Name Converter

If you import another person's genealogy file into your tree, you may find that each file has recorded names differently; your surnames may be in all caps while theirs may not. You can use the convert names tool to format all names in your tree at once.

1 Choose **Tools>Convert Names**. The Convert Names dialog opens.

2 To capitalize the first letter in each name, select **First Middle Surname**. To capitalize the first letter of the first and middle names and capitalize the entire surname, select **First Middle SURNAME**.

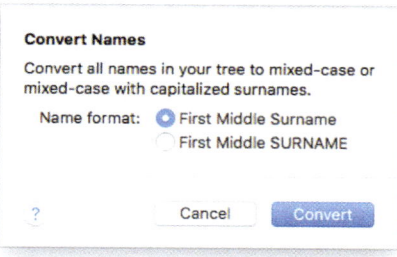

3 Click **Convert**.

Find Individual Tool

You can use any fact in your tree (such as occupation or burial) to locate either a specific individual or a group of individuals who fit specific criteria. For example, you can search for everyone in your tree who lived in Illinois at the time of the 1850 census. Or, you can find out which individuals are buried in the same cemetery.

Note: The Find Individual tool searches Place and Description fields; Date fields cannot be searched.

1 Choose **Edit>Find Individual**. The Find Individual dialog opens.

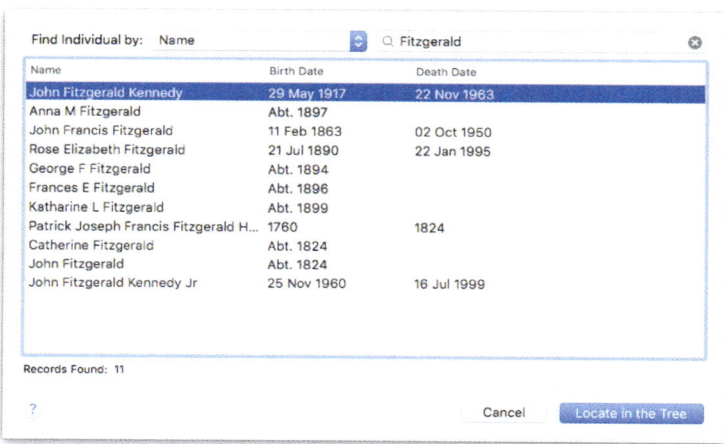

280 Part 4: Managing Your Trees

2   Choose the type of fact you want to search from the pop-up menu. Then type a search term and click the search icon (magnifying glass).

3   To view a specific individual, select him or her in the search results and click **Locate in the Tree**.

Automatic Reference Numbers

Some family historians use reference numbers to identify people in their trees, particularly if the tree contains individuals with identical names. Family Tree Maker can assign reference numbers to individuals (Person ID), relationships (Relationship ID), or both.

Note: If you have entered your own reference numbers, Family Tree Maker will not overwrite them.

1   Choose **Tools>References**. The References dialog opens.

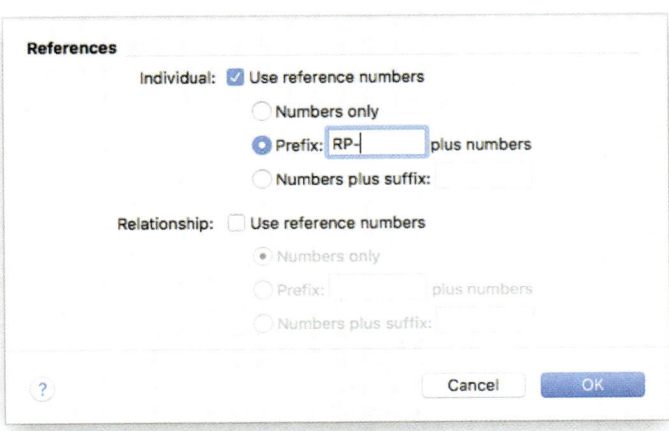

2   Select **Individual** to choose how numbers are assigned to individuals; select **Relationship** to choose how numbers are assigned to relationships.

3 Select **Numbers only** to assign numbers, starting with 1. Select **Prefix** to add a prefix before the number (you can enter numbers, letters, and/or symbols). Select **Numbers plus suffix** to add a suffix after the number (you can enter numbers, letters, and/or symbols).

4 Click **OK**.

Global Birth Order Tool

In the family group view, you can change the order in which children are displayed in a family by clicking the Move up and Move down buttons. If you always want to display children in your tree by birth order, you can use this tool to change them all at once.

1 Choose **Tools>Sort All Children by Birth**.

2 If you want to back up your tree file before you sort children, select the **Backup file before sorting** checkbox (recommended).

3 Click **Sort**.

Research To-Do List

Whether you're a new user or an experienced family historian, the to-do list can help you keep track of the research you've already done and create tasks for your next steps. You can add research tasks for specific individuals or general tasks for your entire tree; tasks can be as simple as sending an email to a cousin or as complicated as locating an entire family in the 1940 census.

Creating a To-Do Task

When you create a task, you can choose the priority of the task, the category it fits in, and its due date.

Note: This section explains how to add tasks for specific individuals. You can also add tasks to the tree's to-do list on the Current Tree tab on the Plan workspace.

1. Go to the **Person** tab for a specific individual (on the People workspace). Click the **Tasks** tab.

2. Click the **New** button in the Tasks toolbar. The Task dialog opens.

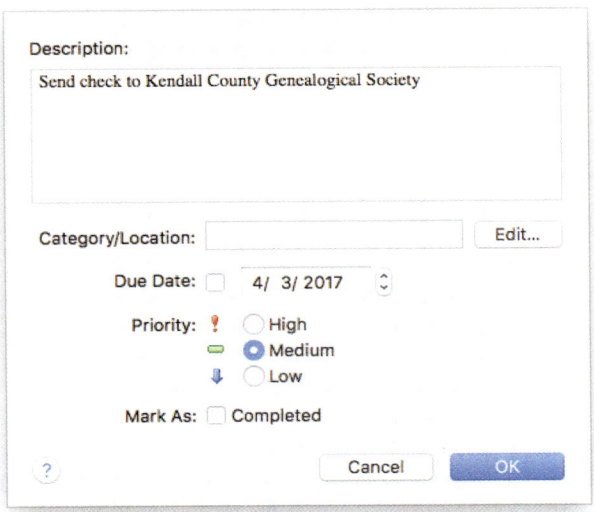

3. Type a task in the **Description** field.

4. Click **Edit** to select a category for the task. Select a category or create a category and click **OK**. (For more information see "Creating Task Categories" below.)

5. Choose a deadline for the task using the **Due Date** arrows. Then select a priority. (Assign a high priority to the tasks you want to accomplish first.) When you're finished, click **OK**.

   Tip: You can print the to-do list for this individual by clicking the Print button in the Tasks toolbar. To print a list of all tasks in your tree, use the Task List Report on the Publish workspace.

Creating Task Categories

Each task you create can be assigned to a category. You can add categories that are useful to your research.

1. Go to the **Current Tree** tab on the Plan workspace. Click the **Tasks** tab to see your current to-do list.
2. Click **New**. The Task dialog opens. Click **Edit**. The categories dialog opens, showing all available categories.

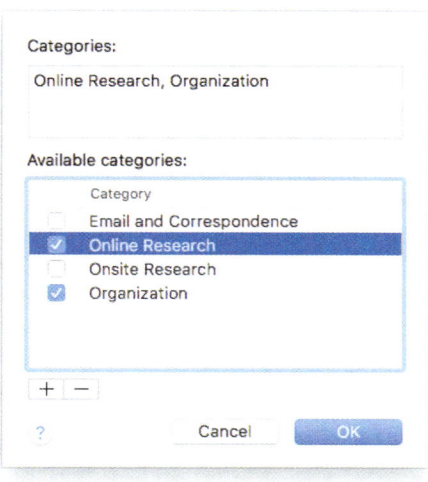

3. Click the **Add (+) button**.
4. Type a name in the New Ca**tegory** field and click **OK**.

Marking a Task as Complete

When you finish a task on your to-do list, you'll want to mark it as complete. Go to the **Current Tree** tab on the Plan workspace. In the Tasks section, select the checkbox next to the task.

Tip: To delete a task, select the task and click the **Delete task** (X) button in the Tasks toolbar.

Sorting the To-Do List

You can filter the to-do list in various ways. For example, you can sort the list to show which tasks are done or still pending.

1   Go to the **Current Tree** tab on the Plan workspace.

2   In the Tasks section, click the **Filter tasks** button and choose one of these commands from the pop-up menu:

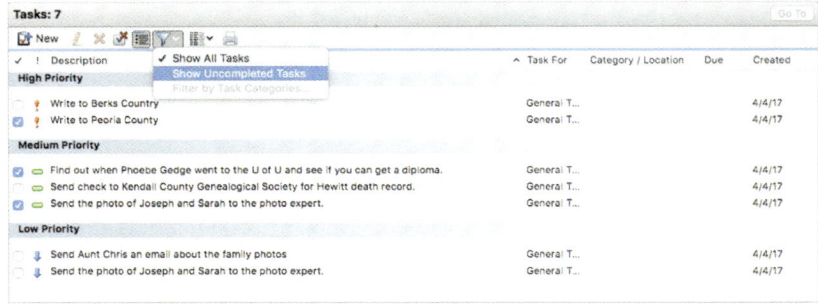

- To show every task you've entered, choose **Show All Tasks**.
- To show unfinished tasks, choose **Show Uncompleted Tasks**.
- To show tasks that belong to a specific category, choose **Filter by Task Categories**.

Tip: You can change what information is displayed for each task. Click the **Show/Hide columns** button in the Tasks toolbar. Then, from the pop-up menu, select or deselect specific columns.

Setting Up Preferences

Family Tree Maker is a powerful program with many features and options. To get the most out of the software, you might want to take a minute and define a few key preferences.

General Preferences

You can set some preferences that affect the interface and general workings of Family Tree Maker.

1   Choose **Family Tree Maker 2019>Settings** (**Preferences** on macOS 12 Monterey or earlier). The **General** tab is selected.

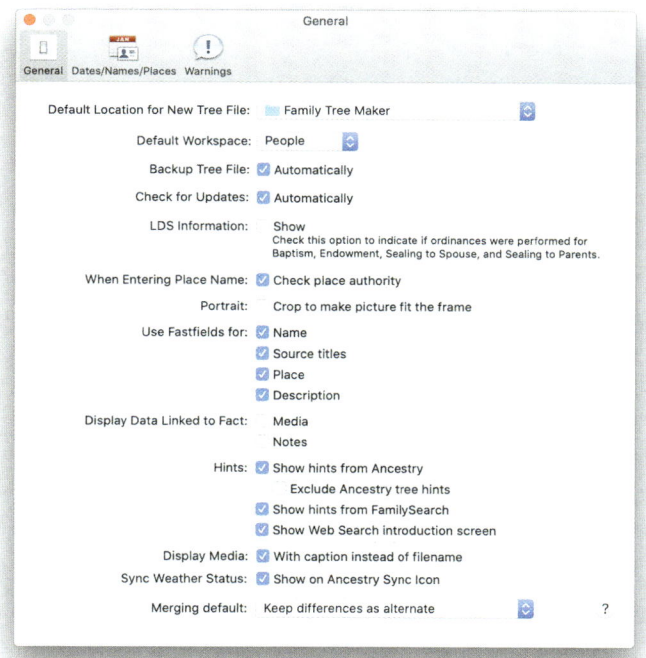

2   Change these preferences as necessary:

- **Default Location for New Tree File.** To change the default location where trees are saved on your hard disk, click **Choose** in the pop-up menu and choose a new folder.

- **Backup Tree File: Automatically.** Select this checkbox to create backups of your trees (without media) automatically when you quit the application. If your original tree is ever lost or damaged, you can use the backup to restore your information.

- **Check for Updates: Automatically.** Select this checkbox if you want Family Tree Maker to look for software updates when you're online. You'll be alerted if an update exists.

- **Default Workspace.** Select the workspace that you want to go to first when you open a tree file.

- **LDS Information: Show.** Select this checkbox if you want to display LDS facts such as sealings and baptisms. This will also add two LDS-specific Person reports to the Publish workspace.

- **When Entering Place Name: Check place authority.** Select this checkbox if you want Family Tree Maker to compare each place you enter against its database of locations. This option helps you keep your locations in standard formats and consistent throughout your tree.

- **Portrait: Crop to make picture fit the frame.** Select this checkbox to resize portrait images so that they fill the frame.
  Note: The actual images in your tree will not be modified. Also, you cannot choose to resize individual thumbnails. This option resizes every portrait in your tree.

- **Display Media: With caption instead of filename.** Select this checkbox to sort media items by the captions you've given them; otherwise, media items will be sorted and displayed by file name.

- **Sync Weather Status: Show on Ancestry Sync Icon.** Select this checkbox to display the sync weather status badge on the Ancestry Sync icon.

- **Merging default.** Choose a default method of dealing with differences when merging trees and individuals. The options are to delete them or to keep them as alternate facts.

Online Searching Preferences

You can determine whether or not Family Tree Maker will search FamilySearch and Ancestry for matching records and trees when you're connected to the Internet.

1 Choose **Family Tree Maker 2019>Settings** (**Preferences** on macOS 12 Monterey or earlier). The **General** tab is selected.

2 Change these preferences as necessary:

- **Show hints from Ancestry.** Select this checkbox to have Family Tree Maker search Ancestry for individuals in your tree when an Internet connection is available.

  You'll see a green leaf (or hint) next to an individual when possible matches have been found. If you deselect this option, you can still search Ancestry for your family members on the Web Search workspace.

- **Exclude Ancestry tree hints.** Select this checkbox to exclude hints from family trees submitted by other Ancestry users.

- **Show hints from FamilySearch.** Select this checkbox to have Family Tree Maker search FamilySearch.org for individuals in your tree when an Internet connection is available.

  You'll see a blue square (or hint) next to an individual when possible matches have been found. If you deselect this option, you can still search FamilySearch for your family members on the Web Search workspace.

- **Show Web Search introduction screen.** Select this checkbox to display Web Search help when you begin an online search.

> **Fastfields**
>
> Fastfields save you time by automatically filling in some types of information. Perhaps you noticed as you typed an individual's name that the last name was completed for you. This is because name fields, among others, are Fastfields.
>
> Location Fastfields remember the places you've entered in a tree. As you type a location, Family Tree Maker suggests possible matches. Use the keyboard arrows, mouse or trackpad to highlight the correct location and press **Return** to select it. You can also keep typing a name to override the Fastfields suggestion.

Fastfields Preferences

Fastfields speed up data entry by automatically filling in repetitive data as you type. For example, if you type "San Jose, California, USA" into a place field then go to another place field and begin to type "San," Family Tree Maker will recognize the similarity and suggest "San Jose, California, USA." By default, all Fastfields are used, but you can turn off any you wish.

1. Choose **Family Tree Maker 2019>Settings (Preferences** on macOS 12 Monterey or earlie**r)**.
2. To turn off Fastfields for a specific field type, deselect the corresponding **Use Fastfields for** checkbox.

Fact Display Preferences

The person editing panel on the Person tab includes a Sources tab. If you want, you can also display media and notes tabs.

1. Choose **Family Tree Maker 2019>Settings (Preferences** on macOS 12 Monterey or earlier).
2. Select the **Display Data Linked to Fact** checkbox for each type of tab you want to display on the person editing panel.

Date Preferences

Family Tree Maker lets you change how dates are formatted.

1 Choose **Family Tree Maker 2019>Settings** (**Preferences** on macOS 12 Monterey or earlier), and then click **Dates/Names/Places**.

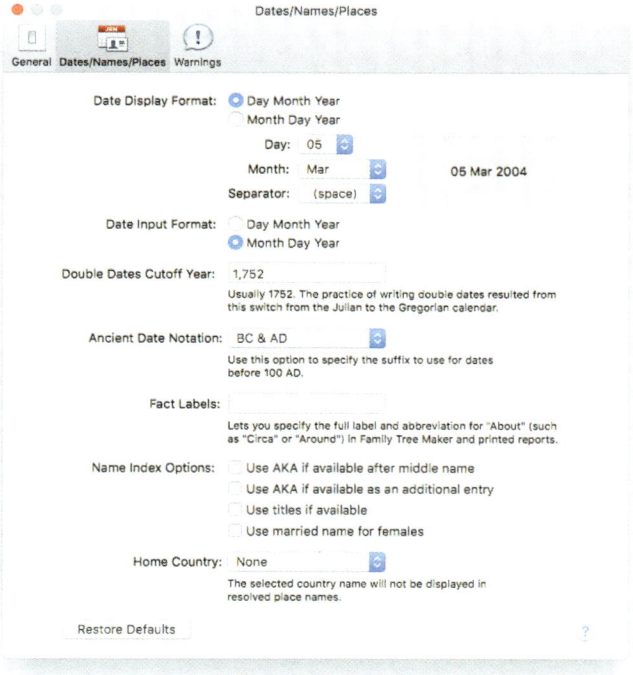

2 Change these date preferences as necessary:

- **Date Display Format.** Choose how dates are displayed. Select **Day Month Year** to show the day before the month (10 September 2019). By default, Family Tree Maker displays dates in this accepted genealogical date standard. Select **Month Day Year** to show the month before the day (September 10, 2019).

Use the pop-up menus to choose different formats for the day, month, and date separator.

- **Date Input Format.** Choose how Family Tree Maker interprets dates you type: day, month, year, or month, day, year. For example, if you type "6/7/2019" Family Tree Maker can read this as June 7th or July 6th.

- **Double Dates Cutoff Year.** Change the year in this field to change the default double date cutoff year (for explanation, see below). If you do not want double dates to print, set the double date cutoff year to zero.

- **Ancient Date Notation.** Choose whether dates before 1000 AD are displayed with BC/AD or BCE/CE.

- **Fact Labels.** To display a different abbreviation for the term "About" (meaning "circa"), type your preferred label.

> **Double Dates Cutoff Year**
>
> January 1 has not always been the first day of the year, and different countries chose to start the year on that date at different times (e.g., Spain in 1556, Scotland in 1600, Russia in 1725). England and its colonies, including those that would go on to form the United States, did so in 1752 when they switched the calendar from Julian to Gregorian. Previously, each new year had officially begun on March 25 (Annunciation Day). So dates that fall within the period January 1 through March 24 in years before 1752 can be interpreted in two ways, and some genealogists prefer to show both dates. For example, February 22 1750 under the old system would fall in the year 1751 using the modern calendar, so the date would be noted as 22 February 1750/51.

Name Preferences

Family Tree Maker lets you determine how names are displayed in the Index on the People workspace. You can include titles, alternate names, and married names for females.

1   Choose **Family Tree Maker 2019>Settings** (**Preferences** on macOS 12 Monterey or earlier), and then click **Dates/Names/Places**.

2   Change these preferences as necessary:

  - **Use AKA if available after middle name.** Select this checkbox to have Also Known As names included with the preferred name (for example, Bobbitt, Mary Eliza "Mollie").

  - **Use AKA if available as an additional entry.** Select this checkbox to give Also Known As names their own entries in the Index (for example, Hannah Willis and Anna Willis).

  - **Use titles if available.** Select this checkbox to have titles included with the preferred name (for example, Hoyt, Captain Samuel).

  - **Use married name for females.** Select this checkbox to list women by their married (and maiden) names (for example, Hoyt, Maria Hitchcock).

3   If most events recorded in your tree occur in the same country (for example, if most of your ancestors were born and died in England), you may not want to include that country's name in place fields and charts and reports. To keep a country's name from appearing, choose it from the **Home Country** pop-up menu.

Warning and Alert Preferences

Family Tree Maker can automatically check your tree for errors and alert you if it detects a possible problem, such as unusual dates.

1 Choose **Family Tree Maker 2019>Settings** (**Preferences** on macOS 12 Monterey or earlier); then click **Warnings**.

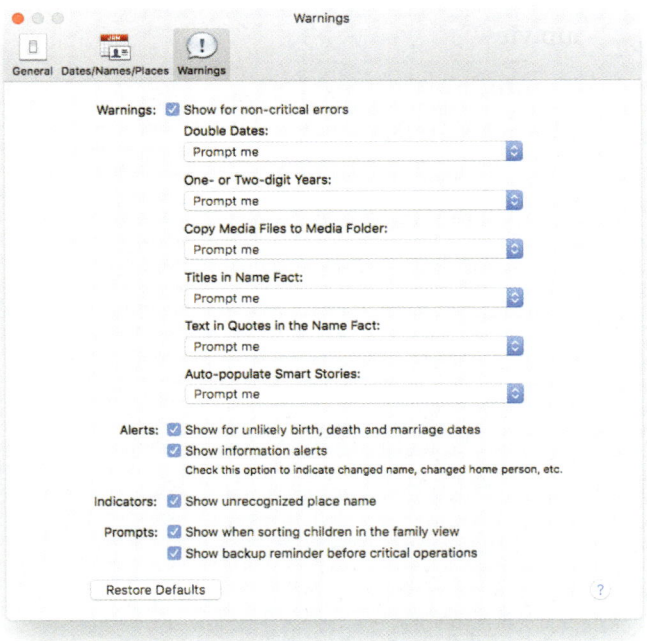

2 Change these warning preferences as necessary:

- **Show for unlikely birth, death, and marriage dates.** Select this checkbox to get alerts when you enter dates that seem to be inaccurate (for example, a death date that occurs earlier than a birth date).

- **Show information alerts.** Select this checkbox to get alerts when you update your tree (for example, when you change the home person or edit an individual's name).

- **Show for unrecognized place name.** Select this checkbox to get alerts when Family Tree Maker doesn't recognize a location you've entered.
  Note: This option is not available if you've deselected the "Check Place Authority" checkbox on the General tab.
- **Show when sorting children in the family view.** Select this checkbox to get alerts when you manually sort children in the family group view.
- **Show backup reminder before critical operations.** Select this checkbox to be reminded to back up your tree before performing an operation which may result in data loss.

3 Determine how Family Tree Maker handles minor errors:
- **Double Dates.** If Family Tree Maker detects double dates, you can leave the dates as they are, use formatting to show both dates, or be prompted for instructions.
- **One- or Two-digit Years.** If Family Tree Maker detects years entered with one or two digits, you can accept the date as it is, change the date to the year of recent century, or be prompted for instructions.
- **Copy Media Files to Media Folder.** When you add a media item to your tree, you can choose whether or not to automatically copy the file to a Family Tree Maker media folder or be prompted for instructions.
- **Titles in Name Fact.** If Family Tree Maker detects a title such as Reverend, Captain, or Sir in a Name fact, you can leave the title in the Name fact, move the title to the Title fact, or be prompted for instructions.
- **Text in Quotes in the Name Fact.** If Family Tree Maker detects nicknames (indicated by quotes) in a Name fact, you can leave the nickname in the Name fact, move the nickname to the AKA fact, or be prompted for instructions.

- **Auto-populate Smart Stories.** When you create a Smart Story, you can start with a blank page, a page populated with information about the individual and his or her family, or be prompted for instructions.

Managing Facts

Facts are the essential building blocks of your tree, where you record the details about your family. In order to capture the information you care about, you might want to create your own facts or change which fields appear in predefined facts.

Creating a Custom Fact

You can create custom facts that work for your family tree. For example, if you are tracking your ancestors by census records, you can make a custom fact for each census year.

1. Choose **Edit>Manage Facts**. The Manage Facts dialog opens.
2. Click the **Add (+)** button. The Add Custom Fact dialog opens.

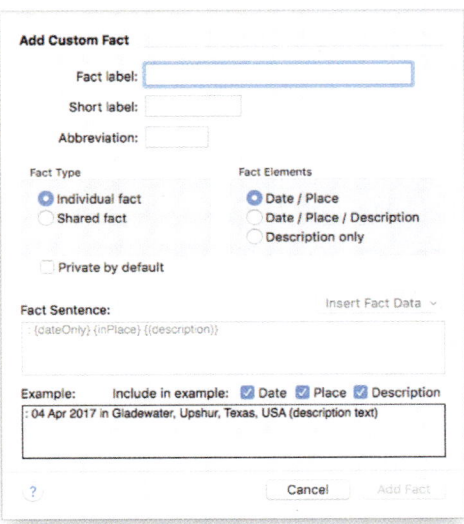

3 Change the fact as necessary:
- **Fact label.** Type the name of the fact as it will appear on the Person tab.
- **Short label.** Type a short name (up to six characters) for the fact that will appear on the Tree tab editing panel.
- **Abbreviation.** Type an abbreviation (up to three characters) for the fact that will appear in reports.
- **Fact Type.** Select **Individual fact** if the fact applies to one person, such as birth or death. Select **Shared fact** if the fact applies to more than one individual, such as marriage.
- **Fact Elements.** Select the fields that you want to appear for the fact: Date and Place; Date, Place, and Description; or Description only.
- **Fact Sentence.** To change the default sentence, see "Modifying a Fact Sentence" on page 296.

4 Click **Add Fact**.

Modifying a Predefined Fact

While you can't rename or delete predefined facts, you can choose which fields are included as part of the fact. For example, you can modify the Cause of Death fact so that only the Description field is included.

1 Choose **Edit>Manage Facts**. The Manage Facts dialog opens.

2 Select the predefined fact that you want to modify. Then click **Properties**. The Fact Properties dialog opens.

3   In **Fact Elements**, select which fields you want for the fact.

4   Select the **Private by default** checkbox to make this fact type private. You can change privacy for a specific fact on the Person tab.

5   Click **Apply**.

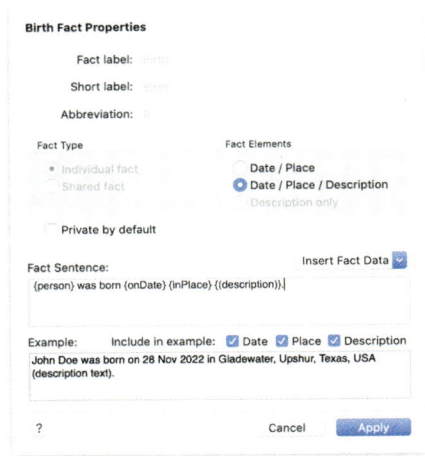

Modifying a Fact Sentence

When you create an Ahnentafel, descendant report, or Smart Story, Family Tree Maker generates descriptive sentences for each fact or event. You can change the wording and choose what info is included. For example, the default burial sentence looks like this: Robert Gedge was buried on 1 Sep 1888 in Attleborough, England. If you record cemetery names, you could include this and change the order of the sentence: Robert Gedge was buried in All Saints Cemetery, Attleborough, England, on 1 Sep 1888.

1   Choose **Edit>Manage Facts**. The Manage Facts dialog opens.

2   Click the **Add (+)** button or select the fact you want to modify and click **Properties**. The Fact Properties dialog opens. The Fact sentence field displays the current sentence—a combination of text and predefined data variables.

3   To change the text, simply add, delete, or type over it. To change which variables are in the sentence, delete the variable or choose a new one from the **Insert Fact Data** pop-up menu.

Tip: If you don't like your changes and want to use the default sentence, click **Insert Fact Data** and choose **Reset Fact Sentence**.

The Example field shows what the fact sentence will look like. For example, if you deselect the Description checkbox, you can see what the sentence will be if the Description field for the fact is blank.

Managing Relationships

The Manage Relationships tool lets you filter relationships by type and change one relationship type to another, whether that is for a single relationship or in bulk.

1. Click **Edit>Manage Relationships**. The **Manage Relationships** dialog opens.
2. Choose the type of relationship you want to change from the **Show relationships** pop-up menu.
3. The **Relationship Instances** list shows all relationships of the selected type. The total number of instances appears next to the list heading.
4. Select the checkbox next to each of the relationships you want to change the type of. To change all the relationships in the list, select the **Select all** checkbox.
5. From the **Change selected relationships to this type** pop-up menu, choose the new relationship type you want the selected relationships to have.
6. Click **Apply**.
7. When you're finished, click **Close**.

Tip: The **Show relationships** filter can help you make bulk changes and repairs. For example, you can use the filter to find all couples who have a **Marriage fact but whose relationship type is "Unknown"**, and then change them all at once to "**Spouse**".

Managing Historical Events

An individual's timeline and the Timeline report can include historical events. You can edit or delete any historical event. You can also add entries that are relevant to your family history, such as international events that caused your ancestors to emigrate.

1 Click **Edit>Manage Historical Events**. The Manage Historical Events dialog opens.

2 To delete an event, click the entry; then click **Delete**.

3 To add an event, click the **Add (+)** button. The Add/Edit Historical Events dialog opens.

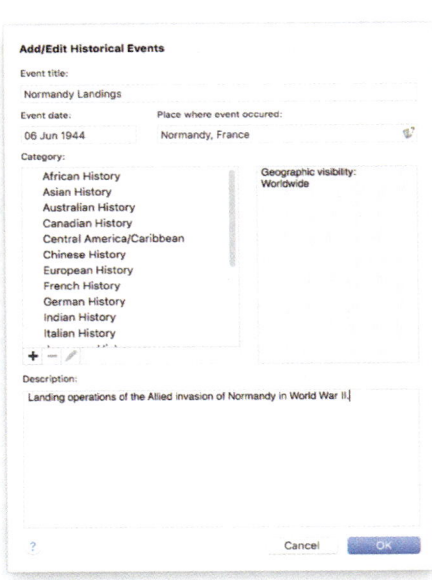

4 Change the historical event as necessary:

- **Event title.** Enter a short title for the event.
- **Event date.** Enter the date or date range of the event.
- **Place where event occurred.** Enter the location of the event.
- **Category.** Choose a historical category from the list or add your own categories. You can also edit and delete the default categories.
- **Description.** Enter a summary of the historical event.

5 Click **OK**.

Customizing the Tree Tab Editing Panel

By default, these facts appear on the editing panel of the Tree tab in the People workspace: name, sex, birth date and place, death date and place, and marriage date and place. If you often record burials or christenings, you can add these facts to the editing panel so you can enter the information more easily.

1. Go to the **Tree** tab on the People workspace. The editing panel appears with its default facts.

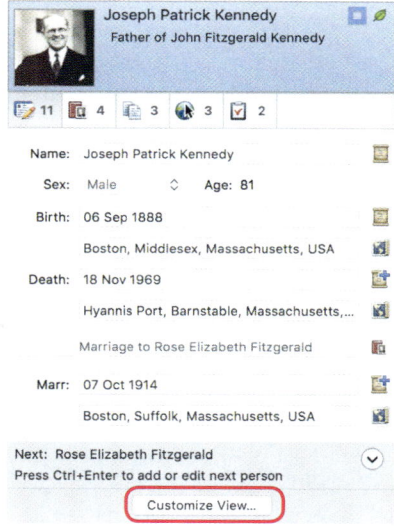

2. Click **Customize View**. The Customize View dialog opens.

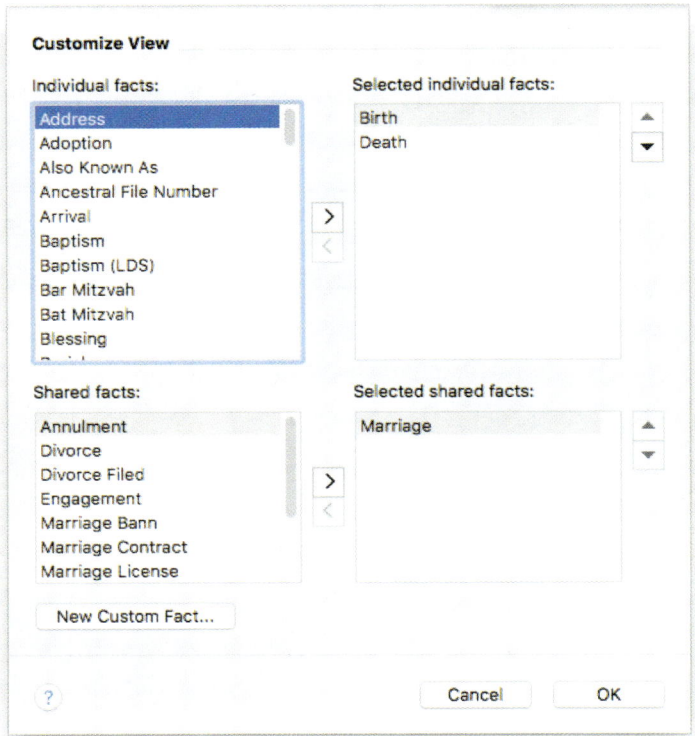

3 In the Individual facts section or the Shared facts section, select a fact; then click the right arrow button to add the fact to the Selected facts sections.

4 To change the order in which the facts display on the panel, select a fact and click the up or down arrows.

5 Click **OK**. The editing panel now includes the new fact.

Entering User Information

You can enter information that identifies you as the creator of a tree. This info is automatically added to your tree file if you export and send it to another family member or researcher.

1 Choose **Tools>User Information**. The User Information dialog opens.

2 Type your information and click **OK**.

Chapter Fifteen
Family Tree Problem Solver

No matter how organized you are or how carefully you enter data, errors can creep into your tree. Whether you've added a child to the wrong family or spelled your ancestor's name incorrectly, Family Tree Maker makes it easy to clean up your tree.

Straightening Out Relationships

At some point in your research you may discover that a certain individual doesn't belong in your tree and you need to delete him or her. Or maybe you added a child to the wrong family. Cleaning up relationship issues as soon as you find them keeps them from multiplying.

Merging Duplicate Individuals

After months and years of gathering names and dates, your family tree may become a bit disorderly. You might discover that Flossie and Florence are actually the same person. If you've entered duplicate individuals, you should merge them together (instead of deleting one) so that you don't lose any information.

Family Tree Maker can assess your tree and show you individuals who might be duplicates.

Note: Before you merge individuals, make a backup of your tree. If you need help, see "Backing Up a Tree File" on page 246.

304 Part 4: Managing Your Trees

Finding Duplicate Individuals

After adding a lot of new information or merging a family member's tree with yours, it's a good idea to check for duplicate individuals.

1 Choose **Edit>Find Duplicate People**. The Find Duplicate List opens.

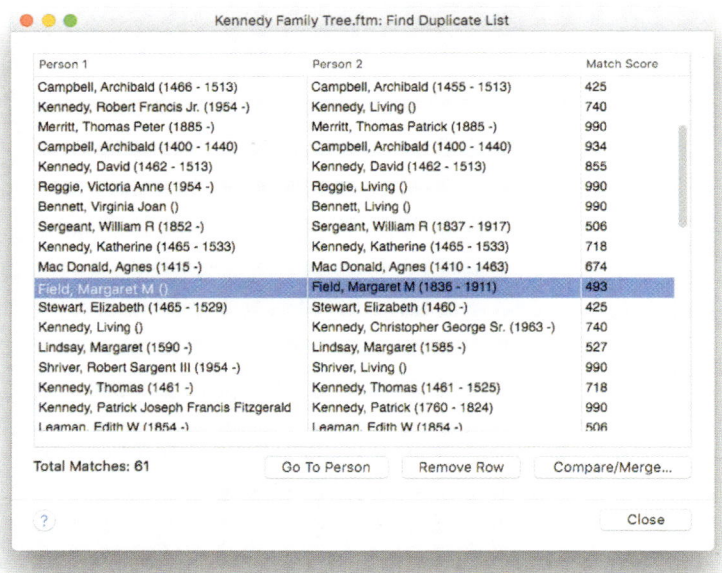

In the Person 1 and Person 2 columns you'll see the individuals who might be duplicates. (You can click a column header to sort a column alphabetically.) In the third column you'll see a match score—the higher the number the more likely the individuals are a match; a 1,000 means the individuals are almost exact matches.

2 To merge a pair of individuals (or just compare the two), select a row and click **Compare/Merge**. The Individual Merge dialog opens. To complete the merge, continue with step 5 in the "Merging Individuals" section on page 306.

Merging Individuals

If you discover that two individuals in your tree are actually the same person, you can merge the two together and retain all the facts and sources associated with each person.

1. Go to the **Tree** tab on the People workspace and select one of the duplicate individuals in the Index.

2. Click the down arrow next to the **People** button on the main toolbar and choose **Merge Two Specific Individuals** from the pop-up menu. The Index of Individuals opens.

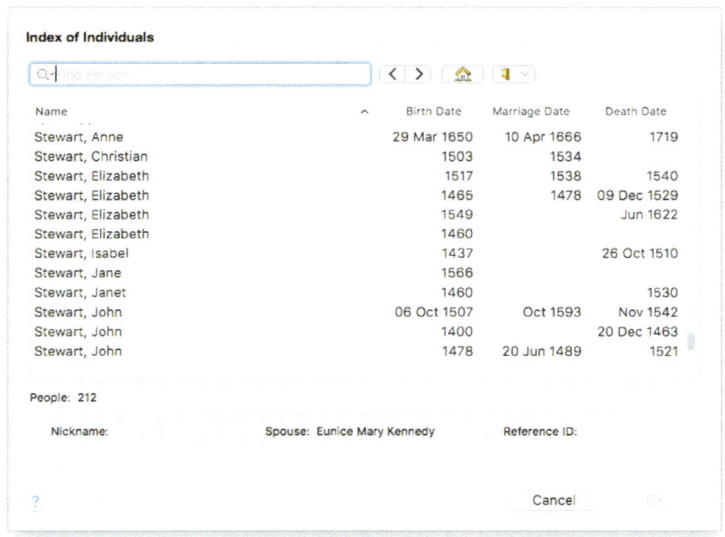

3. Select the name of the other duplicate individual. You can use the scroll bar to move up and down the list, or type a name (last name first) in the search field.

4. Click **OK**. The Individual Merge dialog opens.

The two columns show the facts attached to each individual.

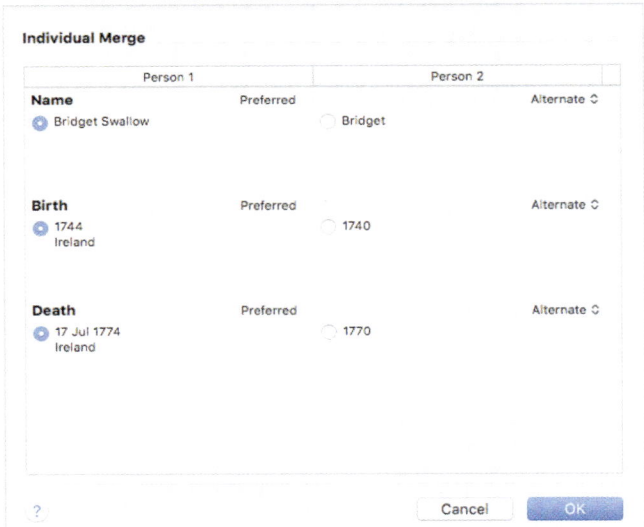

5 Use the buttons next to the facts to determine how each fact will be merged:

- To keep a fact and mark it as preferred, select the button next to the fact. The corresponding fact for the other individual will be merged as an alternate fact unless you discard it.

- To remove a fact, click the **Alternate** arrow and choose **Discard** from the pop-up menu. Though you may discard any fact you like, it is usually a good idea to keep all facts in case they turn out to be relevant. If you discard a fact, you can keep its sources, media items, and notes by clicking the corresponding checkbox in the **Keep** group.

    Note: To learn more about preferred and alternate facts, see "Adding Alternate Facts" on page 53.

6 Click **OK** to complete the merge.

Removing an Individual from a Tree

If you've mistakenly added an individual who isn't related to you, don't worry. Family Tree Maker makes it easy to delete any individual and his or her information from your tree.

1 Go to the **Tree** tab on the People workspace.

2 In the Index or family group view, Control-click the individual you want to delete.

3 Choose **Delete Person** from the shortcut menu.

All notes, tasks, and media links associated with the person will be permanently deleted.

Note: Whenever you want to remove someone permanently from your tree, always use the Delete Person command. If you try to delete someone by removing his or her name from the Name fact, you won't actually delete the individual—or any of his or her facts or relationships.

Removing a Marriage

As you continue your research you might find that you've connected a couple incorrectly. You'll need to delete any marriage facts you've entered and also detach the individuals from each other.

1 Go to the **Tree** tab on the People workspace and select the appropriate couple.

2 Click the **Person** tab for one of the individuals. Then click **Facts** to open the Individual & Shared Facts pane.

3 Control-click the **Marriage** fact and choose **Delete Fact** from the shortcut menu.

Note: If you don't delete the Marriage fact, the individual will still be considered married to an unknown person.

4 To detach the individual from the current spouse, click the down arrow next to the **People** button on the main toolbar and choose **Attach/Detach Person>Detach Selected Person** from the pop-up menu.

5 Select the checkbox for the incorrect spouse. If the couple has children, you can select their checkboxes to detach them from the selected individual too.

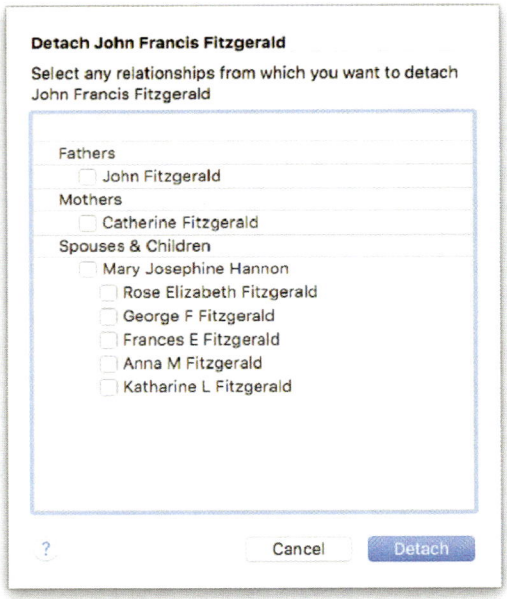

6 Click **Detach**.

Detaching a Child from the Wrong Parents

If you've added a child to the wrong parents, you can detach the child from the family without deleting them from your tree.

1   Go to the **Tree** tab on the People workspace.

2   Make sure the correct family is the focus of the family group view.

3   Select the child.

4   Click the **People** button on the main toolbar and choose **Attach/Detach Person>Detach Selected Person** from the shortcut menu.

5   Select the checkboxes next to the father and/or mother.

6   Click **Detach**.

Attaching a Child to a Father and Mother

If you've added an individual and his or her parents to your tree, but you did not know they were related when you entered them, you can still link them together.

1   Go to the **Tree** tab on the People workspace.

2   Make sure the individual you want to attach to his or her parents is the focus of the Index or family group view.

3   Click the **People** button on the main toolbar, click the down arrow next to the button, and choose **Attach/Detach Person>Attach Mother/Father** from the people menu.

4 Select the father or mother from the list and click **OK**. If the father or mother has multiple spouses, you'll need to choose which family the child belongs to.

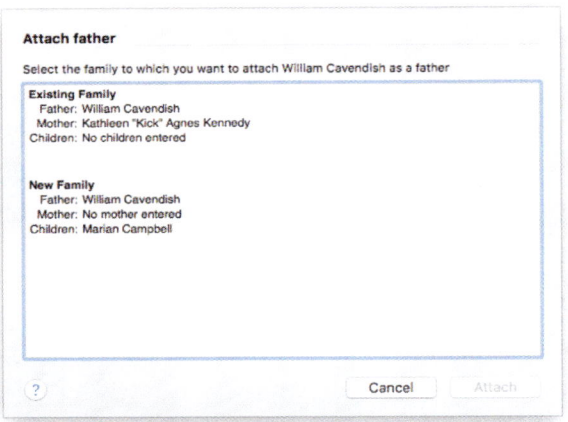

5 Choose the appropriate family and click **Attach**.

Fixing Text Mistakes

It's easy to introduce errors into your tree. Perhaps you transcribed a record too quickly or imported incorrect notes from a family member's tree. Family Tree Maker has several tools that can help look for misspellings, inaccurate dates, and duplicate facts.

Global Spell Checker

The global spell checker lets you search for errors in your tree.

1 Choose **Tools>Global Spell Check**.

2 Change these options as necessary:

- **Fact descriptions.** Select this checkbox to check spelling in fact descriptions.

- **Notes.** Select this checkbox to check spelling in all notes.
- **Media.** Select this checkbox to check spelling in media captions and descriptions.
- **Tasks.** Select this checkbox to check spelling in all tasks in the research to-do list.
- **Sources.** Select this checkbox to check spelling in citation detail and citation text fields.

3 Click **Begin Checking**. If the spell checker finds a potential error, it displays the word in the "Not in dictionary" field.

4 Replace or ignore the word using the spell check buttons. A message tells you when the spell check is complete. Click **OK**.

Find and Replace Tool

You may have mistakenly spelled an individual's name wrong throughout your tree or perhaps you abbreviated a place name that you want to spell out now. You can use Find and Replace to correct these mistakes—one by one or all at the same time.

1 Choose **Edit>Find and Replace**.

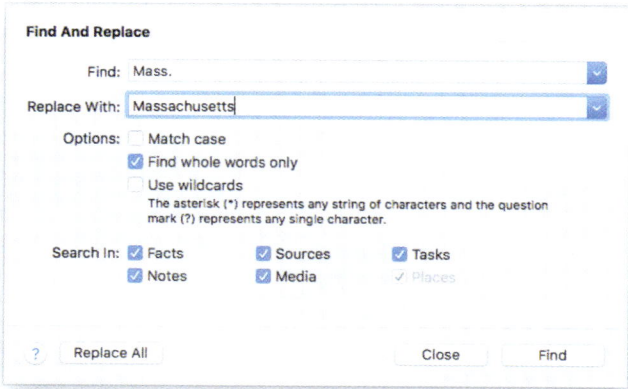

2. Type the term you want to search for in the **Find** field. Then type the new term you want to use in the **Replace With** field.

3. Select one or more of these options:
   - To find words that match your search exactly (uppercase and lowercase), select the **Match case** checkbox.
   - To find entire words that match your search, select the **Find whole words only** checkbox. (For example, a search for Will would not show results for William or Willton.)
   - To search using wildcards, select the **Use wildcards** checkbox. Wildcards allow you to search for one or more missing characters. An asterisk (*) replaces multiple characters; a search for "Mas*" could find Massachusetts, Masonville, or Masterson. A question mark (?) replaces one character; a search for Su?an would find Susan and Suzan.

4. Select the checkbox for each part of the tree you want to search. If you're not sure where the information is, you might want to select all of the checkboxes.

5. Click **Find**. The first result that matches your terms appears.

6. If you want to replace the current match, click **Replace**.

   Tip: You can replace all matching search results by clicking the **Replace All** button. Before you do, you may want to back up your tree. However, you always can roll back the changes using the Turn Back Time feature. See page 248.

7. To find the next matching term, click **Find Next**.

8. Continue searching and replacing terms, as necessary. When you're finished, click **Close**.

Merging Duplicate Facts

If you have multiple versions of the same fact, you can merge them together. You can choose only one date and place for the fact. If you have multiple descriptions, they will be combined into one.

1 Go to the **Person** tab on the People workspace and select the appropriate individual.

2 Click **Facts**. Then Control-click one of the duplicate facts and select **Merge Duplicate Facts**.

3 Select the checkboxes next to the facts you want to merge and click **Next**.

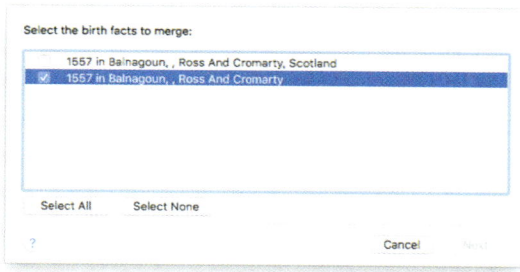

4 Select the date and location you want to keep.

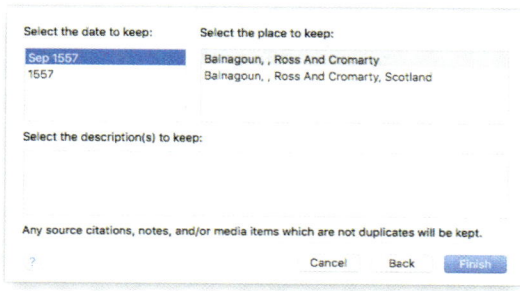

5 Click **Finish**.

Running the Data Errors Report

Family Tree Maker can search your tree and identify potential errors. For example, it can look for blank fields or date problems, such as an individual being born before his or her parents were born. It's a good idea to run the Data Errors Report periodically to make sure your tree is as error free as possible.

1. Go to the **Collection** tab on the Publish workspace. In **Publication Types**, select **Person Reports**.

2. Double-click the **Data Errors Report** or select the report icon and click the **Detail** tab.

3. To determine which errors the report lists, click the **Errors To Include** button on the editing toolbar.

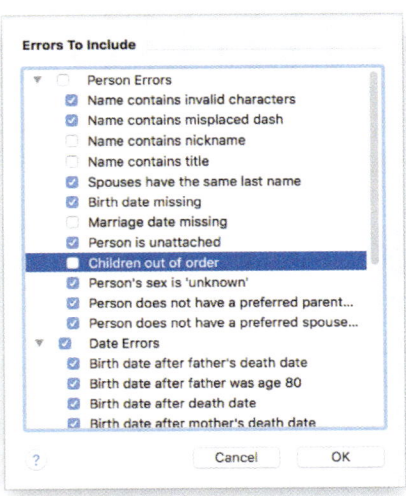

4. Select the checkboxes next to the errors you want to search for. Then click **OK**. The Data Errors Report opens.

5. To fix an error immediately, click an individual's name in the report. An editing dialog will open.

Standardizing Locations

When you import a tree or manually enter a location, Family Tree Maker checks the location against its database of three million places. If any misspellings are found, or if the place doesn't match any sites in the database, a location is considered "unidentified."

You'll want to examine these "unidentified" locations occasionally and make any necessary changes. In some cases, you'll want to leave the name exactly as it is. For example, if a town or city no longer exists, or the county boundaries have changed over the years, you'll want to keep the location's name as it is. However, in most cases, you'll want to identify locations to keep your tree consistent and to make sure that locations are grouped together correctly on the Places workspace.

Identifying a Single Location

If you see a question mark icon next to a place name in your tree, you can try to identify the place in the locations database.

1 Click the **Places** button on the main toolbar.
2 Control-click the unidentified location (with a question mark icon) in the Places panel and choose **Resolve This Place Name**.

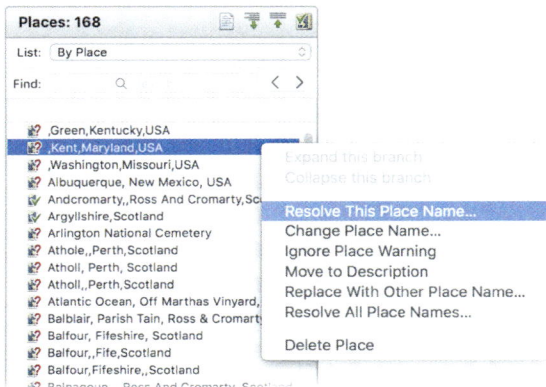

3 Do one of the following:

- If a suggestion matches the location in your tree, click its name in "Suggested place names" and click **Replace**.

- If only part of the place name matches an entry in the list, move the unmatching portion to the **Place detail** field by clicking the **Move first segment to place detail** button; then click **Replace**. This will let you keep the entire place name as it is while resolving the matching portion. (You can also click **Ignore** to leave the location as it is.)

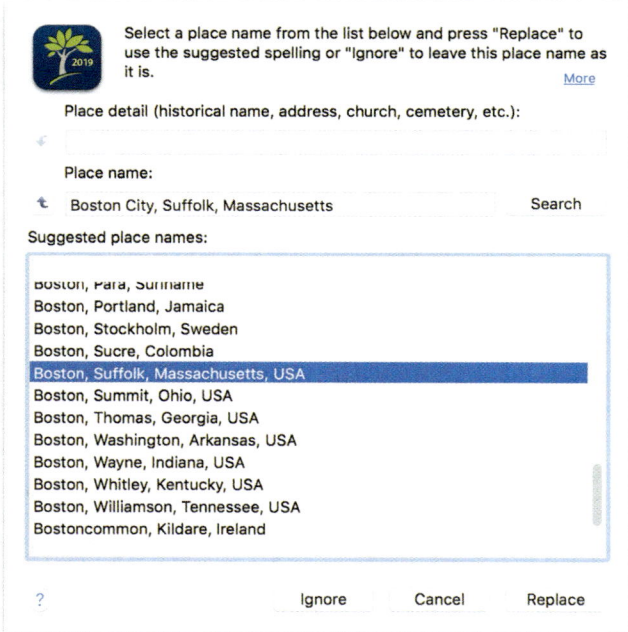

Note: Ignoring part of a location doesn't change how it is displayed in your tree; it simply allows the location to be grouped correctly on the Places workspace.

Identifying Multiple Locations

If you've imported a tree or merged someone's tree into your own, you'll likely have many place names that don't match the other locations in your tree. Instead of updating each location one at a time, you can identify multiple locations at once.

1   Choose **Tools>Resolve All Place Names**.
2   To back up your tree file before you update your locations, click **Backup**. The Backup dialog opens. Change any options as necessary and click **Backup**.

The Resolve All Place Names dialog opens. Each unidentified location is listed, along with a suggested replacement location.

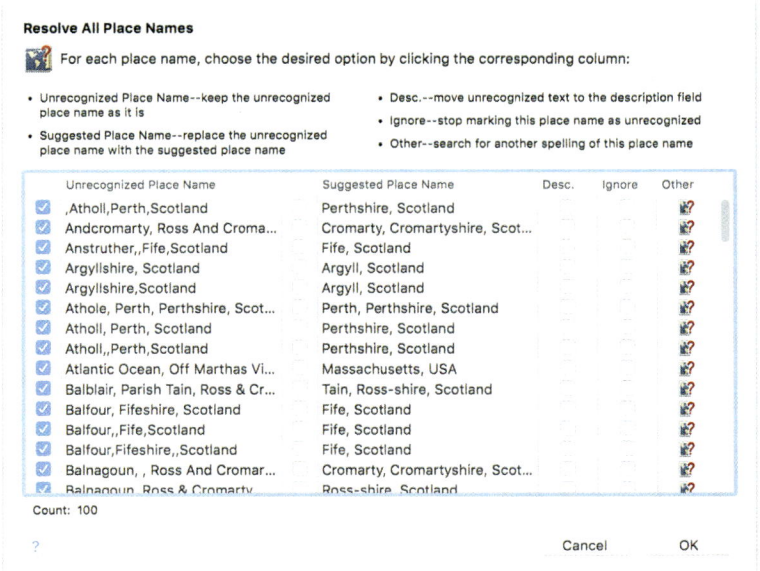

3 For each listed location, select the checkbox for the option you want to use:

- **Unrecognized Place Name.** Select this checkbox to leave the location as it is.
- **Suggested Place Name.** Select this checkbox to change the current location to the suggested location.
- **Desc.** Select this checkbox to move the location's name from the Place field to the Description field.
- **Ignore.** Click this checkbox to leave the location as it is. The location name will no longer be "unidentified."
- **Other.** To see other locations that might match the current place name, or to ignore only part of a location, click **Other**. The Resolve Place Name dialog opens. When you identify a matching location, click **Replace**.

4 When you've chosen an option for each location, click **OK**.

Finding Missing Media Items

If you move a media item on your computer after you've added it to a tree, you won't be able to view, print, or export the item until it is relinked to your tree. You can search for missing media items individually or all at once.

Finding a Single Missing Media Item

On the Media workspace, the editing panel shows the media item's name and location on your computer. If a media item is no longer linked to your tree, you'll see a red "File not found" message. To relink the media item, click the link and locate the item.

Finding All Missing Media Items

Family Tree Maker can search for missing media items and help you relink them to your tree.

1 Click the **Media** button on the main toolbar. Then click the down arrow next to the button and choose **Find Missing Media** from the pop-up menu.

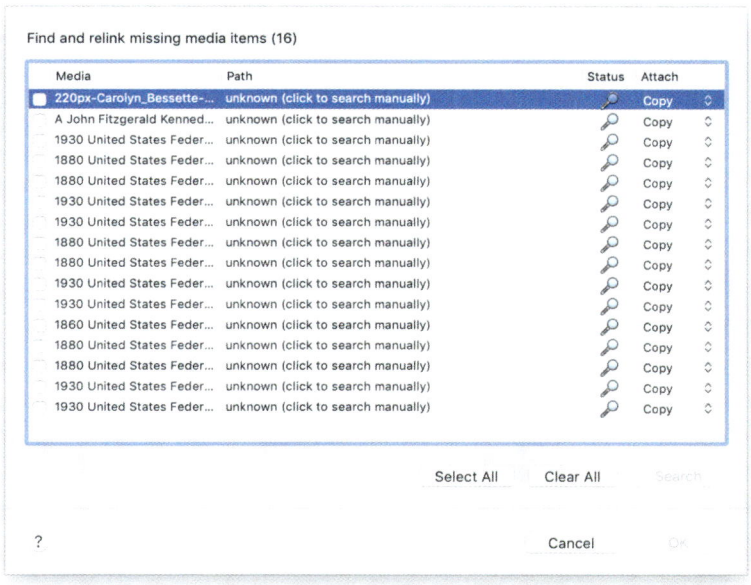

2 Select the checkboxes next to the items you want to locate or click **Select All** to find all broken media links.

3 Click **Search**. If Family Tree Maker finds the file, its current location is displayed in the Path column; a check mark appears in the Status column. If Family Tree Maker can't find the file, click its row in the Path column to search for it yourself.

4 When you're finished, click **OK**.

Glossary

Ahnentafel   German for ancestor table. In addition to being a chart, it also refers to a genealogical numbering system.

ancestor   A person you descend from—parent, grandparent, great-grandparent, etc.

Ancestry hint   The green leaf indicating that a person might have matching records on Ancestry.

Ancestry Member Tree (AMT)   Same as Ancestry tree.

Ancestry tree   An online family tree you have created on or uploaded to Ancestry.

Antenna tree   See *TreeVault Antenna tree*.

blended family   A family composed of a couple and their children from previous relationships and/or marriages, as well as any children they have together.

combined family view   An option in the family group view that lets you view blended families.

CSV   Comma Separated Values. A file format that organizes information into fields and can be imported into a spreadsheet.

descendant   A person who descends from you—your child, grandchild, great-grandchild, etc.

editing panel A section of a workspace that lets you easily edit and view information for a specific individual or item.

export To transfer data from one computer to another or from one computer application to another.

family group sheet A chart or report that displays information about a single family—father, mother, and children.

family group view Shows a single family—father, mother, and their children—in Family Tree Maker.

family view One of the display options for the tree viewer on the People workspace. Similar to the vertical pedigree chart.

FamilySearch hint The hollow blue square indicating that a person might have matching records on FamilySearch.org. If there are hints to historical records for the matched person on FamilySearch, the center of the hint turns dark blue.

FamilySync A feature that lets you link trees from Family Tree Maker and Ancestry so that changes made to an FTM tree will be reflected in the Ancestry tree and vice versa.

Fastfields A feature that reminds you of locations and people you've entered previously so that when you type a new place or name, you'll see possible matches.

FTM tree A family tree you have created in or downloaded to Family Tree Maker.

FTM Source tree An FTM tree used to create a TreeVault Antenna tree. Changes to the FTM Source tree are automatically and continuously applied to the Antenna tree.

GEDCOM   GEnealogical Data COMmunication. A standard designed by the Family History Department of The Church of Jesus Christ of Latter-day Saints for transferring data between different genealogy software applications.

genealogy report   A narrative-style report that details a family through one or more generations and includes basic facts about each member.

generation   The period of time between the birth of one group of individuals and the next—usually twenty-five to thirty years.

given name   The first (and middle) name given to a child at his or her birth. Also known as a Christian name.

hint   See Ancestry Hint and FamilySearch hint.

home person   The main individual in your tree.

HTML   HyperText Markup Language. The standard language for creating and formatting Web pages.

icon   A small picture or symbol that represents a program, file, or folder on your computer. Double-clicking an icon causes the application to run, the folder to open, or the file to be displayed.

import   To bring a file into an application. The file may have been created in the same or a different application.

maternal ancestor   An ancestor on the mother's side of the family.

media item   Photographs, scanned documents, audio files, or videos that you can add to a tree.

paternal ancestor   An ancestor on the father's side of the family.

PDF   Portable Document Format. A file format that retains printer formatting so that when it is opened it looks as it would on the printed page.

pedigree chart   A chart that shows the direct ancestors of an individual. Also known as an ancestor tree.

pedigree view   One of the display options for the tree viewer on the People workspace. Similar to the standard pedigree chart.

preferred   A term Family Tree Maker uses in reference to parents, spouses, or duplicate events indicating that you want to see the preferred selection first or have it displayed in charts and reports.

primary person   The individual who is currently the focus of the workspace, chart, or report.

RTF   Rich Text Format. A basic text file format that can be opened in almost all word-processing programs.

siblings   Children of the same parents.

Smart Stories   A tool that helps you compose stories using facts, sources, notes, and images from your tree.

Soundex   A system that assigns a code to a surname based on how it sounds rather than how it is spelled.

source   A place where you found specific information, such as a historical records, a book, or an interview.

source citation   The individual details about where information is located within a source.

Source tree   See *FTM Source tree*.

surname   The family name or last name of an individual.

TreeVault Antenna tree   A tree created with TreeVault cloud services that contains all the data from one of your FTM trees (see *FTM Source tree*).

Web clipping   The ability to "clip" text or images from a Web page and add them elsewhere, like to your Family Tree Maker tree.

Web Dashboard   A feature on the Plan workspace that lets you view your Ancestry account and trees.

Web Merge   A feature that lets you take records you've found on Ancestry and FamilySearch and add them to your Family Tree Maker tree.

workspace   A major grouping of Family Tree Maker features. Each workspace can be opened from the main toolbar.

Index

A

addresses, entering, 51
adoptions, indicating, 68
aerial maps, 123
ages, calculating, 277–278
Ahnentafel reports, 193–194
AKA (Also Known As) names
    entering, 51
AKA names, including in Index, 291
AlbumWALK Connection, 273
alerts, preferences for, 292–294
alternate facts, entering, 53
ancestor reports, 202
ancestors
    reports of, 202
Ancestry
    hints from, 135–137
    hints from, turning off and on, 287
    records, adding to trees, 148–151
    records on, 139
    searching, 138–141
    searching automatically, 287
    search results, merging into trees, 148–152
    search tips, 142
Ancestry Hints
    ignoring, 138
    turning off and on, 287
    viewing, 136
    viewing ignored hints, 138
Ancestry trees. See trees (Ancestry)
    comparison with FTM trees, 254–256
    inviting others to view, 264–266
    privacy options, 253
Ancestry Web Dashboard, 11
anniversary lists, 197
annotated bibliographies, 206
Antenna tree, 269
audio files. See media items

B

backgrounds
    for charts, 175–176
    for reports, 213–214
backups
    automatic, preferences for, 285
    creating, 245–247
    reminders, turning off and on, 293

restoring files from, 247
bibliographies, 206
biographies, creating with Smart Stories, 72–73
bird's-eye-view maps, 124
birth dates
    calculating, 277
    entering, 43
birthday lists, 197
birth order, sorting children by, 281
birthplaces, entering, 44
blended families, viewing, 62–63
book-building tool
    overview, 221
Bookmarks button, 13
books
    chapters in, reordering, 232
    charts, adding, 228
    creating new, 221–222
    exporting as PDF, 233
    footers, changing, 222–223
    headers, changing, 222–223
    images, adding, 226–227
    index of individuals, adding, 230
    in linked trees, 255
    place holders, adding, 228–229
    printing, 233
    reports, adding, 228
    saved, accessing, 222
    settings, changing for items, 231–232
    table of contents, adding, 229
    text item
        adding manually, 223–225
        importing, 225
    titles, adding, 222
borders, adding to charts, 184–186

bow tie charts, 169
boxes (text), adding to charts, 184–186

C

calculators
    for dates, 277
    for relationships, 276–277
    Soundex, 275
calendars, 208
call numbers, 86
captions for media items, 103
categories
    for media items, 115
    for to-do lists, creating, 283–284
causes of death, entering, 51
cemeteries, locating on maps, 127
censuses available on Ancestry, 139
changes, rolling back, 248–250
charts
    adding embellishments to, 178
    adding photographs to, 175–177
    adding text boxes, 179
    adding to books, 228
    backgrounds for, 175–176
    borders for, 184–186
    bow tie, 169
    boxes for, 184–186
    centering on pages, 182
    Charting Companion plug-in, 191
    choosing facts to include, 172–174
    creating, 172
    about descendants, 168

displaying everyone in tree, 170–171
display names for locations entering, 134
emailing, 190
family group sheets, 200–201
family tree, 169
fan, 170
fonts for, changing, 186
footers for, changing, 180–181
headers for, changing, 180–181
hourglass
    horizontal, 167
    standard, 165–167
including sources in, 175
in linked trees, 255
pedigree
    standard, 164
    vertical, 164–165
photographs of individuals in, assigning, 105–106
printing, 189–190
about relationships, 171
saving
    in Family Tree Maker, 188–189
    as files, 189
spacing of columns, changing, 181–182
titles for, 174
children
    adding to trees, 47–48
    adopted, indicating, 68
    attaching to parents, 309–310
    biological, indicating, 68
    detaching from parents, 308–309
    foster, indicating, 68
    order for, changing, 48
christenings, entering, 51
churches, locating on maps, 127
Citation detail field, 87
citations. See source citations
Citation text field, 87
Collection tab (Publish), 26
color coding, 59
combined family view, 62–63
Compact File tool, 251
Companion Guide (PDF), 7
contact lists, 197
contributors in Ancestry trees, 265
Convert Names tool, 278
courthouses, locating on maps, 127
CSV format, saving reports in, 218–219
custom facts
    creating, 294–295
    sentences for, modifying, 296–297
custom reports, 195
custom templates (for charts)
    creating, 187
    using, 187–188

D

Data Errors Report, 314
Data Errors Reports, 195
Date Calculator, 277
dates
    of births, entering, 43
    calculating, 277
    errors in, 292–293
    guidelines for entering, 44
    inaccurate, locating, 314
    preferences for, 289–290

deleting individuals from tree, 307
descendant reports, 194, 202
descendants
    charts displaying, 168
    reports of, 194, 202
Detail tab (Media), 24
Detail tab (Publish), 26
divorces, indicating, 67
Documented Facts Reports, 207
double dates, preferences for, 290
downloading
    Ancestry trees, 32–35
duplicate individuals
    finding, 304
    merging, 305–306

E

editing panel (People workspace)
    overview, 21
editing panel (Tree tab)
    customizing facts on, 299–300
    customizing tabs on, 288
editing photos, 107–108
editors in Ancestry trees, 265
emailing
    charts, 190
    reports, 219
embellishments, adding to charts, 178
emigration information, entering, 51
errors
    creating reports of, 195, 314
    data entry, 310–314
    File Not Found (media items), 318–319
    finding and replacing, 311–312
    missing media items, 318–319
    preferences for alerts, 292–294
    for unidentified locations
        resolving, 315–318
        setting up, 293
    for unlikely dates, 292–293
    Unrecognized Place Name, 315–318
events. See facts
exporting
    books, 233
    trees, 242–245
extended family charts, 170–171

F

facts
    adding source citations for, 87–93
    adding sources for, 81–86
    alternate, 53
    associated with locations, viewing, 129–130
    copying and pasting, 52
    custom, creating, 294–295
    duplicate, merging, 313
    entering, 49–51
    including in charts, 172–174
    including in reports, 209–212
    in linked trees, 254
    making private, 54–55
    media items for, adding, 100–102
    online, saving to trees, 152–153
    predefined, modifying, 295–296
    preferred, 53–54
    privacy for, 296

sentences for, modifying, 296–297
sourced, reports of, 207
transferring between Family Tree Maker and Ancestry, 254–255
using in Smart Stories, 73
families
    blended, viewing, 62–63
    combined, viewing, 62–63
    locations associated with, 132–133
    step, viewing, 62–63
Family Book Creator, 234
Family Book Creator plug-in, 234
family group sheets, 200–201
family group view
    displaying blended families, 62–63
    overview, 21
    sorting children in, 48
FamilySearch
    hints, 136
    hints, turning off and on, 287
    matching a person with, 144
    searching, 144
    search tips, 143
FamilySync
    comparison between Ancestry and FTM trees, 254–255
    conflicts between trees, resolving, 261–262
    downloading Ancestry trees, 33–34
    log of changes, 258–259
    options for, 257–258
    privacy for linked trees, changing, 262–263
    status of linked trees, 259
    syncing trees manually, 260
    unlinking trees, 262
    uploading trees to Ancestry, 252–253
family tree charts, 169
family view, 20
fan charts, 170
Fastfields
    overview, 288
    preferences for, 288
favorite websites
    adding to, 158–159
    sorting, 159
feedback, providing, 7
File Not Found errors (media items), 318
files
    backing up, 246–247
    compressing, 251
    exporting, 242–245
    importing, 30–31
    media items, changing names of, 113
    media items, missing, 318–319
    restoring from backups, 247
file sizes
    reducing, 251
    viewing, 240–241
filters
    adding conditions to, 17–18
    managing saved, 18
    saving, 14
Find and Replace tool, 311–312
Find Individual tool, 279–280
fonts

changing in charts, 186
changing in reports, 215
in books, 226
footers
    for books, 222–223, 231–232
    for charts, 180–181
    for reports, 214
foster children, indicating, 68
FTM Source tree, 269

G

GEDCOMs
    importing, 30–31
    overview, 244
    saving trees as, 242–244
GPS (Global Positioning System) coordinates
    entering, 133–134
Gregorian calendar, 290
guests in Ancestry trees, 265
guide, organization of, xxii

H

headers
    for books, 222–223, 231–232
    for charts, 180–181
    for reports, 214
Help
    Companion Guide (PDF), 7
    Help Tags, 6
    onscreen, 5–6
    technical support, contacting, 7
hierarchy list, for groups, 129–130
hints. See Ancestry Hints, Family-Search hints
historical events for timelines,
    creating or editing, 298
History button, 13
home person, 38–39
horizontal hourglass charts, 167
hospitals, locating on map, 127
hourglass charts
    horizontal, 167
    standard, 165–167
HTML, saving reports as, 218

I

ID numbers, 280–281
images. See media items; photographs
immigration information, entering, 51
importing
    trees, 30–31
Index
    including
        married names, 291
        titles, 291–292
    overview, 12
indexes, adding to books, 230
index of individuals
    including in books, 230
    reports of, 197
Index of Individuals Reports, 197
individuals
    adding media items for, 100–102
    addresses, entering, 51
    causes of death, entering, 51
    christenings, entering, 51
    default photo for, assigning, 105–106
    duplicate

Index

finding, 304
merging, 305–306
emigration information, entering, 51
entering basic information for, 43–45
entering information about marriage, 46–47
finding specific people, 279–280
immigration information, entering, 51
locations associated with, 131–132
media items for, choosing sort order, 113–114
physical descriptions, entering, 51
reference numbers for, 280–281
removing marriages, 307–308
reports about, 196
slide show of media items, 116–119
installation
registering software, 4
system requirements, 3

J

Julian calendar, 290

K

Kinship Reports, 201

L

layout
changing for charts, 181–184
poster, 182
LDS options, displaying, 286
LDS Ordinances Reports, 196
LDS Ordinance Summary Reports, 197
libraries, locating on maps, 127
linked trees
comparison between Ancestry and FTM trees, 254–255
conflicts between, 261–262
inviting others to view, 264–266
log of changes, 258–260
multiple FTM trees to Ancestry, 256–257
privacy for, changing, 262–263
status of, 259
synchronization options, 257–258
syncing manually, 260
unlinking, 262
uploading to Ancestry, 252–253
locations
associated with families, 132–133
associated with individuals, 131–132
completing with Fastfields, 288
display name for, 134
entering, 45
facts associated with, 129–130
finding nearby places of interest, 127–128
GPS coordinates for, entering, 133–134
guidelines for entering, 45
reports of usage, 204

standardizing, preferences option for, 286, 315–318
transferring between Family Tree Maker and Ancestry, 255
troubleshooting, 315–318
unidentified
    resolving multiple, 317–318
    resolving one at a time, 315–316
unrecognized
    warnings for, 293
viewing for individuals, 131–132
viewing in groups, 129
log of sync changes, 258–259

M

main toolbar, 10
maps
    GPS coordinates for locations, entering, 133–134
    printing, 128
maps (Microsoft Bing Maps)
    aerial, 123
    bird's-eye, 124
    road, 124
    Streetside, 126–127
    viewing, 121–127
    zooming in and out of, 125
Marriage Reports, 201
marriages
    entering, 46–47
    multiple, 64–66
    removing from individuals, 307–308
    reports of, 201
    statuses of, 67
married names
    including in Index, 291
media categories, creating, 115
Media Item Reports, 205
media items
    adding
        for facts, 100–102
    adding to Smart Stories, 76
    categories for, 115–116
    choosing sort order, 113–114
    display of, changing, 102–103
    editing within Family Tree Maker, 113
    entering details about, 103–104
    file names, changing, 113
    linking to
        source citations, 92
    linking to individuals, 109–110
    missing, troubleshooting, 318–319
    notes for, 104–105
    online, adding to trees, 154–155
    printing, 119
    privacy for, 104
    reports about, 204–206
    scanning into Family Tree Maker, 101–102
    slide show of, 116–119
    Smart Stories, 69–76
    transferring between Family Tree Maker and Ancestry, 254
    types of, 99
Media Usage Reports, 206
Media workspace, 24
medical conditions, entering, 51

merging
    Ancestry records into trees, 148–152
    duplicate facts, 313
    duplicate individuals, 305–306
migration paths
    maps of, 131–133
    printing, 128

N

names
    completing with Fastfields, 288
    guidelines for entering, 46
    including AKA names in Index, 291
    including married names in Index, 291
    nicknames, entering, 51
    standardizing tool, 278
    titles in, 51
Next of Kin certificate, 270
nicknames, entering, 51
notes
    adding for individuals, 55
    create using online information, 155–156
    display size, changing, 57
    for media items, 104–105
    personal, 56
    printing, 57
    privacy for, 58–59
    reports of, 198
    research, 56
    for source citations, 93
    spell checking, 310–311
    transferring between Family Tree Maker and Ancestry, 255
    using in Smart Stories, 75
Notes Report, 198

O

online facts, adding to trees, 152–153
online images, adding to trees, 154–155
online trees. See Ancestry trees
Outline Ancestor Reports, 202

P

page numbers
    in books, 222–223
    including in charts, 180
    including in reports, 214–215
parents
    adding to trees, 48–49
    attaching children to, 309–310
    detaching children from, 308–309
    reports about, 203
partner relationships, indicating, 67
PDFs
    of charts, creating, 189–190
    Companion Guide, accessing, 7
    of books, creating, 233
    of reports, creating, 218–219
pedigree charts
    standard, 164
    vertical, 164–165
pedigree view, 20
People workspace, 12–20
personal notes, 56
Person tab, 22

photo albums, 204
Photo Darkroom, 107–108
photographs. See also media items
    adding to books, 226–227
    assigning default for individuals, 105–106
    available on Ancestry, 139
    for charts, 175–177
    missing, troubleshooting, 318–319
    printing, 119
    scanning into Family Tree Maker, 101–102
physical descriptions, entering, 51
place holders, adding to books, 228–229
places. See locations
Places workspace, 23
Place Usage Reports, 204
Plan workspace, 10–11
plug-in
    Charting Companion, 191
    Family Book Creator, 234
portraits
    assigning to individuals, 105–106
    cropping in workspaces, 286
    defaults for charts, 105–106
    including in charts, 177–179
poster layout, 182
predefined facts
    modifying, 295
preferences
    for alerts, 292–294
    for automatic backups, 285
    for dates, 289–290
    for errors, 292–293
    for Fastfields, 288
    general, 285–287
    for names, 291
    for online searching, 287
    for tab displays, 288
preferred spouses, 65–66
preferred facts, 53–54
printing
    charts, 189
    large charts, 190
    maps, 128
    media items, 119
    notes for individuals, 57
    reports, 219
privacy
    for Ancestry trees, 253
    for Family Tree Maker trees, 242
    for facts, 296
    for linked trees, changing, 262–263
    for media items, 104
    in linked trees, 255
    making facts private, 54–55
    making notes private, 58
    roles in Ancestry trees, 265
problem solver. See errors; troubleshooting
public trees, 253
Publish workspace, 26

R

reference notes, 88
reference numbers, automatic, 280–281
registering software, 4
Register reports, 194
Relationship calculator, 276–277

relationships
    charts about, 171
    between children and parents, 68
    between couples, 67
    details about, entering, 46–47
    managing, 297
    media items for, adding, 46–47
    reference numbers for, 280–281
    removing marriages, 307–308
    reports about, 200–203
    status of, 67
    troubleshooting, 303–311
    viewing for individuals, 63–64
removing individuals from tree, 307
reports
    adding to books, 228
    Ahnentafels, 193–194
    of ancestors, 193–194
    of anniversaries, 197
    of birthdays, 197
    choosing facts to include, 209–212
    choosing individuals to include, 212
    of contacts, 197
    creating, 209
    custom, 195
    customizing, 209–215
    default settings for, changing, 216
    of descendants, 194, 202
    display names for locations entering, 134
    of documented facts, 207
    emailing, 219–220
    of errors, 195, 314
    fact sentences for, 296–297
    fonts for, changing, 215
    about individuals, 196
    about kinship, 201
    about LDS Ordinances, 196–197
    in linked trees, 255
    about locations, 204
    about marriages, 201
    about media items, 205–206
    of notes, 198
    about parentage, 203
    printing, 219
    Register, 194
    about relationships, 200–203
    of research tasks, 199
    saving, 216–218
    of sources, 206–208
    of surnames, 198
    timelines, 199
    titles for, 213
repositories, 86, 94
    adding, 94
    deleting, 98
    editing information, 97
    managing, 95–98
    replacing, 96
    reviewing usage of, 95
requirements, system, 3
research notes, 56–57
roles in Ancestry trees, 264–266
RTF (Rich Text Format), saving reports in, 218

S

saving
    charts
        as files, 189

338 Index

    in Family Tree Maker, 188
  reports
    as files, 218
    in Family Tree Maker, 216–217
scanning photograph into Family Tree Maker, 101–102
searching
  Ancestry, 138–142
  FamilySearch, 144
  online with Family Tree Maker, 151–152
  for specific people, 279–280
search results
  excluding Ancestry trees from, 252
search tips
  for Ancestry, 142
  for FamilySearch, 143
sentences for facts, modifying, 296–297
separations (marriage), indicating, 67
settings, default
  for book items, changing, 231–232
  changing for reports, 216
sharing trees
  online, 264–266
slide show, creating, 116–119
Smart Stories
  adding facts, 73–74
  adding images, 76–77
  adding notes, 75
  adding sources, 74–75
  creating biographies with, 72–73
  creating timelines with, 76–77

  overview, 69–71
  text, editing, 77–78
Smart Weather Sentences, xxii
software
  closing, 9
  opening, 9
software updates
  preferences for, 286
sorting children by birth order, 281
Soundex calculator, 275
soundtracks, adding to slide shows, 118
source citations
  adding notes about, 93
  attaching media items to, 92–93
  copying, 90–91
  creating new, 87–89
  explanation of, 79–80
  using multiple times, 89–91
source repositories, 94
sources
  adding, 81–82
  basic format, 85–86
  explanation of, 79–80
  including in charts, 175
  reports of, 206–208
  repositories for, 86
  spell checking, 310–311
  templates for, 82–85
  transferring between Family Tree Maker and Ancestry, 255
  using in Smart Stories, 74–75
Sources workspace, 25
source templates, 82–85
Source tree. See FTM Source tree
Source Usage Reports, 208
spell checker

using, 310–311
spouses
    adding to tree, 45–46, 64–65
    multiple, 64–66
    preferred, 65–66
    switching between, 66
standard hourglass charts, 165–167
status (sync), viewing, 259
stepfamilies, viewing, 62–63
stories, transferring between Family Tree Maker and Ancestry, 255
Streetside view, 126–127
support, contacting, 7
Surname Reports, 198
syncing trees. See FamilySync
Sync Weather Report, 260–261
system defaults
    location for trees, 285
    searching Ancestry, 287
system requirements, 3

T

table of contents, creating for books, 229
tabs
    Collection (Publish), 26
    Current Tree, 10–11
    Detail (Media), 24
    Detail (Publish), 26
    displaying on editing panel, 288
    New Tree, 10
    Person, 22
    Tree, 12
task lists, 199
technical support, 7
templates (chart)
    creating, 187
    preferred, 187
    using, 186–187
templates (source), 82–85
text
    adding to books, 223–225
    adding to charts, 179
    finding and replacing, 311–312
    formatting in books, 226
    online, adding to notes, 155–157
    Smart Stories, editing, 77–78
    spell checking, 310–311
timelines
    creating in Smart Stories, 76
    historical events for, creating or editing, 298
    viewing, 68–69
titles
    changing for books, 222–223
    changing for charts, 174
    changing for reports, 213
    including in Index, 291
titles (in names)
    fact for, 51
to-do lists
    adding tasks, 281–282
    creating task categories, 283
    marking tasks as complete, 283
    sorting, 284
toolbars, 10
tools
    book-building, 221
    Compact File, 251
    Convert Names, 278
    Date Calculator, 277
    Find and Replace, 311–312

Find Individual, 279–280
Finding Duplicate People, 304
managing historical events, 298
relationship calculator, 276–277
Soundex calculator, 275
Web clipping, 152–156
Tree Browser, 237–239
tree charts. See charts
trees (Ancestry). See also Ancestry trees, linked trees
    downloading, 32–34
trees (Family Tree Maker)
    adding
        children, 47–48
        notes, 55–57
        parents, 48–49
        spouses, 45–46, 64–65
    backing up files, 246–247
    comparison with Ancestry trees, 254–255
    creating, 29–38
    default directory for, 285
    deleting, 241
    exporting, 242–245
    guidelines for creating, 32
    home person of, 38–39
    importing, 30–31
    linking multiple FTM trees to Ancestry, 256
    number of generations in, viewing, 240–241
    number of individuals in, viewing, 240–241
    opening, 240
    removing individual from, 307
    renaming, 241
    securing, 242
    size of file, reducing, 251
    statistics about, 240–241
    uploading and linking to Ancestry, 252–253
Tree tab
    customizing fields on editing panel, 299–300
    family group view on, 21–22
    Index on, 12–13
    tree viewer on, 20
TreeVault cloud services
    AlbumWALK Connection, 273
    Emergency Tree restore service, 269
    Family Tree Maker Connect, 271
    Historical Weather, 272
    Next of Kin, 270
tree viewer, 20
    background color, 20
troubleshooting
    accessing onscreen help, 5–6
    conflicts between linked trees, 261–262
    contacting technical support, 7
    data entry errors, 310–314
    Data Errors report, 314
    Data Errors Reports, 195
    marriages, removing, 307–308
    missing media items, 318–319
    reducing file size, 251
    relationships issues, 303–310
    unidentified locations, 315–318

U

unlinking trees, 262

unmarried couples, indicating, 67
Unrecognized Place Name error, 315–318
unrelated individuals, adding to trees, 68
uploading
    trees to Ancestry, 251–255
user information, entering, 301

V

vertical pedigree charts, 164–165
videos. See media items

W

Web clipping tool, 152–157
Web links, adding for an individual, 58
Web Merge Wizard, 148–151
Web pages. See also websites
Web Search
    merging result into trees, 148–151
    preferences for, 287
    results, ignoring, 138
Web Search workspace, 27
websites
    archiving specific pages, 157–158
    favorites
        adding to, 158–159
        sorting, 159
    searching with Family Tree Maker, 151–152
    for sources, 87–88
wildcards
    in Ancestry searches, 142
    in FamilySearch searches, 143
workspaces
    Media, 24
    People, 12–21
    Places, 23
    Plan, 10–11
    Publish, 26
    Sources, 25
    Web Search, 27

About the Original Author

Tana L. Pedersen
Tana has been writing and editing in the technology industry for more than twenty years. She has earned several awards for her writing, including the Distinguished Technical Communication award from the Society for Technical Communication. Tana is author of *Beyond the Basics: A Guide for Advanced Users of Family Tree Maker 2012*, five editions of *The Official Guide to Family Tree Maker*, and co-author of *The Official Guide to RootsWeb.com*.